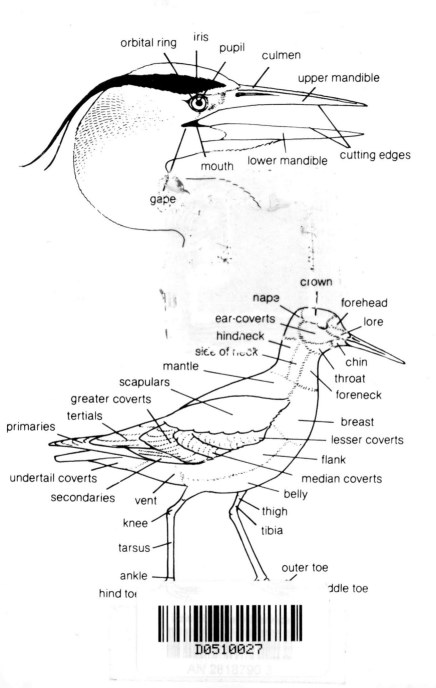

orbital ring • iris • pupil • culmen • upper mandible • cutting edges • lower mandible • mouth • gape

crown • nape • forehead • ear-coverts • lore • hindneck • side of neck • chin • mantle • throat • scapulars • foreneck • greater coverts • breast • tertials • primaries • lesser coverts • flank • undertail coverts • median coverts • secondaries • vent • belly • knee • thigh • tarsus • tibia • ankle • outer toe • hind toe • middle toe

THE
RSPB GUIDE TO
BRITISH
BIRDS

NY
10/09

Peter Holden, well known for his success in introducing young people to the pleasures of birdwatching, is the Head of the RSPB's Youth and Volunteer Department and appears frequently on children's television programmes.

Dr J.T.R. Sharrock was Managing Editor of the monthly journal *British Birds* for 25 years and is the author of a number of distinguished books, including *The Atlas of Breeding Birds in Britain and Ireland* and *Rare Birds in Britain and Ireland*.

Hilary Burn is a member of The Society of Wildlife Artists and has illustrated many books on birds, including *Wildfowl – An Identification Guide to the Ducks, Geese and Swans of the World*, *Crows and Jays*, *The Handbook of Bird Identification* and *The Handbook of Birds of the World*.

THE
RSPB GUIDE TO
BRITISH
BIRDS

Peter Holden · J.T.R. Sharrock

Illustrated by Hilary Burn

MACMILLAN

First published 2002 by Macmillan
an imprint of Pan Macmillan Ltd
Pan Macmillan, 20 New Wharf Road, London N1 9RR
Basingstoke and Oxford
Associated companies throughout the world
www.panmacmillan.com

ISBN 0 333 90751 5

A CIP catalogue record for this book is available from
the British Library

Typeset by SX Composing DTP, Rayleigh, Essex
Printed and bound by Butler and Tanner, Frome, Somerset

Contents

Introduction, ix

Glossary of Terms, 1
Divers, 2–3
Grebes, 4–7
Fulmar/Shearwaters, 8–9
Petrels/Gannet, 10–11
Cormorant/Shag, 12–13
Herons/Spoonbill, 14–15
Swans, 16–17
Geese, 18–21
Ducks, 22–37
Raptors, 38–47
Gamebirds, 48–55
Rails, 56–9
Waders, 60–83
Skuas, 84–5
Gulls, 86–93
Terns, 94–7
Auks, 98–101
Doves, 102–5
Parakeet/Cuckoo, 106–7
Owls, 108–9
Owls/Nightjar, 110–11
Swift/Hoopoe/
    Kingfisher, 112–13
Woodpeckers, 114–15

Larks, 116–17
Swallows/Martins, 118–19
Pipits, 120–1
Wagtails, 122–3
Waxwing/Dipper/
    Wren, 124–5
Dunnock/Thrushes, 126–7
Thrushes, 128–37
Warblers, 138–47
Crests, 148–9
Flycatchers, 150–1
Tits, 152–7
Nuthatch/
    Treecreeper, 158–9
Oriole/Shrikes, 160–1
Crows, 162–7
Starling, 168–9
Sparrows, 170–1
Finches, 172–9
Finches/Buntings, 180–1
Buntings, 182–5
Rarities, 186–93

Maps, 194
RSPB Reserves, 222
Ornithological Organisations, 254
Index, 255

Introduction

It is now more than 20 years since the two authors and the artist of this guide planned what was deliberately intended to be a different approach for a bird book.

At a time when bird guides were widening their horizons to Europe and beyond, we all believed in the need for a book for people, especially beginners, who wanted to know more about British birds. We also believed that the growing emphasis on identification in most other field guides was overlooking much of the interesting information about common and not-so-common species that we three find fascinating and that we believed would appeal to a much wider audience. We also developed the idea that we would not follow the growing trend and illustrate the birds, like stamps, side by side on the page, but would depict them in scenes that an observer was likely to encounter.

Three editions and 200,000 copies later, it seems that those decisions were correct. It has been a constant source of pleasure for us to meet readers of previous editions of this book who have been inspired with the series of facts that were incorporated into the text. Many of the especially favourable comments relate to Hilary's detailed artwork that not only successfully captures the character of each species, but also conjures up the atmosphere of the places where they live.

Part of the fascination of getting to know and understand our native bird population is the discovery that nature does not stand still: populations change, either naturally or as a reaction to human influence on the environment. This new edition has provided an opportunity to draw attention to some of those changes and to incorporate new information that was not available to us 20 years ago.

The title has been changed to include the word 'Guide' in recognition that the biggest change to this new edition is the incorporation of a gazetteer of RSPB reserves. Many of these are simply the best places to go to see most of the species mentioned in our book. Reserves differ widely. Some, such as Fowlmere and Forsinard, have minimal interpretation, allowing the observer to 'capture' the wildness of the habitat. Others. such as Minsmere and Leighton Moss, have a shop and tea room and cater for the family days out, as well as providing the hides and trails that bring people closer to birds. Reserves such as Sandwell Valley and Rye Meads are also very different, as they provide an oasis for wildlife in an urban environment.

Other successful features of the original edition remain unchanged. The species are still arranged in the usual scientific order so that related species appear close to one another. The text is intended to be easy to read with no abbreviations, and the very few 'technical terms' are usually explained in the text and also included in the Glossary. The normal symbol ♂ has been used for male and ♀ for female on the colour plates. The average size of a bird from the tip of its tail to the tip of its bill (assuming it is lying on its back!) has been included, but we urge newer observers to use the more helpful size comparison with a familiar species which we have incorporated into each description. Since the first edition there has been some standardization of bird names, and we have included the new names, usually in brackets, in our text.

Finally, we hope readers will enjoy this book and have pleasure watching the wide variety of species that it covers. Many of these birds face problems in a rapidly changing world, so we hope that you will also want to support the RSPB in its work to protect them.

Glossary of Terms

Brood Young birds in or just out of nest, all from one clutch

Camouflage *cryptic*: blending with the background; *disruptive*: bold patterning which helps to disguise shape

Clutch Eggs in nest all laid by one bird

Courtship A bird's special behaviour when attracting or keeping a mate

Crèche A group of young ducks from different families which are still dependent on an adult, but not necessarily one of their own parents

Dabbling ducks Species of ducks which usually feed on or near the water surface

Display Visual signals given by a bird, often associated with courtship

Drumming Instrumental noise. Woodpeckers use their bill to drum on wood. A Snipe's tail feathers make a bleating sound during display, which is called drumming

Eclipse The camouflage plumage which is grown by male ducks while moulting their flight feathers

Feral Living wild, although originally having been released, or having escaped from captivity

Field mark A plumage feature which aids identification (e.g. white wing-bars)

Genus A scientific grouping of closely allied species which is indicated by the first word of the scientific name (e.g. all divers are in the genus *Gavia*)

Gizzard Part of a bird's digestive system, where food is broken up

Gliding Flying on a straight course with no wingbeats

Habitat Area with distinct vegetation in which bird species (and other animal species) are also usually distinct

Immature A bird which has left the nest but which is not yet in its fully adult plumage; depending on the species, it may be from a fledgling to four years old

Introduction A bird deliberately released by man, now breeding wild

Invasion A large movement of birds into an area for a relatively short period

Irruption Some species have an irregular one-way movement away from an area of high population or food shortage – this is known as an eruption. Their arrival in a new area is known as an irruption

Jizz Characteristic postures, stance or actions of a bird which help identify it

Juvenile A young bird which has left the nest but retains some of its first plumage

Migration The movement from one area to another, followed, at a different season, by a return to the original area

Moult The natural loss and replacement of feathers

Moult migration Migration to and from a special area for the moult period

Nocturnal Active at night

Passage migrant A bird which passes through the British Isles on its migration

Pellet A solid mass of indigestible food ejected through a bird's mouth rather than passed as droppings

Plumage A bird's covering of feathers

Race A subspecies (see below)

Raptor Bird of prey – not an owl

Resident Bird which remains in the same area throughout the year

Roost To rest or sleep; a gathering of birds at their communal sleeping place

Sawbill A member of the merganser family. The name is derived from tooth-like projections along the edge of the bill which help the bird hold fish

Soaring Circling, effortless flight, often in thermals

Species Animal or plant of one sort (e.g. House Sparrow) which can produce a new generation identical to itself

Speculum The coloured patch on a duck's wing

Subspecies Subdivision of a species, the individuals of which all look similar (but different from those of other subspecies) and breed in a distinct geographical area

Territory An area, usually (but not always) around a nest-site, which is defended by a bird or pair of birds from others of the same species

Red-throated Diver *Gavia stellata*

This, the most common of Britain's divers, breeds on small, remote, upland lochs, where there are few fish, and regular flights are made by the parents to bring food for their young from lowland lochs, estuaries or the sea.

On their breeding grounds these divers are quite noisy. Calls include harsh, barking warning-calls and weird wails. They have exciting displays and fly over their territories calling, a habit once thought to predict rain!

Divers are easily disturbed while breeding and bird-watchers wanting to see Red-throats should look on larger lochs, where they fish, and avoid visiting breeding sites.

In August, they leave their upland homes to winter in our coastal waters with others from Scandinavia, Iceland and Greenland. Usually seen singly, they may gather in small flocks. Here, they are endangered by pollution and fishing nets. After winter gales or hard weather, a few may be found on inland lakes.

Black-throated Diver *Gavia arctica*

Like the previous species, the Black-throated Diver is a summer visitor to remote lochs in northern Scotland; it usually nests on islands in larger lochs. Unfortunately, breeding divers are sometimes disturbed by tourists and birdwatchers. Fluctuating water levels may flood the nests and predators also reduce breeding success. To avoid these hazards, conservationists build artificial, floating islands to help this endangered species.

Black-throated Divers may stay underwater for as long as two minutes, but the average dive for fish lasts about 45 seconds.

Although silent for most of the year, a variety of calls may be heard in spring, including a drawn-out wail.

Great Northern Diver *Gavia immer*

Known as the Common Loon in North America, this large diver is sometimes seen around the coast of Scotland in summer, but nesting has only once been proved in Britain. The nearest breeding population is in Iceland and it is from there that they come to winter around Britain and Ireland. The chief threat is oil pollution.

Beautifully adapted, it can slip underwater with barely a ripple. When alarmed it swims low in the water with only head and neck visible.

The **Yellow-billed Diver** *Gavia adamsii* is sometimes seen in British waters, chiefly in winter. It is much rarer than the similar Great Northern, from which it is distinguished by its wholly pale and usually upswept bill.

Red-throated Diver
Size of Mallard – 60 cm. In breeding plumage (**1**) has dull red throat, grey head, dark back and white underparts. Brown and white in winter (**2**) with white around eye. Slender bill often tilted upwards. Hunch-backed and thin-necked in flight.
Breeds on small lochs in north and west Scotland. A few pairs nest in Ireland. Seen around the coast in winter, also visits inland lakes and reservoirs.
(Map: page 195)

Black-throated Diver
Slightly larger than Mallard – 65 cm. Grey head, black throat bordered with white stripes, and white patches on back in summer (**3**). In winter (**4**) appears darker than Red-throat with dark cap to level of eye and pale thigh patch. Dagger-like bill held horizontal.
Breeds on large lochs in northwest Scotland. Seen in coastal waters in winter and sometimes on inland lakes. (Map: page 195)

Great Northern Diver
Larger than Mallard – 80 cm. Powerful head and bill, steep forehead and thick neck usually obvious. In summer (**5**) has black head and neck with white collars; back is chequered black and white. In winter (**6**) has ragged merger of light and dark areas on face and neck. Thick neck and relatively slow wingbeats aid identification in flight.
Seen around coast of Scotland in summer and more southern coasts in winter, rarely coming inland.
(Map: page 195)

Black-throated Diver

Great Northern
Diver

Red-throated Diver

Cormorant

2 Red-throated
Diver
winter

6 Great Northern
Diver
winter

4 Black-throated Diver
winter

5 Great Northern
Diver
summer

1 Red-throated
Diver
summer

3 Black-throated
Diver
summer

Hilary Burn.

Great Crested Grebe *Podiceps cristatus*

With legs situated under its tail, the Great Crested Grebe is ungainly and rarely seen on land, but supreme under water. It feeds mainly on fish, which it chases below the surface, usually at a depth of 2–4 m, and regularly stays submerged for 26 seconds or more.

The ritual of this grebe's courtship has been much studied as it is beautiful, highly stylized and quite easily observed. A pair will display their crests and 'tippits' to each other by repeatedly shaking their heads. Sometimes both will dive, bring up weed and adopt an upright position while pressing their breasts together and shaking their heads from side to side.

The nest is usually a floating raft of vegetation, anchored to a branch or to aquatic plants. Both sexes incubate the eggs. When the adults leave the nest they generally cover the eggs with weed to conceal them from crows and other predators.

Young grebes frequently ride on the backs of their parents as this gives them protection from their main enemy, the pike. Adult grebes can frequently be seen feeding their young with feathers and will also eat feathers themselves; it is likely that this helps grebes to form pellets of the indigestible items – the fish bones being ejected wrapped up with feathers.

In the 19th century, the Great Crested Grebe was rare and was almost exterminated as a breeding species in Britain because its dense fur-like breast feathers were used for making muffs for Victorian ladies. Protection laws, the construction of gravel pits and reservoirs and, perhaps, milder winters have fortunately resulted in the species becoming more common again. This grebe suffers from the increasing use of lakes for water sports which may reduce its breeding success in areas where it is most numerous.

Great Crested Grebe

Slightly smaller than Mallard – 48 cm. Long, slender, white neck; dagger-like bill; grey-brown back and blackish crown and crest in winter (**1**). Chestnut frills around head when breeding (**2**). Dives frequently. Seldom seen in flight. Juveniles (**3**) have dark stripes on sides of neck. Most common call is growling 'gorr'.

Breeds on freshwater lakes, reservoirs, gravel pits and sometimes on rivers. Present in most parts of Britain, rarer in northern Scotland and southwest England. These grebes may leave small lakes in autumn and join flocks of several hundred others on larger lakes and reservoirs. Often seen on the sea in winter especially in estuaries. (Map: page 195)

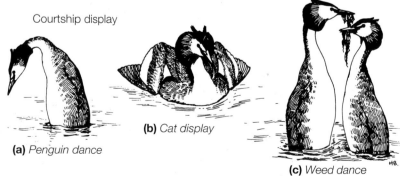

Courtship display

(a) *Penguin dance*

(b) *Cat display*

(c) *Weed dance*

4

1 *winter*

3 *juvenile*

2 *summer*

display

Great Crested Grebes

Little Grebe *Tachybaptus ruficollis*

A loud trilling or 'whinnying' is a typical sound of summer around many ponds or lakes. The call tells us that a Little Grebe or 'Dabchick' is not far away, but seeing it may be difficult.

Once a Little Grebe is disturbed, it slips underwater with hardly a ripple, and usually emerges again out of sight, often among nearby vegetation, or swims with just its head showing above the water.

Little Grebes are at home in a variety of habitats, from remote moorland tarns to town park ponds or even on the sea in winter. They prefer relatively shallow water, where they feed on insects, shellfish and small fish, which they catch up to 2 m below the surface.

Red-necked Grebe *Podiceps grisegena*

A winter visitor to Britain from Denmark and north-eastern Europe, arriving in small numbers in October and moving back in March. Usually seen on the sea, often in estuaries, but sometimes on inland waters.

In some winters, when the weather is particularly severe in northern Europe, many more Red-necked Grebes suddenly appear in British waters. Recently, small numbers have summered here and there have been several attempts to nest.

Slavonian Grebe *Podiceps auritus*

Like other members of this family, the Slavonian Grebe catches most of its prey underwater. The food includes small fish such as sticklebacks, and aquatic insects.

This species was first found nesting in the Scottish Highlands in 1908 and gradually increased to the 40 or so pairs which now nest annually. The number of young reared each year is often limited by changing water levels in breeding lochs, illegal egg-collecting and disturbance by holidaymakers, sometimes birdwatchers.

Black-necked Grebe *Podiceps nigricollis*

In the past hundred years, the Black-necked Grebe has colonised parts of Northern Europe. It first bred in Britain in 1904, but remains a rare bird, with only about 40 pairs nesting each year.

Food usually consists of insects or their larvae, but small fish and shellfish are also eaten. Some food is taken from the surface of the water by skimming the bill from side to side. Other food is found by diving; dives usually last about 30 seconds.

It is less often seen on the sea than Slavonian Grebes and may, in winter, visit reservoirs.

Little Grebe
Smaller than Moorhen – 27 cm. Smallest grebe. Appears dumpy and blunt-tailed. In summer (**1**) has yellow base to bill, dark brown plumage with chestnut neck, throat and cheeks. Paler in winter (**2**) with dusky neck and face. *Widespread on lakes, quiet rivers and ponds.*
(Map: page 195)

Red-necked Grebe
Smaller than Mallard – 45 cm. Chestnut neck, white cheeks, black crown to level of eye and yellow base to bill in summer (**3**). Grey and white in winter (**4**) with black crown to level of eye and dusky neck. *Winter visitor, mainly to east coast of England.*
(Map: page 195)

Slavonian Grebe
Smaller than Mallard – 35 cm. In summer (**5**) has chestnut neck and flanks, black head and yellow tufts. In winter (**6**) is like Black-necked, but has flatter head, straight bill and whiter cheeks, contrasting with dark cap. *A winter visitor to coastal waters and inland lakes. A few nest in Scotland.*
(Map: page 195)

Black-necked Grebe
Smaller than Mallard – 31 cm. Black head and neck with gold feathers behind eye in summer (**7**). Bill often noticeably upturned. In winter (**8**) similar to Slavonian, but more rounded head and dark crown extending lower, especially behind eye, and merging with pale cheeks. *Rare breeding species. Winter visitor to coasts and inland lakes.*
(Map: page 195)

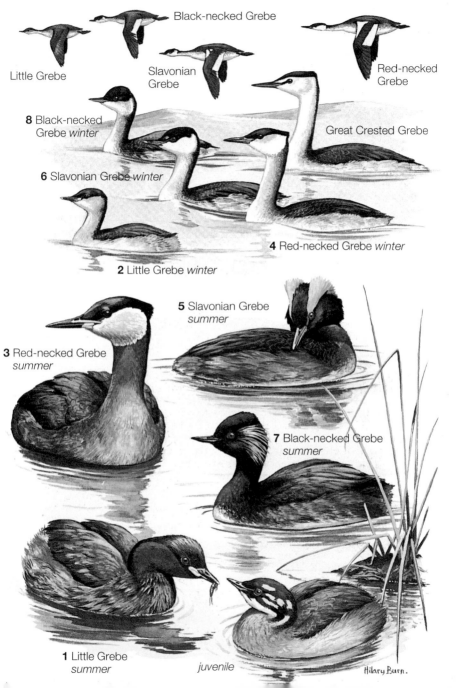

Black-necked Grebe

Little Grebe

Slavonian
Grebe

Red-necked
Grebe

8 Black-necked
Grebe *winter*

Great Crested Grebe

6 Slavonian Grebe *winter*

4 Red-necked Grebe *winter*

2 Little Grebe *winter*

5 Slavonian Grebe
summer

3 Red-necked Grebe
summer

7 Black-necked Grebe
summer

1 Little Grebe
summer

juvenile

Hilary Burn.

(Northern) Fulmar *Fulmarus glacialis*

Wheeling Fulmars are now a common sight around most sea cliffs in Britain or Ireland, but this has not always been so. The numbers of Fulmars have undergone an amazing expansion during the last hundred years or so. Before 1878, the only British colony was on the remote island of St Kilda, 200 km from mainland Scotland, but since then they have spread right around our coasts. They may have been helped by the fishing industry because they feed on offal thrown from boats.

Fulmars do not breed until at least six years old and lay only one egg each year, but they have long lives, regularly reaching 30 years or more.

Great Shearwater *Puffinus gravis*

Staring out to sea from a vantage point on the west coast of Britain or Ireland in August or September is the way one is most likely to see this master of flight.

Great Shearwaters are summer visitors to the Northern Hemisphere. They breed on a few remote islands in the South Atlantic and then migrate into the North Atlantic, moving first north and then west towards Europe. Often found near whales and porpoises.

Cory's Shearwaters *Calonectris diomedea* sometimes appear off our coast, especially from July to September. Brown above, merging to white below, lacking dark cap.

Sooty Shearwater *Puffinus griseus*

Equally at home around the Antarctic pack ice or in the English Channel, the Sooty Shearwater is one of the world's greatest travellers. Its breeding colonies are on islands in the South Atlantic and Pacific Oceans and it visits the Northern Hemisphere between April and November. Searching the horizon through binoculars in rough weather is the way to find this species (but beware dark skuas, p. 84).

Manx Shearwater *Puffinus puffinus*

Vikings in long-boats heard the weird calls of Manx Shearwaters and included them among the 'evil spirits' of their sagas. On summer nights, those same sounds can still be heard as the birds approach their cliff-top colonies having spent the day feeding at sea. Shearwaters are clumsy and vulnerable on land, so darkness saves them from predators such as Great Black-backed Gulls. After nine weeks, the young are deserted by their parents and eight days later make their way down to the sea, where they start their long migration to a wintering area off the coast of South America.

Fulmar (1)
Smaller than Herring Gull – 47 cm. Gull-like, with stiff, straight wings. Shallow wingbeats and long glides. Thick neck and short, thick bill. Grey back, wing-tips and tail. Dark smudge around eye. White underparts. *Breeds in colonies on sea cliffs.* (Map: page 195)

Great Shearwater (2)
Body shorter than Herring Gull – 47 cm, but longer wings. Large shearwater with brown back and white underparts; dark cap; white collar. Strong wingbeats and long glides. *Seen mainly off western coasts, August–October.* (No map)

Sooty Shearwater (3)
Smaller than Herring Gull – 46 cm. Torpedo-shaped body, long Swift-like wings and small head. Dark brown above and below except for white stripe on undersides of wings. Flies close to sea, often far out on horizon. *Seen off our coasts in August and September.* (No map)

Manx Shearwater (4)
Smaller than Herring Gull – 34 cm. Black above, white below. Hurried, stiff wingbeats followed by glide over waves is typical, but also banks and glides. *Mostly seen around western coasts in summer.* (Map: page 196) *The closely related* **Balearic Shearwater** *P. mauretanicus* (**5**) *is browner above and duskier below, some like Sooty without wing-stripe. Some occur in British waters June–October.*

2 Great Shearwaters

3 Sooty Shearwaters

5 Balearic Shearwater

4 Manx Shearwaters

1 Fulmars

(European) Storm-petrel *Hydrobates pelagicus*

This tiny seabird may sometimes be seen fluttering along behind a ship while searching for small fish, tiny sea creatures and even scraps thrown overboard. Feeding at sea by day, it approaches land only after dark.

Almost one-third of the world population may breed on islands off the north and west coast of Britain and Ireland and some colonies number 10,000 pairs or more. Nests may be in holes in walls or in tunnels. Purring calls of adults and a musty scent make these nests easy to locate. Some tunnels are dug by the petrels, others by Puffins or by rabbits. It is vital that rats are prevented from reaching islands with petrel colonies as they eat both eggs and young.

Leach's Storm-petrel *Oceanodroma leucorhoa*

Gales in September are likely to bring these elusive seabirds to inshore waters, mainly on the western side of the British Isles. In some years, a few are found even on inland lakes and reservoirs.

Leach's Storm-petrels visit their underground nest-sites only after dark and, because they prefer remote islands, only a few colonies have been found in Britain so far, although others may still await discovery.

(Northern) Gannet *Morus bassanus*

Over half the world's Gannets nest in colonies around Britain and Ireland. Almost all of them are on cliffs or steep slopes of small isolated islands. The 'gannetry' on St Kilda, northwest of the Scottish mainland, has almost 40,000 pairs and is the largest colony in the world.

A gannetry is a fantastic seabird city: the sloping cliffs, from which a Gannet can launch itself into the air, are densely packed with nests, each being only about 80 cm (pecking distance) from the next.

When they first leave their nests, young Gannets cannot fly, but they begin their journey to the West African coast by swimming southwards where they may stay until their second or third summer. When they do return, they group around the edge of the breeding colonies, but do not nest until five or six years old. Gannets are long-lived, and often survive for 20 years or more if they do not get caught in fishing nets or die as a result of oil pollution or some other man-made accident.

Gannets plunge-diving for fish from 9 m or more are an exciting sight, hitting the water at 100 km per hour to catch fish at a depth of 3 m or more.

The Gannet is the emblem of the British Trust for Ornithology.

Storm-petrel (1)
Sparrow-sized – 16 cm. Black with white rump, rather like House Martin with square tail. Pale, often white, stripe on underwing. Weak fluttering flight near water, often patters surface with feet.
Most often seen in summer. Nests on remote islands in north and west Britain and Ireland. Sometimes follows boats. (Map: page 196)

Leach's Storm-petrel (2)
Larger than sparrow – 20 cm. Brownish-black with white rump which, at very close range, shows a dark line down the middle. Longer, more pointed wings than those of Storm. Tail is forked. Pale stripe on upperwings. May bank, glide and sometimes hover.
Nests on a few remote islands. Seen mainly in summer. (Map: page 196)

Gannet
Larger than any gull – 95 cm. Long, narrow wings almost 2 m across. Pointed tail. Adults (**3**) are white with black wing-tips and yellow on back of head. Juveniles (**4**) vary from slate-grey on leaving nest, to white with black marks in their 2nd, 3rd or 4th years (**5**). Often glides close to waves, also seen in wheeling flocks. Feeds by plunge-diving into water.
Found in the open ocean at all times of year. Breeds on islands and rocky cliffs. (Map: page 196)

Gannets

adults

4 *juvenile*

juvenile

2 Leach's Storm-petrels

5 4th-year

1 Storm-petrels

3 Gannet *adult*

Hilary Burn

(Great) Cormorant *Phalacrocorax carbo*

A Cormorant standing on a rock or breakwater with wings outstretched is a familiar sight anywhere around our coasts. The reason for this behaviour is, however, disputed: is it drying its wings after a fishing expedition, or does this position assist in the digestion of fish? Ornithologists are uncertain.

Cormorants feed on fish – especially flat-fish, such as flounders, that live on the sea bed – which they catch by diving underwater for between 15 and 60 seconds in areas of relatively shallow water.

These birds are often seen in loose flocks, usually when moving between feeding and roosting areas. Where they are common, groups can often be seen standing around, sitting in trees, or even perched on pylons.

In Britain, they nest on cliff ledges usually near the sea and the only territory which they defend is immediately around the nest, although in some colonies conditions are so cramped that nests are actually touching. In parts of Europe, they nest inland in trees and these trees are sometimes killed by their droppings.

In recent years Cormorants have moved up British rivers, especially in winter. Some stay all year and inland breeding, usually in trees, is being reported from several localities.

(European) Shag *Phalacrocorax aristotelis*

Around British and Irish coasts, Shags outnumber Cormorants by almost ten to one, and in some places their numbers continue to increase.

A typical nest-site is sheltered, near the bottom of a cliff, or between boulders, safely above the highwater mark. Shags usually nest in loose colonies.

Although similar in appearance to Cormorants, Shags fill a separate niche in the ecology of our coasts and the two species do not really compete for food: Shags prefer free-swimming fish and generally hunt in deeper water. Prey is often caught by diving from a swimming position although they will, like Cormorants, sometimes spring out of the water as they dive. A favourite food is sand-eels.

Shags can be found around rocky coasts throughout the year, but only after particularly severe gales are they seen on inland waters. Although not truly migratory, some – especially from colonies in the west – do make their way southwards to French or even Spanish waters.

Cormorant

Heron-sized – 90 cm. Large, blackish with long thick neck and heavy bill. Throat and part of cheeks white. Some adults have more white on their head and neck. Breeding adults (**1**) have shaggy crest on back of head and white thigh patch which are lost in winter (**2**). Juvenile and 1st-winter birds (**3**) are brown, often with pale neck and belly. Stands upright or swims, often with head and bill up-tilted like Red-throated Diver. *Found on rocky coasts, mainly in the west, and always near shallow bays. Also seen inland on lakes and rivers.* (Map: page 196)

Shag

Smaller than Cormorant – 75 cm. Finer bill and thinner neck than Cormorant. In flight, notice smaller head and faster wingbeats. Iridescent green feathers of adult (**4**) usually appear blackish. Crest only in spring, when breeding starts. Base of bill yellow. Adults in winter (**5**) are more brown, with pale chin and throat. Juveniles (**6**) are brown, less white on belly than young Cormorants, but have white patch on chin. *Found along rocky coasts and islands. Rarely seen inland.* (Map: page 196)

Cormorant

6 Shag *juvenile*

Shag

4 Shag *spring*

3 Cormorant *juvenile*

5 Shag *winter*

1 Cormorant *spring*

2 Cormorant *winter*

(Great) Bittern *Botaurus stellaris*

Large reedbeds are the home of this rare and secretive bird. By 1868, Bitterns had ceased to breed in Britain because many wetlands had been drained, they were hunted as food and, as they became rarer, collectors shot them to preserve their skins and took their eggs. They recolonised and numbers rose to about 80 'booming' males by 1954, but have since fallen to around 20.

Although fish are the chief food, amphibians, insects, worms, small mammals and even young birds are also eaten. The spring call is a famous 'boom' similar to someone blowing across the top of an empty bottle.

Bitterns have cryptic camouflage and blend with reeds. When alarmed, they stretch their neck, point their bill upwards and sway like reeds in the wind.

In winter, Bitterns from the Continent reach Britain and it is then that they visit more open, but still marshy habitats. In severe winters, many of these wandering birds fail to find sufficient food and die.

Grey Heron *Ardea cinerea*

Unless you have seen a 'heronry', you may find it hard to believe that these birds are at home in trees, only rarely nesting on the ground or on cliff ledges.

Herons may lay eggs as early as February. Eleven weeks later, young Herons are trying out their wings and clambering around the heronry. After leaving the nest, the young often wander far from the colony – a way of ensuring they do not compete for food.

Herons often stand motionless in slow-moving water, neck stretched forward, waiting to strike at a passing fish. But not only fish are eaten: the diet includes amphibians, small mammals, insects, worms and birds. When not feeding, Herons often roost at traditional 'standing grounds' where sometimes several will gather. It is not unusual to see one or more Herons standing motionless in open fields.

Although North European Grey Herons are long-distance migrants, ours seldom leave Britain and Ireland; in severe winters, many do not find enough food, and die.

The rare **Purple Heron** *Ardea purpurea* is smaller, more slender and is tinged rufous; a few occur as vagrants from May to September. (*See also* pages 186–7.)

(Eurasian) Spoonbill *Platalea leucorodia*

Long ago, Spoonbills nested in England. A few visit Britain in summer, and in 1999 a pair successfully reared two young. Their curiously shaped bills are swept from side to side in shallow waters in the search for prey.

Bittern (1)

Smaller than Grey Heron – 75 cm. Golden brown with darker marks. Black 'moustache' and crown. Dagger-like bill. Neck often withdrawn, but can appear long and thin. In flight, head is drawn back on to shoulders and wings are broad and rounded.
Very secretive. Nests in dense reedbeds. In winter may visit open marshy areas.
(Map: page 196)

Grey Heron

Very large – 94 cm. Adult (**2**) has grey back, white underparts, long thin white neck with black marks. Wispy crest, long legs. Often stands hunched up on one leg. Flies with head drawn back, large broad wings and trailing legs. Juvenile and 1st-winter (**3**) have smaller crest, dark crown and darker neck. Usual call is loud, harsh 'frank'.
Nests in trees in most parts of Britain and Ireland. Feeds by water but sometimes stands in fields and other dry areas. (Map: page 196)

Spoonbill

Smaller than Grey Heron – 85 cm. Graceful, long-necked white bird with long legs and long 'spoon-shaped' bill. Adult in breeding plumage (**4**) has crest and yellow breast band. Juvenile (**5**) has pink bill and black wing-tips.
Rare visitor to eastern and southern Britain. Mainly marshes near the coast and estuaries. (No map)

heronry

5 *juvenile*

Spoonbills
4 *adult*

Grey Heron

1 Bitterns

3 Grey Heron
juvenile

2 Grey Heron

4 Spoonbill

Mute Swan *Cygnus olor*

The Mute Swan is one of the world's heaviest birds. Its long neck allows it to reach plants up to one metre underwater. It also picks up grit from river bottoms.

Swan meat was once considered a delicacy and Mute Swans were semi-domesticated. To prove ownership some bills were marked – a tradition still carried out on the River Thames in the famous 'swan upping' ceremony.

The Mute Swan is not totally silent: it has a variety of calls, especially snorts or hisses when defending a territory. In flight the wings make a rhythmic whistling.

Downy young are regularly carried on their parents' backs which keeps them warm and protects them from predators such as pike. Males are often seen with wings raised and head back when driving off an intruder.

Bewick's Swan (Tundra Swan) *Cygnus columbianus*

Named after the 18th-century engraver Thomas Bewick, who was responsible for many bird portraits, this is the smallest swan to visit the British Isles.

One-third of the world's Bewick's Swans migrate to Britain from Siberia each autumn. Large flocks winter at Slimbridge, Gloucestershire, and the Ouse Washes, Cambridgeshire, but they also visit other lowland lakes and river valleys.

Each individual has its own bill pattern. From this, we know that pairs stay together for years and 'divorce' is rare. If one of a pair dies, the other may take three years to find a new mate. We also know that family groups migrate together, spend the winter together and begin their return to Siberia together. Unfortunately many are shot at during their migration.

Whooper Swan *Cygnus cygnus*

In autumn, about three-quarters of the Whooper Swans in Iceland migrate to Britain and Ireland. During the breeding season the swans live on lakes and streams, rich in iron-compounds which stain the head and neck of many of them. This colouring is lost during the winter when old feathers are moulted.

Whooper Swans also breed in Scandinavia and northern Russia, but it is likely that only a few from these areas ever reach us. Some Whoopers summer in Scotland and occasionally breed there successfully.

Swans fly high when migrating. A flock of 30 swans, probably Whoopers, was seen by the pilot of a plane flying at a height of 8,000 m.

Mute Swan
Very large – 150 cm. Long thin neck with graceful curve. Adults are white with orange-and-black bill; the male or cob (1) has larger black knob on bill than the female or pen (2). Juveniles or cygnets (3) are brown with pale bills. *Found on fresh water almost everywhere in Britain and Ireland. Occasionally on the sea.* (Map: page 196)

Bewick's Swan
Smaller than Mute – 120 cm. Adult (4) is all white with relatively short straight neck and domed head. Bill is black with yellow base forming variable pattern, but yellow mark generally rounded, not wedge-shaped. Often makes a musical honking, especially when in flocks. Juvenile (5) is grey with black-and-pinkish bill. *Winter visitor to inland lakes in southern Britain and Ireland.* (Map: page 197)

Whooper Swan
Size of Mute Swan – 150 cm. Adult (6) all white with wedge-shaped yellow patch on black bill. Straight neck with base often resting on back giving 'kinked' effect. Larger bill than Bewick's. Some adults (7) have rust-coloured staining on neck. Juvenile (8) is brown with pink-and-black bill. Loud trumpeting call. *Winter visitor mainly to northern Britain and Ireland with a few remaining in Scotland in summer.* (Map: page 197)

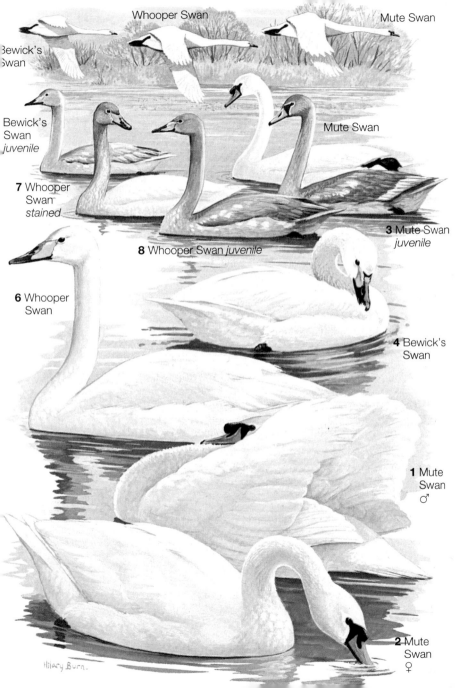

Whooper Swan

Mute Swan

Bewick's
Swan

Bewick's
Swan
juvenile

Mute Swan

7 Whooper
Swan
stained

8 Whooper Swan *juvenile*

3 Mute Swan
juvenile

6 Whooper
Swan

4 Bewick's
Swan

1 Mute
Swan
♂

2 Mute
Swan
♀

Hilary Burn

Bean Goose *Anser fabalis*

Breeds in northern Europe and Russia. Within the vast area inhabited by this goose, different subspecies or races have evolved, and some even nest in dense forests. In winter, Bean Geese migrate to various parts of Europe, but only about 400 reach Britain.

Pink-footed Goose *Anser brachyrhynchus*

The evening flight of Pinkfeet from their farmland feeding grounds to the safety of a nearby estuary or lake is one of the most spectacular winter sights.

The Pinkfeet which migrate to the British Isles in late September breed in Iceland or even Greenland. The numbers of these geese have increased dramatically in recent years, especially in Scotland. This is attributed to the increase in barley-growing. The geese traditionally graze grass, but also feed on other growing shoots, especially cereals. Although there is some conflict with farming interests, these geese do comparatively little damage.

White-fronted Goose *Anser albifrons*

Two separate races of White-fronts visit us in winter. One, from Russia, migrates into Europe and reaches England or Wales, especially around Slimbridge on the Severn Estuary; the other race, from Greenland, winters mainly in Scotland and Ireland.

Geese migrate in family groups, and juvenile White-fronts stay with their parents during their first winter.

In some areas, these geese have moved from traditional wet meadows or bogs on to farmland, although the main food remains grasses. Research has shown that White-fronts are able to select the most nutritious grasses from a field.

Greylag Goose *Anser anser*

Once, this goose nested in the fenland of East Anglia. The name Greylag is probably derived from the fact that this was the grey goose which lagged behind the others: the one which lingered in spring, with some remaining to breed. Now, owing to drainage and changes in agriculture, our only native breeding population is in northern Scotland, especially the Outer Hebrides, although feral Greylags breed commonly in other areas. In winter, Greylags from Iceland reach Britain, where they feed on farmland by day and roost on pools, lakes or estuaries.

The large bill of the Greylag is used, not only for grazing grasses, but also for digging up and eating roots or cutting through tough vegetation.

Bean Goose (1)
Larger than Pink-foot – 68–84 cm. Dark brown plumage with orange legs. Head and neck very dark, almost black on forehead. Large bill with variable pattern. In flight, head appears long and neck is longer and darker than on other 'grey geese'. *Scarce winter visitor to farmland.* (Map: page 197)

Pink-footed Goose (2)
Smaller than Bean – 60–75 cm. Pinkish-brown plumage and pink legs. Bill has variable pink-and-black pattern. Short dark neck, short bill and rounded head are obvious in flight, as are pale grey forewings. *Winter visitor to Scotland and parts of England near coasts.* (Map: page 197)

White-fronted Goose
Larger than Pink-foot – 65–78 cm. Adult (**3**) has greyish-brown plumage and wide, white surround to pink or orange bill. Legs are orange. Black bars and blotches on belly. Relatively short neck and long wings in flight. Juvenile (**4**) lacks white on face and bars on belly. *Winter visitor to low-lying grassland.* (Map: page 197)

Greylag Goose (5)
Large grey-brown goose 75–90 cm. Large pale head, thick pale neck, heavy orange bill, pink legs. Orange ring around eye. Broad wings with large bluish-grey patches. *Wild Greylags nest in north and west Scotland, others visit in winter. Feral Greylags now breed in many parts of Britain.* (Map: page 197)

Pink-footed Geese

Greylag Goose

Bean Goose

White-fronted Goose

Pink-footed Goose

1 Bean Geese

2 Pink-footed Goose

4 White-fronted Goose *juvenile*

5 Greylag Goose

3 White-fronted Goose

Canada Goose *Branta canadensis*

Introduced from North America in the reign of Charles II, since when it has become a common bird in parks, and also nests wild in many areas. In some places, it has become so numerous that it is considered a nuisance because of the damage it does to crops.

During their annual moult, geese become flightless. Many Canada Geese in North America migrate to traditional areas where they can moult safely. Now, in Britain, some Yorkshire Canadas make a regular moult migration to the Beauly Firth in northern Scotland.

In North America, there may be more than 15 different races of Canada Geese, varying considerably in size and colour. They are highly migratory: some Canadas fly to Greenland to moult, and there they sometimes mix with flocks of Barnacle Geese and occasionally migrate with them to Britain; so there are genuine records of wild Canada Geese in Britain as well as the feral ones.

Barnacle Goose *Branta leucopsis*

Those Barnacle Geese which migrate to Britain for the winter come from either Spitsbergen or Greenland. Spitsbergen birds visit the Solway Firth and those from Greenland fly to western Scotland or Ireland. The two populations do not mix, but both have increased in recent years.

Like the other geese, a Barnacle is white above and below the tail, which is a visual signal and helps to keep birds together, especially when flying in 'V' formation or in diagonal lines.

Back on their breeding grounds, these geese often nest on inaccessible cliff-faces, which gives them protection from predators such as Arctic foxes.

Brent Goose *Branta bernicla*

The Arctic tundra is where Brent Geese breed. Dark-bellied Brents breed in Siberia; the light-bellied race comes to us from Spitsbergen, Greenland and northern Canada. Food is plentiful in the Arctic, but the summer is short: nesting starts before the snow and ice melt and the geese must leave within 100 days. In bad summers, hardly any young are reared.

In the 1930s, numbers of Brent Geese fell dramatically following disease in their chief winter food, eel-grass *Zostera*, which grows on mud-flats.

Protection, a succession of good breeding summers and the recovery of the eel-grass have resulted in a remarkable improvement. Even more surprising is the recent change in the habits of the geese, which now often graze on arable farmland.

Canada Goose (1)
Largest goose – 95 cm. Black head with white chin-strap, long black neck, brown body, pale breast. Call is a noisy, trumpet-like honking.
Found near lakes, reservoirs and park ponds. Widespread in England and parts of Wales, and increasingly in Scotland. (Map: page 197)

Barnacle Goose (2)
Smaller than Canada – 58–70 cm. White face. Crown, back of head, neck and breast are black. Grey back and pale underparts. Appears black-and-white in flight.
Winter visitor to western coasts of Scotland and Ireland. (Map: page 197)

Brent Goose
Size of Mallard – 56–61 cm. Small goose with short neck and small head. Dark back. Black head and neck, with white patches on neck of adult. Dark-bellied race (**3**) has very dark grey underparts, pale-bellied race (**4**) has much lighter underparts. Fast and manoeuvrable in flight. Juveniles (**5**) of both races lack white patches on necks and have pale wing-bars.
Winter visitor to coastal areas: dark-bellied in southern and eastern England; pale-bellied in Ireland and Northumberland. (Map: page 197)

Canada Goose

Barnacle Goose

Brent Goose

2 Barnacle Geese

1 Canada Goose

3 Brent Goose
dark-bellied race

5 Brent Goose
juvenile
pale-bellied race

4 Brent Goose
pale-bellied race

Egyptian Goose *Alopochen aegyptiacus*

More closely related to the Shelduck than to the geese. Egyptian Geese are native not only to Egypt, but to most of Africa, especially the sub-tropics, where they may nest at any time of year, especially the rainy season. The bird has escaped from wildfowl collections or been introduced to several parts of Britain. The largest population, numbering a few hundred, is to be found around lakes and rivers in Norfolk.

(Common) Shelduck *Tadorna tadorna*

Found all around our coast, except where the cliffs are steepest, but even there some will probably be found nearby in a tidal inlet or estuary.

Ducks' bills have tooth-like projections called lamellae along each side, which the Shelduck uses when filtering wet sand or mud during its search for *Hydrobia ulvea*, a tiny snail which is its most important food.

Shelducks nest in many different sites: under buildings, in trees, on stacks of straw and, most common of all, in rabbit burrows in old sand dunes. Newly hatched young travel with their parents to suitable feeding areas, but after about a week the family often splits up and the young band together in crèches of as many as 100 or more, with only a few adults in attendance. The young later become more independent, and may even brood one another.

From July, adults leave their breeding grounds and fly to traditional moulting areas where they will be flightless for about four weeks. Many European Shelducks gather off the coast of the Netherlands and Germany, and smaller numbers moult in Bridgwater Bay in Somerset and on some smaller estuaries.

Britain and Ireland is now the winter home for about one-third of the western European population of Shelducks.

Mandarin Duck *Aix galericulata*

This attractive duck was, as its name suggests, first brought from China or Japan as an ornamental species for parks and gardens. In the 20th century, escapes started to breed and feral populations became established.

Mandarins are very secretive and are usually found on lakes fringed with trees and shrubs which overhang the water. They are more at home in woodland than are our other ducks; in flight they can easily manoeuvre between trees, and regularly perch on branches. Mandarins usually use holes in trees as nest-sites.

Outside the breeding season, in places where Mandarins are common, they occur in flocks.

Egyptian Goose

Larger than Shelduck – 68 cm. Unlike either typical duck or goose. Has long legs and upright stance. Heavy bill. Adult (**1**) has brown smudge around eye, dark collar, brown patch on breast and green speculum. Back is either red-brown or grey. Large white wing-patches in flight. Young in their 1st winter (**2**) are duller, without eye-patch and breast spot. *Found near inland lakes in East Anglia.*
(Map: page 198)

Shelduck

Larger than Mallard – 62 cm. Adult is white with red bill and legs, dark green head, and brown breast band. Black wing-tips obvious in flight. Green speculum. Male (**3**) has knob on bill. Female (**4**) has less well defined pattern and narrower breast band. Juvenile (**5**) is grey-brown above with white face. *Found in coastal areas, especially estuaries. Will visit inland lakes and sometimes nests inland.*
(Map: page 198)

Mandarin Duck

Smaller than Mallard – 45 cm. Adult male (**6**) is very striking with crest, broad white eye-stripe, multi-coloured plumage, red bill, long orange neck feathers and orange 'sails'. Female (**7**) has grey-brown upperparts, spotted flanks and white 'spectacles'. Male in eclipse resembles female. Whistling call. In flight, both sexes show white belly and green speculum. *Around wood-fringed lakes mostly in parts of central and southern England.*
(Map: page 198)

Shelduck

Egyptian Goose

Mandarin Ducks

♀

♂

1 Egyptian Geese

2 Egyptian Goose *juvenile*

3 Shelduck ♂

5 Shelduck *juvenile*

7 Mandarin Duck ♀

6 Mandarin Duck ♂

4 Shelduck ♀

Hilary Burn

Mallard *Anas platyrhynchos*

The most widespread duck in the world: found throughout the Northern Hemisphere and has been introduced to Australia and New Zealand. It has been domesticated for over 2,000 years and there are now many breeds which are kept for eggs or for eating.

The Mallard is one of several duck species which find much of their food on or near the surface of the water and are known as 'dabbling ducks'. The Mallard's food is varied and includes seeds and other vegetable matter, insects and their larvae, small shellfish and even frogs. To find their food, they will often 'up-end' and occasionally dive; often they will fly to nearby fields to feed after dark.

Like other ducks, the male, or drake, is more colourful than the female, or duck. The drake's bright plumage is used in courtship, but he plays no part in nest-building, incubation or rearing the young. The duck is cryptically camouflaged with her mottled plumage and dark line disguising her eye. The nest is made from grass, leaves and down, plucked from the duck's own breast. Although usually situated on the ground, the nest may be in a tree, 10 m or more from the ground.

Young Mallards leave the nest within 24 hours of hatching and can swim and feed themselves straightaway. If danger threatens, the duck will make a noisy getaway and the young will scatter and dive; with luck, the family will join up again when the danger is past.

Feathers must remain in good condition and all birds must moult and grow new feathers at least once a year. Mallards, like other ducks, moult at the end of their breeding season and drakes grow a drab camouflage-plumage and resemble the ducks; they are then said to be 'in eclipse'. For about two weeks they are flightless, but after their flight feathers are regrown they gradually moult their body feathers again and the drakes reappear in their breeding plumage.

Most Mallards in Britain and Ireland are resident, but in winter are joined by others from Iceland or northern Europe.

Mallard
50–65 cm. Male (**1**) has bottle-green head, white collar, purple-brown breast, grey body and black tail with two curly feathers. Purple speculum. Female (**2**) is mottled brown with purple speculum and dark stripe through eyes. Males in eclipse (**3**) (June–September) resemble females but have yellow bills and darker crowns. Call of female is familiar 'kwark-kwark', male's call is quieter 'arrk'. *Common throughout Britain and Ireland on ponds, lakes, reservoirs, rivers and coastal marshes. Often seen on the sea in winter.*
(Map: page 198)

Domesticated Mallards have a variety of colours. They sometimes mix with wild ducks.

♂

♀

♂ up-ending

juvenile

3 eclipse
♂

2 ♀

1 ♂

Mallards

Hilary Burn.

(Eurasian) Wigeon *Anas penelope*

Only small numbers of Wigeons breed in Britain; the flocks which appear in winter are mainly migrants from Iceland, northern Europe or even Russia.

Once, Wigeons were seen regularly only on salt marshes and estuaries, but following disease in an important food, eel-grass, in 1930, they started to range wider and are now frequent visitors to inland lakes, flood meadows, marshes, gravel pits and reservoirs.

The Wigeon is vegetarian and may often be seen grazing on grass, and picking up food from the water's edge or from the surface of a lake. Sometimes, it follows swans and picks up food which has been pulled out of deeper water and would normally be out of reach for a Wigeon. This is known as 'commensal feeding', one species' activities benefiting another.

(Eurasian) Teal *Anas crecca*

The Teal is the smallest European duck. In flight, a flock can resemble waders as they twist and turn with rapidly beating wings.

Teals may breed near fresh water in many localities, but it is the rushy moorland pools of northern Britain where breeding numbers are greatest.

In winter, Teals from Iceland, Scandinavia and Russia migrate to Britain and Ireland. The largest numbers are seen around our coast, but many come inland where they feed in shallow water using their bills to filter mud in their search for seeds. Most feeding takes place at night, when there are fewer predators around. During the day, Teals can be seen roosting on water, often close together in small groups.

Garganey *Anas querquedula*

The Garganey is the only duck which migrates to Europe for the summer. In autumn, it returns to its winter quarters in West Africa. On its 5,000-km journey, it will cross the Mediterranean, the North African coast and the Sahara in a single flight. Some travel south through Spain, but return, the following spring, through Italy: this is known as loop migration.

The largest populations of Garganeys are in eastern Europe and Russia; Britain is on the edge of the species' range. Most of the small number which breed are found in southern and eastern England. Once there were many more wet fields and marshes and more nest sites for Garganeys. Now it is important that the few remaining sites are not drained.

Wigeon
Smaller than Mallard – 48 cm. Small bill and rounded crown. Male (**1**) has chestnut head with buff stripe, grey body and pale breast. In flight, has white belly and shoulder patches. Female (**2**) has dark green speculum. 1st-winter male is like adult without white shoulders. Commonly seen in flocks. Call is far-carrying whistle, 'whee-oo'.
Breeds mainly in the north. Winter visitor to variety of wetlands farther south, particularly coastal marshes.
(Map: page 198)

Teal
Much smaller than Mallard – 36 cm. Small short-necked duck. Male's (**3**) chestnut-and-green head often appears dark. Grey body, white stripe above wing and yellow patch near tail. Female (**4**) like small Mallard with green speculum. Rapid wingbeats, pale belly and white stripe on wings in flight. Piping call.
Breeds near reed-fringed lakes mainly in the north. Widespread in winter liking shallow lakes, flooded fields and coastal marshes.
(Map: page 198)

Garganey
Smaller than Mallard, slightly larger than Teal – 39 cm. Male (**5**) has white stripe over eye and, in flight, blue-grey forewing. Female (**6**) like Teal, but dark eye-stripe, pale stripe over eye and, in flight, grey forewing with duller speculum.
Summer visitor, March to September. Likes shallow, reedy pools.
(Map: page 198)

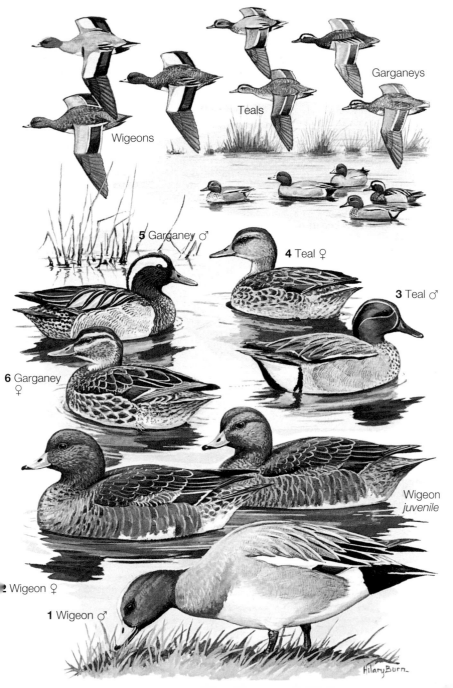

Garganeys

Teals

Wigeons

5 Garganey ♂

4 Teal ♀

3 Teal ♂

6 Garganey ♀

Wigeon
juvenile

2 Wigeon ♀

1 Wigeon ♂

HilaryBurn

Gadwall *Anas strepera*

The Gadwall was introduced into Britain around 1850 and is now established as a regular breeding species. The Brecklands of East Anglia were the original stronghold, but further areas have now been colonised. In winter, about three-quarters of the British population remains in its breeding areas, and numbers are increased by additional Gadwalls arriving from Iceland and northern Europe.

The food of the Gadwall is mainly plants or seeds which are picked up from the water-surface, or obtained by 'up-ending' and reaching 30 cm or so below the surface. Sometimes Gadwalls follow species which feed in deeper water, such as Coots, Goldeneyes or Mute Swans, in order to pick up any food which floats to the top of the water.

(Northern) Pintail *Anas acuta*

This very attractive duck is a rare breeding species in Britain and Ireland, but it is far more numerous in winter, when others fly in from Iceland, northern and eastern Europe.

A variety of animal and vegetable food is picked from the surface water or taken when the birds 'up-end' to reach the bottom of deeper water. The long neck enables the Pintail to find food out of the reach of other 'dabbling ducks'. Male Pintails have slightly longer necks than do the females, which enables them to feed in even deeper water.

(Northern) Shoveler *Anas clypeata*

Inside the long, broad bill of the Shoveler are rows of tiny spines called lamellae which are a most efficient filter for trapping the minute animals and plant remains which make up its diet. Although some food may occasionally be found by diving or by 'up-ending', the most usual method is for the bill to be used for filtering the surface water. Groups of Shovelers may feed close together and sometimes swim in circles or in lines, which stirs up the water and brings more food to the surface.

By October, most of the Shovelers which breed in Britain and Ireland have moved south to France or Spain, while a few may reach the North African coast. They are replaced on our lakes, however, by others which migrate here from northern and eastern Europe.

In areas where Shovelers breed, the males can often be seen chasing each other and displaying with a comical head-bobbing. Often these displays are accompanied by sharp 'took, took-took' calls.

Gadwall
Smaller than Mallard – 51 cm. Male (**1**) is grey with black tail and white speculum. Female (**2**) resembles female Mallard, but has white speculum, orange sides to bill and brown tail. Both sexes show white bellies in flight. Male has croaking call, female, soft 'quack'. In eclipse, male is like dark female.
Breeds mainly in East Anglia, around freshwater lakes. Visits inland lakes in other areas in winter.
(Map: page 198)

Pintail
Mallard-size – 50–66 cm. Graceful, long-necked duck. Male (**3**) has 10 cm-long pointed tail, white breast, brown head with white stripe and grey body. Female (**4**) is like female Mallard, but has longer neck, greyer plumage and grey bill. Long neck and tail obvious in flight. Male in eclipse is like grey female.
Mainly a winter visitor to estuaries or inland lakes. A few pairs breed near shallow water. (Map: page 198)

Shoveler
Smaller than Mallard – 48 cm. Male (**5**) has green head, huge bill and white body with chestnut flanks and belly. Female (**6**) like female Mallard, but with large bill. In flight, wings appear set far back on body and both sexes show blue-grey patch on forewings: male brighter than female. In eclipse, male is similar to female.
In summer likes shallow marshy areas. Widespread in winter. (Map: page 199)

Shovelers

Mallard

Pintails

Gadwalls

Mallard ♀

2 Gadwall ♀

1 Gadwall ♂

6 Shoveler ♀

5 Shoveler ♂

Shoveler ♂
partial eclipse

4 Pintail ♀

3 Pintail ♂

Hilary Burn

Red-crested Pochard *Netta rufina*

Small numbers of this attractive diving duck breed in Europe. Also Red-crested Pochards are common in collections of waterfowl and many have been introduced to ornamental lakes. In autumn, a few truly wild ones may reach Britain from the Netherlands, but are usually impossible to distinguish from free-flying escapes.

(Common) Pochard *Aythya ferina*

The number of wintering Pochards has increased in recent years, helped by new flooded gravel pits and reservoirs, but only a few hundred breed in Britain.

It eats mostly plants which grow underwater, especially stoneworts (*Chara*). It usually dives for about 15 seconds and feeds at a depth of 3 m. Males often feed in deeper water than females. Much feeding takes place at night and they roost during the day.

Like other diving ducks, Pochards are seldom seen alone outside of the breeding season and often large flocks can be seen on lakes where food is plentiful.

The **Ferruginous Duck** *Aythya nyroca* is a rare winter visitor from eastern Europe. Its chestnut plumage, white patch under the tail and domed head help to single it out from all other wildfowl, except some warm-coloured female Tufted Ducks with white under their tails.

Tufted Duck *Aythya fuligula*

Watch a family of Tufted Ducks and you will notice the young chasing midges or looking for seeds on the water surface, but sometimes diving to find midge larvae underwater. The adults dive deeper, as they feed mainly on molluscs, at a depth of 7 m or more.

This, our commonest diving duck, first colonised Britain 150 years ago. In some areas, they nest among colonies of gulls, which helps give protection to the sitting females.

Tufted Ducks are present throughout the year, and some visit lakes in towns and cities. In winter, many more migrate here from Iceland and northeast Europe.

(Greater) Scaup *Aythya marila*

This species has occasionally nested in Britain, but never regularly. The flocks which visit some of our estuaries are made up of winter migrants from Iceland or northern Europe. The chief food is shellfish. Once, large flocks formed to feed at traditional sites on mussel-beds and where raw sewage was discharged into the sea, but with cleaner coasts the flocks are usually smaller and dispersed. Where food is plentiful, most feeding takes place at night.

Red-crested Pochard
Size of Mallard – 55 cm.
Male (**1**) has large orange head, red bill, black neck and belly, and white flanks.
Female (**2**) is brown with pale cheeks and dark crown, grey bill with pink edges. White wing-bar shows in flight.
Introduced into parks.
A few wild individuals visit eastern Britain in winter.
(Map: page 199)

Pochard
Smaller than Mallard – 45 cm. Short neck and steep forehead. Male (**3**) has grey back, black breast and reddish-brown head. Female (**4**) is grey-brown with blotchy cheeks.
Found on freshwater lakes in winter. Breeds in small numbers, but scarce in Ireland. (Map: page 199)

Tufted Duck
Smaller than Mallard – 43 cm. Male (**5**) is black with white flanks and belly, and drooping crest on back of head. Female (**6**) is dark brown with pale brown flanks. Male in eclipse resembles female. Both male and female show white wing-bar in flight.
Breeds and winters on inland lakes or slow-flowing rivers.
(Map: page 199)

Scaup
Larger and more bulky than Tufted Duck – 47 cm. Rounded head and white wing-bar. Often leaps when diving. Male (**7**) has black head, breast and tail, white flanks and grey back. Female (**8**) is dark brown with large white patch at base of bill. (Female Tufted may have similar patch.)
Winter visitor to coastal waters, especially estuaries.
(Map: page 199)

Scaups

Red-crested Pochards

Pochards

Tufted Ducks

Ferruginous Duck ♂

2 ♀

♂

1 Red-crested Pochards

8 Scaup ♀

7 Scaup ♂

6 Tufted Ducks ♀

4 Pochard ♀

♀

3 Pochard ♂

Tufted Duck ♂ *eclipse*

Hilary Burn

5 Tufted Duck ♂

(Common) Eider *Somateria mollissima*

These are 'sea ducks', a term used to describe species of duck which spend most of their lives on the open sea.

Eiders nest in the open, often on rocky islands. Nests are lined with downy feathers plucked from the female's breast. The female incubates her four to six eggs for 27 days; she seldom leaves the nest, and by the end she will have lost more than one-third of her body weight. As soon as the young have hatched and dried, they make their way to the sea. This journey is dangerous as the tiny ducklings are easy prey for predators such as gulls, but once on the water they can escape by diving.

For a few days the young are guarded by their mothers, but the ducklings can feed only in shallow water, while adults need deeper water: soon, the young of various families join together in crèches with a few ducks in attendance, while the rest of the adults go off to feed.

The powerful bill of the Eider is used for pulling mussels and other shellfish off rocks; these molluscs are swallowed whole and ground up in the bird's gizzard.

Long-tailed Duck *Clangula hyemalis*

There can be few more exciting and beautiful sights than a flock of Long-tailed Ducks on a stormy sea in winter. The spectacular winter plumage of the male is, however, only one of three distinct plumages, but the others are usually only seen on the Arctic breeding grounds.

This species regularly breeds farther north than any other species of duck. It feeds on shellfish which are found by diving up to 20 m underwater.

Ruddy Duck *Oxyura jamaicensis*

This small diving duck belongs to a group of ducks known as 'stiff-tails'. It is native to North America and those seen wild in Britain are descended from about 70 young which escaped from the Wildfowl Trust's collection at Slimbridge in Gloucestershire between 1956 and 1963. They then colonised parts of the English Midlands and have now spread to new areas. Some have reached Spain, where there is a concern that the Ruddy Duck will threaten the endangered population of the closely related, native White-headed Duck with which it hybridises.

When displaying, the male Ruddy Duck cocks his tail, raises two tufts of feathers on his head and inflates an air-sac in his neck; he then rapidly drums on his swollen neck with his bill, which creates a hollow sound and also produces many air bubbles on the surface of the water.

Eider

Size of Mallard – 60 cm. Large, wedge-shaped bill. Male (**1**) is white with black underparts and black crown. Green marks on back of head and rosy flush on breast. Female (**2**) is brown. Young males and males in moult (**3**) have a variety of dark brown and white plumages.
Breeds around rocky coasts in northern Britain. Also seen around southern coasts mainly in winter.
(Map: page 199)

Long-tailed Duck

Smaller than Mallard – 44 cm, but tail of male may be extra 13 cm. Small, neat duck with small bill. Male (**4**) is brown in summer with pale flanks and white face patch. Largely white in winter (**5**) with dark patch on cheek. Female (**6**) has dark body, pale head with dark smudge on cheeks. No wing-bar in flight.
Visits inshore waters in winter mainly in Scotland, northern England and Ireland.
(Map: page 199)

Ruddy Duck

Much smaller than Mallard – 39 cm. Male (**7**) is reddish-brown with darker head, white cheeks, white undertail and blue bill. Female (**8**) is brown, has buff cheeks with dark line under the eye. Both sexes have stiff projecting tails which may be cocked or lowered on to the water.
Breeds on inland lakes mainly in central England.
(Map: page 199)

Long-tailed Ducks

Ruddy Ducks

Eiders

5 winter ♂   **4** *summer* ♂   *immature* ♂

Long-tailed Ducks

6 ♀

1 Eider ♂   **3** Eider ♂ moulting

2 Eider ♀

7 ♂

8 ♀

Ruddy Ducks

Hilary Burn.

Common Scoter (Black Scoter) *Melanitta nigra*

On looking out to sea in winter it is not unusual to see flocks of dark brown and black ducks swimming, diving and flying low over the waves. These are Common Scoters, mostly winter migrants from Iceland and northern Europe.

Common Scoters are true 'sea duck' and feed by diving for shellfish. Underwater, they use their feet for propulsion, but their wings are partly opened, which helps to steady them in their search for food on the sea bed.

As scoters spend so much time on the open sea, especially in the North Sea and in busy shipping lanes, they regularly fall victim to oil-slicks.

The Common Scoter was first discovered nesting in Scotland in the last century, since when a few new nesting sites have been discovered, especially in Ireland. It remains a rare breeding duck here and less than 200 pairs nest in Britain and Ireland each year.

Velvet Scoter *Melanitta fusca*

The Velvet Scoters which visit our coastal waters in winter come from their breeding grounds in Scandinavia or Russia. After breeding, in late July, a concentration of many thousands gathers off the coast of Denmark for their annual moult.

They visit our coasts in winter, especially between January and March. Numbers are small, but a few Velvet Scoters often join larger flocks of Common Scoters, the largest numbers often being in the Moray Firth.

(Common) Goldeneye *Bucephala clangula*

The species gets its name from its beautiful golden eyes which are usually difficult to see unless one happens to get very close. Most Goldeneyes are winter visitors from northern Europe, but since 1970 increasing numbers have nested in Scotland. The nest is usually 10–15 m off the ground in a hole in a tree-trunk. They will also readily adopt nest-boxes; the erection of these in coniferous forests close to water in central Scotland has helped the species to colonise.

During late winter and early spring, it is not unusual to see Goldeneyes displaying. Groups of several drakes gather with one or more ducks in attendance. The drakes throw back their heads, displaying their brilliant white breasts while they make a low growling call.

The curious hump on a Goldeneye's head contains chambers of air, which, it is thought, give the bird a reserve air supply to enable it to dive for longer periods. They can dive to over 4 m and stay under for 30 seconds or more.

Common Scoter

Smaller than Mallard – 49 cm. Male (**1**) is only all-black duck, with yellow and black bill with a knob at its base. Female (**2**) is dark brown with paler cheeks, throat and neck. Neither sex shows any wing-bar in flight.
Flocks seen in coastal waters in winter. A few pairs nest in western Scotland and Ireland. (Map: page 200)

Velvet Scoter

Size of Mallard – 55 cm. White wing-patches very noticeable in flight. On the water male (**3**) is black with white wing-patch sometimes visible, white mark under eye and orange side to its large bill. Female (**4**) is dark brown with white wing-patch and often pale patches on head.
Seen on the sea in winter, often with Common Scoters and Eiders. (Map: page 200)

Goldeneye

Smaller than Mallard – 46 cm. Male (**5**) is black-and-white, with glossy green sheen to its black, domed head, white patch between bill and eye, and black back. Female (**6**) is greyish with brown head and white collar. 1st-winter male (**7**) is like female, but browner with no collar. Wings make whistling noise in flight. Both sexes show white wing-patches in flight.
Seen around coasts and on inland lakes between October and March. About 100 pairs breed in Scotland. (Map: page 200)

Goldeneyes

Common
Scoters

Velvet
Scoters

Eider ♀

3 Velvet Scoter ♂

4 Velvet Scoter ♀

1 Common Scoter ♂

2 Common Scoter ♀

7 Goldeneye
1st-winter ♂

5 Goldeneye
♂ displaying

6 Goldeneye ♀

Hilary Burn.

Smew *Mergellus albellus*

The Smew, or 'White Nun' as the male of this beautiful winter visitor from Russia and northeast Europe used to be called, is a member of a group of ducks known as 'sawbills' (see below). Of the three sawbills likely to be seen in Britain, the Smew is the rarest.

The crest on the drake's crown is raised during courtship. Like other sawbills, Smews eat fish, but they also feed on insect larvae and shellfish, which they find by diving to a depth of up to 4 m.

Red-breasted Merganser *Mergus serrator*

Although Red-breasted Mergansers have nested in Scotland and Ireland for centuries, they started nesting in England only in 1950 and in Wales in 1953, and more recently have spread farther south.

Unlike other ducks, sawbills chase fish underwater, and their long, narrow bills with serrated edges help them to catch and hold their slippery prey. When fishing they often look for prey by submerging their bill and eyes below the surface. Sometimes a group of mergansers will fish together, hunting in circles or semi-circles and diving at the same time: a profitable method if a shoal is discovered.

Red-breasted Mergansers nest on the ground, and line their nests with grey breast feathers. Goosanders, which nest in holes, use paler feathers as a nest-lining as they have less need for camouflage. After hatching, large groups of young from different broods sometimes gather together with a few females, known as 'aunties', to look after them.

Goosander *Mergus merganser*

The Goosander, our largest sawbill, is a relative new-comer, being only a rare winter visitor 130 years ago; it was first found nesting in 1871 in Scotland and in England in 1941. Its arrival was not welcomed by fishermen who were concerned about the possible effect on fish stocks, but, in spite of persecution, it became established and continues to expand its range in Britain, recently reaching Wales and Devon.

Where there are trees, the Goosander regularly nests in holes up to 18 m from the ground, and from these nests the newly hatched, flightless ducklings must jump. In treeless areas, the female nests among rocks near water. Once in the water, young ducklings are often carried on the female's back when in danger.

Like other ducks, the drake has an eclipse plumage, and from July to late September he resembles the female.

Smew
Much smaller than Mallard – 26 cm. Male (**1**) is white with black mask and other black lines. Female (**2**) is grey with reddish-brown head and contrasting white cheeks and throat. Black-and-white wing-pattern shown by both sexes in flight.
A few visit inland lakes in winter. Occasionally seen on the sea. (Map: page 200)

Red-breasted Merganser
Mallard-sized – 55 cm. Long, thin bill and wispy crest. Male (**3**) has green head, chestnut breast and white collar. Female (**4**) has grey body, pale throat blending into brown, and brown head merging with brownish-grey neck. In flight, white wing-patches shown by both sexes, but larger patch of male is crossed by black bars.
Breeds in northern and western parts of British Isles, often on lakes or rivers away from the coast. Generally seen on or near the coast in winter. (Map: page 200)

Goosander
Larger than Mallard – 62 cm. Long body and long, thin red bill. Male (**5**) is pinkish-white, with dark green head and black back. Female (**6**) has drooping crest, well-defined white throat and marked division between brown head and grey neck. Male has black-and-white wings in flight, female shows square, white wing-patches.
Breeds on lakes and rivers in northern Britain. Visits southern lakes and reservoirs in winter. (Map: page 200)

Red-breasted Mergansers

Goosanders

Smews

6 ♀

Goosanders
1st-winter

5 Goosander ♂

4 Red-breasted
Merganser
♀

4 ♀

3 ♂

Red-breasted Mergansers

1 Smew ♂

2 Smew ♀

Hilary Burn.

Marsh Harrier *Circus aeruginosus*

Once, when there were many large fens and marshes in Britain, Marsh Harriers were common, but, gradually, reedbeds were drained to make more farmland, and these spectacular birds of prey became rare. As they declined, their eggs were taken by collectors and many were shot, stuffed, mounted and displayed in glass cases; eventually, they ceased to nest here. Several years passed before they returned to Norfolk where, under protection, they survived and spread to a few other marshes.

The chief prey is small mammals and waterbirds. Males are sometimes polygamous, having more than one mate. Like other harriers, the male will often call the female off the nest; she will then rise, fly behind and below him and catch the prey which he drops.

Although some Marsh Harriers are seen in Britain in winter, most are summer visitors and migrate to Africa in autumn. Many never complete the journey because they are shot by hunters in southern Europe.

Hen Harrier *Circus cyaneus*

A male Hen Harrier quartering moorland stirs emotions. For the birdwatcher, it is an exhilarating sight. For most gamekeepers, it is a traditional enemy. Tolerated on some shooting estates, but ruthlessly and illegally exterminated on others, persecution has apparently halted the southward spread of this species from its Orkney stronghold.

When hunting, harriers fly slowly, a metre or two from the ground, taking a zig-zag course into the wind. Ears, as well as eyes, are used to locate a small bird or mammal in the dense vegetation. Harriers are among the few day-flying raptors which use their ears to help them find their prey and it is assumed that their keen hearing is further aided by the owl-like disc round their face.

A male may have a territory of more than a square kilometre and within it have several mates. In winter, Hen Harriers leave their breeding grounds and visit lowland or coastal areas, and groups of a dozen or more may gather at dusk and roost communally.

Montagu's Harrier *Circus pygargus*

First identified by Colonel George Montagu in 1802, this, our rarest harrier, has declined alarmingly since 1950. By the 1970s, very few nested here. Happily, in the past few years more have attempted to breed and, with protection provided by the RSPB and other conservation bodies, young are being successfully reared once again.

Female and young Hen and Montagu's Harriers look very similar; they are jointly known as 'ring-tails'.

Marsh Harrier
Size of Buzzard – 48–56 cm. Largest harrier. Long wings, long tail and long legs. Often flies low with wings in shallow V. Male (**1**) has dark body, yellow head, grey tail and grey on wings. Female (**2**) is dark brown with straw-coloured head and fore-wings. Juveniles (**3**) similar, but may be all-brown. *Mainly a summer visitor breeding in a few reedbeds, and occasionally among arable crops mainly in eastern Britain.* (Map: page 200)

Hen Harrier
Smaller than Buzzard – 44–52 cm. Male (**4**) is silver-grey with white underparts, black wing-tips and a white rump. Female (**5**) is larger, and is brown with white rump. Often hunts low over the ground. Wings held in shallow V when soaring. *Breeds on moorland in northern and western British Isles. Visits open country in other areas in winter, especially near the coast.* (Map: page 200)

Montagu's Harrier
Smaller than Buzzard – 43–47 cm. Male (**6**) is grey with pale underparts and streaks on belly and flanks; has black wing-tips and a black wing-bar. Rump is pale grey. Female (**7**) is similar to female Hen, but less bulky with slimmer, more pointed wings, smaller white rump, pale area behind eye and dark cheeks. Juvenile (**8**) has rufous underparts, sometimes streaked on sides of breast. *Rare summer visitor to arable farmland, mainly in southern Britain.* (Map: page 200)

1 ♂

Marsh Harriers

3 *juvenile*

2 ♀

6 Montagu's Harrier ♂

7 Montagu's Harrier ♀

5 Hen Harrier ♀

8 Montagu's Harrier *juvenile*

4 Hen Harrier ♂

Hilary Burn

(Northern) Goshawk *Accipiter gentilis*

Once virtually extinct as a British breeding bird, the Goshawk now breeds here again and has recolonised many forests.

In Britain, Wood Pigeons and crows are common prey and mammals up to the size of hares may also be killed. Prey is usually seized after a fast, low, short flight.

(Eurasian) Sparrowhawk *Accipiter nisus*

A hunting Sparrowhawk often chooses a flock of small birds. Using the cover of nearby trees, bushes or hedges it will move closer until, suddenly, it makes a short dash to pick on perhaps the slowest bird, which is pursued, seized by a large foot, carried away, plucked and eaten.

This secretive raptor has been persecuted, and also suffered from the effects of harmful pesticides. The population has recovered and Sparrowhawks are now breeding in many of our woods. They also often visit towns where they hunt small birds in gardens.

Birds such as finches and thrushes are the chief prey, but the much larger female may take birds up to the size of a Wood Pigeon. A few mammals are also eaten.

(Common) Buzzard *Buteo buteo*

Whether soaring effortlessly or sitting patiently on a telegraph pole, Common Buzzards are impressive as they are the largest raptor that many of us ever see. Once very common, they were persecuted in the last century and declined, but since then they have recolonised some of their former haunts and are now spreading eastwards. This is likely to continue provided gamekeepers observe the law and resist the temptation to shoot, trap or poison them.

Common Buzzards hunt from a perch, from the ground or while hovering. Rabbits are an important food. In the 1950s, when the disease myxomatosis killed many rabbits, Common Buzzards also decreased for a time. Other food includes small mammals, especially voles, carrion, insects and even earthworms.

In early spring, pairs display near crag or tree nest-sites. They spiral upwards, the lighter male climbing fastest and then diving at the female.

Rough-legged Buzzard *Buteo lagopus*

A buzzard of the Arctic tundra which migrates south in winter and may visit coastal areas of eastern Britain. Occasionally, larger numbers arrive in autumn; these invasions occur when the population level is high and may be triggered by food shortages in the breeding areas.

Goshawk
Much larger than Sparrowhawk – 48–62 cm. Female (**1**) is Buzzard-sized. Male (**2**) is smaller. Relatively short, broad rounded wings and long tail. White stripe over eye and dark cheeks gives hooded appearance. White undertail-coverts. Flies low to ground or soars; when soaring, hind edge of wing is S-shaped.
Rare breeding species in a few large woods.
(Map: page 201)

Sparrowhawk
Smaller than Wood Pigeon – 28–38 cm. Female (**3**) larger than male (**4**). Short, rounded wings, long tail and barred underparts. Typical flight is a dash through woods or along hedges. Also soars.
Lives mainly in woodland.
(Map: page 201)

Common Buzzard (5)
Large raptor – 54 cm. Female slightly larger than male. Broad wings, short neck and short, rounded, barred tail. Variable plumage: upperparts brown, paler underparts with dark wing-patches. Often soars with wings held in shallow V. Has 'mewing' call.
Lives mainly in northern and western Britain and in northern Ireland.
(Map: page 201)

Rough-legged Buzzard (6)
Size of Buzzard – 55 cm, with longer wings and tail. Variable plumage, but usually pale underparts contrasting with dark belly-patch, tail-band, wing-patches and wing-tips.
Sometimes winters in eastern Britain.
(Map: page 201)

Goshawks

1 ♀

2 ♂

♀

♂

Sparrowhawks

Common Buzzards

Rough-legged Buzzard

Common Buzzard

6 Rough-legged Buzzard

4 Sparrowhawk ♂

3 Sparrowhawk ♀

5 Common Buzzard

Red Kite *Milvus milvus*

Once, Red Kites were common scavengers, even on the streets of London, but improved sanitation, loss of suitable habitat and, most important, persecution by man, almost wiped out the species. Only ten pairs remained, all in Wales, at the beginning of the 20th century.

The hanging oak woods in the steep-sided valleys of central Wales are still the Red Kite's stronghold. Special protection has helped the population recover, but egg-collectors still raid nests and upland feeding haunts are lost through planting with conifers.

Recently, young kites have been released in England and Scotland and healthy breeding populations are becoming established. In winter many kites may assemble round a food supply and large numbers will often gather at communal roosts at dusk. Kites eat carrion, small mammals, insects and worms.

Golden Eagle *Aquila chrysaetos*

The Golden Eagle has been cruelly persecuted and the Scottish Highlands are now its only stronghold in Britain. Recently there has been some recolonisation, and one pair nests regularly in the Lake District.

Golden Eagles feed mainly on mammals and birds, especially hares, Ptarmigan and Red Grouse. Carrion is also frequently eaten. When hunting, these eagles range over an area of 4,000–5,000 hectares.

Usually two eggs are laid in the traditional eyrie in March. There is an interval of several days between the eggs hatching, and, if there is not sufficient food for them both, the elder chick kills the younger.

In spite of legal protection, these birds are still killed by some keepers and breeding pairs are often disturbed by climbers, walkers and even birdwatchers.

Osprey *Pandion haliaetus*

Hunted to extinction in Britain in 1916, the Osprey was a rare visitor until 1954 when a pair nested once again. Since then they have been specially protected. The pair at Loch Garten in Inverness-shire has become world-famous and is visited annually by thousands of tourists.

Ospreys feed on fish, which are located from the air and caught after a spectacular aerial dive during which the bird plummets down head first, and at the last moment the feet are thrown forward to seize the fish. The bird is well adapted: its nostrils can be closed, plumage is waterproof, talons are long and curved and there are spines under its toes to grip the slippery prey.

Red Kite (1)

Larger than Buzzard – 63 cm. Long forked tail, long wings with pale patches on undersides. Pale head, dark back and reddish underparts. Very manoeuvrable in flight. Often glides on flat wings and flexes tail.
Breeding restricted to central Wales and also reintroduced elsewhere in Britain. A rare vagrant to other areas. Nests in old oak woods.
(Map: page 201)

Golden Eagle

Much larger than Buzzard – 80 cm, wingspan over 2 m. Large and powerful. Long wings are held in shallow V when soaring, or flat when gliding. Tail is long and head protrudes well in front of wings. Adult (**2**) is dark brown with yellow head and neck. Immature (**3**) has white base to tail and white patches in winter.
Nests on crags, sea cliffs or in trees. Found mostly in Scottish Highlands.
(Map: page 201)

Osprey (4)

Slightly larger than Buzzard – 56 cm, with longer wings. Dark brown above and white below. Streaked breast and dark patches on underside of wings. Dark mask and slight crest. Often soars; wings have bowed appearance resembling those of a large gull. Plunges feet-first for fish.
Usually seen between April and September. Breeds in pines near Scottish lochs and seen farther south mostly on migration in spring and autumn. A few pairs have recently begun to nest in England. (Map: page 201)

1 Red Kite

Osprey

3 Golden Eagle *immature*

2 Golden Eagle *adult*

Common Buzzard

Osprey

4 Osprey

Hilary Burn.

Peregrine Falcon *Falco peregrinus*

The popularity and fortunes of the Peregrine Falcon have changed over the centuries. In the Middle Ages, when hunting with falcons was very common, the Peregrine was a symbol of royalty or nobility and specially protected by severe penalties. Later, when game shooting became popular, Peregrines, like other birds of prey, were treated as vermin and shot and trapped.

During World War II, homing pigeons were released by airmen who crashed and, to protect these pigeons, Peregrines which nested on many sea cliffs were destroyed. After the war, the Peregrine population started to recover, but by the 1960s it had declined again until the numbers were reduced by over 50%. The cause of this reduction was found to be DDT and other chemicals used to protect farm crops from insect pests. These 'pesticides' were being used on seeds which were eaten by small birds which were, in their turn, eaten by Peregrines. The build-up of chemicals in Peregrines resulted either in their death or, at lower concentrations, in unsuccessful breeding: the eggs, which were often infertile, had such thin shells that they frequently broke during incubation.

Following the withdrawal of the most dangerous chemicals, the Peregrine population has slowly increased, although the illegal activities of some pigeon enthusiasts, egg-collectors and falconers prevent the number of Peregrines fully recovering in many areas.

For successful breeding, Peregrines require open country over which to hunt, plenty of birds to feed on, and steep rock for nest sites (although a few have taken to nesting on buildings and on electricity pylons). Outside the breeding season, they generally leave their upland homes and move to land below 600 m, especially coastal areas where food is plentiful.

Increasingly, Peregrines are being seen around some of our cities, where prey, in the form of feral Rock Doves, is readily available.

Although the Peregrine will catch and kill mammals, it specialises in hunting birds, particularly birds in flight. Its prey may vary in size from Blue Tit to Great Black-backed Gull. The best-known method of attack is the 'stoop': Peregrines spot their prey from a high perch or while circling, then they fold back their wings and drop at a very high speed to strike their prey with a foot, often tearing it open with a talon which kills the victim outright or knocks it senseless so that the Peregrine may then recover it from the ground. Sometimes prey is seized in mid-air or occasionally picked skilfully off its perch.

Peregrine Falcon
Large and powerful falcon 36–48 cm. Male (**1**) is much smaller than female (**2**). Broad pointed wings, rather short tail. Adult has blue-black back and buff underparts barred with black. Black head and 'moustache', white cheeks and chin. Juvenile (**3**) has dark brown upperparts. Flight is pigeon-like with long glides. When hunting, often drops from great heights and may reach speeds of over 160 km/h. Most usual call is a chattering 'kek-kek-kek'. *In summer, Peregrines are found on moorland and other open areas usually near crags or sea cliffs. In winter they visit estuaries.*
(Map: page 201)

Carrion
Crow

1 Peregrine Falcon ♂

3 Peregrine
Falcon
juvenile

Rock Doves

Carrion Crow
Hooded race

2 Peregrine Falcon ♀

Hilary Burn.

(Common) Kestrel *Falco tinnunculus*

Equally at home hovering over windswept moors, motorway embankments or noisy town centres, Kestrels must be our most familiar bird of prey. The Kestrel population remained stable when many other birds of prey declined in the 20th century and the species proved itself very adaptable. In recent years, however, it has declined for reasons that are not fully understood.

A Kestrel's diet includes mammals (especially voles), insects, worms and small birds. Hovering, head into the wind, is the most usual method of hunting; when prey is located, the Kestrel glides gently down and, at the last moment, lifts its wings above its back and drops on to the creature. Kestrels often hunt from perches and also catch small birds in flight. They do not limit their hunting to daylight and may hunt at dusk or even after dark, especially on moonlit nights.

Kestrels usually nest in holes in trees, on cliff ledges, on buildings and they will sometimes use nest-boxes.

Merlin *Falco columbarius*

This is Europe's smallest falcon. It feeds mainly on small birds, especially Meadow Pipits and Sky Larks, which it catches in the air, often after a fast and spectacular chase. At other times, Merlins will surprise their prey and the chase will be short. Sometimes, two Merlins will hunt together and they have also been seen to catch birds which were disturbed by other birds of prey. When food is plentiful, it may be stored and eaten later.

Nest-sites are usually on the ground. Sites may be occupied for many years: one site is said to have been used for 19 years, although the adults were killed by gamekeepers each year and no young were reared.

Damage to heather moors by intensive sheep grazing and forestation reduced the Merlin population, although numbers may now be recovering.

Hobby *Falco subbuteo*

This small, spectacular falcon is our only bird of prey to feed regularly on large insects, which it catches in flight with its feet, and feeds as it flies. Dragonflies are its favourite prey, but birds such as Swallows, Swifts and Sky Larks are also often caught in the air.

Hobbies winter in Africa, south of the Sahara, and return to the heathland, downland or farmland of southern and central England in April. They nest in trees, often using unoccupied nests of Carrion Crows.

Kestrel
38 cm. Long, pointed wings and long tail. Wings appear more rounded when soaring. Regularly hovers when hunting. Male and female are similar size. Male (**1**) has chestnut back with black spots and blue-grey head and tail, the tail having a black band above its white tip. Females and juveniles are less colourful with darker, barred backs and tails. *Found in most parts of Britain and Ireland, even beside busy roads and in town centres.* (Map: page 201)

Merlin
Smaller than Kestrel – 27 cm. Male (**2**) has bluish back, reddish striped underparts and black band at end of tail. Female (**3**) is larger with dark brown back and bars on tail, but no dark 'moustache'. Flight is dashing, with rapid wingbeats and short glides. Highly agile when chasing prey. Rarely soars and never hovers. *Lives in open country, especially moorland in summer. Often moves to coastal marshes in winter.* (Map: page 202)

Hobby (4)
Size of Kestrel – 33 cm. Shorter tail than Kestrel and longer, scythe-like wings. Often resembles a large Swift in flight. Dark blue-grey above and heavily streaked below, chestnut flanks and dark 'moustache'. Fast, streamlined and agile in flight, especially chasing large insects or birds. *Summer visitor to open country in southern and central England.* (Map: page 202)

Merlin

Kestrel

Hobby

Sparrowhawk

Kestrel *hovering* ♀

3 Merlin ♀

4 Hobby

1 Kestrel ♂

2 Merlin ♂

Hilary Burn

Red Grouse (Willow Ptarmigan) *Lagopus lagopus*

Large stretches of moorland are carefully managed to ensure that grouse survive in sufficient numbers for good shoots in the autumn and winter. It was to protect this valuable gamebird that many birds of prey were slaughtered by gamekeepers in the past and, in some areas, this persecution continues illegally even today.

Red Grouse are mainly vegetarian, feeding on heather shoots, flowers and seeds; they will also land in trees and bushes to feed on berries. Young grouse eat insects. Although grouse will move to lower-lying farmland in winter, many remain on the moors and burrow in the snow to find food.

All moors may look similar to us, but some are better for grouse than others as these birds require a delicate balance of young shoots for food and old, deep heather for nesting.

Like other young gamebirds, grouse chicks are able to fly before they are fully grown. In summer, while adults are moulting, moors may appear empty as the grouse hide and only occasionally show their heads over the top of the heather.

Very few Red Grouse ever move more than 1.5 km from their breeding areas and it has been proved that the breeding population on any moor is limited to a certain number of cocks which can hold territory; the remaining birds do not move far away, but occupy less favourable habitat where they become weak and easy prey for Golden Eagles, foxes and other predators.

The Red Grouse is the emblem of the journal *British Birds*.

(Rock) Ptarmigan *Lagopus mutus*

These gamebirds live beyond the moors on the high, barren mountain tops where the wind is keenest, snow lies longest and the vegetation is similar to that of the Arctic. Only the severest winter blizzards drive them down to slightly lower, more sheltered places. They feed on shoots, leaves, berries and seeds of low-growing vegetation.

Ski-lifts now take visitors to the mountain tops and in some places Ptarmigan have declined. Elsewhere, they show little fear of man and if approached they are more likely to crouch and 'freeze' than to fly off: their beautifully mottled plumage blends perfectly with the lichen-covered rocks. Their main enemies are Golden Eagles, which regularly search the barren tops.

The Ptarmigan has three distinct seasonal plumages, which is unusual among birds, but each provides it with perfect camouflage which helps it to survive.

Red Grouse

Larger than Grey Partridge – 40 cm. Plump, dark red-brown bird with white stripes on underwings and rounded dark tail. Male (**1**) is redder than female (**2**) and has red wattle over eye. When disturbed, grouse 'explode' from the ground with whirring wings and then glide with bowed wings. Seen in flocks in autumn and winter. Alarm call is a cackling 'kwok-kok-kok'. When displaying, the call sounds like 'Go back-back-back'.
Found on open treeless heather moors and bogs in northern and western Britain and Ireland.
(Map: page 202)

Ptarmigan

Larger than Grey Partridge – 35 cm. Has white wings and underparts and black tail at all seasons, rest of plumage is pure white in winter except that male (**3**) has black mark around eyes. In summer male (**4**) is darker brown than female (**5**) and also has larger red wattle over eye, but in autumn male is grey and female dark brown. Call is a harsh croak and alarm call is a grating sound.
Lives on high, barren mountain tops in central and northern Scotland.
(Map: page 202)

Red Grouse

Ptarmigan

4 ♂ *summer*

3 ♂ *winter*

2 Red Grouse
♀

5 Ptarmigan
♀

1 Red Grouse
♂

Hilary Burn.

Black Grouse *Tetrao tetrix*

Early in the morning, as the sky becomes lighter in the east, the soft crooning calls of the Black Grouse may be heard at the wooded edge of a moor. This is a 'lek', a communal display area where the males, sometimes called 'blackcock', fan their tails, strut around and fight mock battles while the females, or 'greyhens', wait silently nearby. Soon some of them will mate and then the group will melt away.

Black Grouse feed on buds, shoots, leaves, berries and also some insects. They usually feed on the ground, but will also feed in trees, especially when snow covers other plants.

Once the Black Grouse was more widespread, but owing to loss of habitat it has disappeared from most of southern England and is declining in some other parts of its range as well. It does not breed in Ireland, in spite of attempts to introduce it there.

(Western) Capercaillie *Tetrao urogallus*

This giant of the pine forests was once common and widespread in Scotland and Ireland, but as forests were felled it became rare until the last Capercaillie was shot in Scotland in 1785, and the species also became extinct in Ireland. From 1837 Capercaillies were brought from Sweden and reintroduced into Perthshire and other parts of Scotland, although attempts to re-establish it in Ireland failed. Since about 1960 the Capercaillie has been in decline.

In spite of their large size, Capercaillies can be surprisingly difficult to observe as they are secretive, and the females are particularly well camouflaged. They feed on shoots and buds of conifers and will frequently perch in trees in order to reach their food. They also roost in trees at night.

Capercaillies display in the early morning for a few weeks in the spring. Several males fly into a traditional site in a forest and there they sing and fight. Many females may be attracted to the display area and it has been found that the larger males are usually dominant and therefore mate with more females.

Black Grouse

Larger than Grey Partridge – male 53 cm, female 41 cm. Male (**1**) is glossy black with white wing-bar and shoulder patch. The male's tail is black and lyre-shaped: under it are white feathers which are shown off during courtship displays. Female (**2**) is larger and greyer than Red Grouse, and has forked tail and slight double wing-bar. Males make dove-like cooing and bubbling calls during courtship. *Favourite habitats are moorland, young conifer plantations, open pine forests or open birch woods. Sometimes visits nearby farmland to feed. Found in Scotland, Wales, parts of the West Country and northern England.* (Map: page 202)

Capercaillie

Largest gamebird – male 86 cm, female 62 cm. Male (**3**) is huge blackish bird with pale patch on shoulder. Wings are broad and tail quite long and wide. The brown-barred female (**4**) is larger than Black Grouse with reddish patch on breast, pale flanks and rounded tail. Call of male during display is a remarkable series of double notes which end in a loud 'pop'. *Lives in mature Scottish pine forests and conifer plantations.* (Map: page 202)

Black Grouse   Red Grouse

Female grouse in flight

Capercaillie ♀

Black Grouse
♂
♀

Black Grouse
1 ♂
2 ♀

3 ♂ Capercaillies

♀

Hilary Burn

Red-legged Partridge *Alectoris rufa*

This partridge is not native to Britain, but has been introduced into many parts of the country between 1673 and the present day. Many of these introductions failed, but some have been successful and it has colonised the drier parts of Britain, especially in the south and east.

Adults feed on seeds, leaves, roots and small numbers of insects; young birds eat many more insects. Red-legged Partridges often form flocks, or 'coveys', and when danger threatens they sometimes run away rather than fly.

The nest is a shallow scrape, lined with vegetation. Males may build several nests – the female will lay her eggs in one of them and then may lay a second clutch in another nest which will be incubated by the male.

Grey Partridge *Perdix perdix*

These partridges are most numerous in traditional mixed farming areas of Britain where fields are small and hedges thick and well cared for. Such farmland is, unfortunately, disappearing: fields are becoming larger, hedges are being uprooted and the Grey Partridge has declined by 84% in the last 25 years. Pesticides, which kill the insect food of young partridges, cold weather in spring, and the sowing of cereal crops in autumn are all thought to have contributed to the decline of the Grey Partridge.

When feeding or at rest, Grey Partridges appear dumpy and may easily be mistaken for large stones or lumps of soil. When alarmed, they will squat, relying on their camouflage to blend in with their surroundings, and only at the last moment take to the air.

Although these partridges feed out in the open, they breed more successfully if their nest is under the cover of a thick hedge or among other dense vegetation. They regularly dust-bathe in dry soil which helps with feather care. Although they are mainly vegetarian, the young eat many more insects than do their parents.

(Common) Quail *Coturnix coturnix*

The distinctive song of a male Quail, until he attracts a mate, is usually the only clue that this rare and highly secretive breeding bird is present. In some summers, they are far more abundant than in others.

Quails were once widespread, and their decline is not fully understood. Changes in farming practices may have contributed, but being migrants they face many dangers during their flights to and from Africa, not least from southern European hunters.

Red-legged Partridge (1)

Larger than Grey Partridge – 33 cm. Colourful at close quarters. Wax-red legs and bill and striped flanks. Black-and-white face pattern may be seen from a distance. Tail is reddish. Runs swiftly. Often seen in small flocks. Usual call is a repetitive 'chuck-chucker'.
Found on farmland. Most common in southern and eastern England. Also likes dry, sandy places, downland and even open areas in woods. (Map: page 202)

Grey Partridge

30 cm. Plump, rounded body and domed head. Body is brown-and-grey with an orange-brown face. Male (**2**) has dark horseshoe mark on lower breast; female (**3**) has similar but less distinct mark. Tail is reddish. Call is a grating 'krr-ick' or 'skee-er'. Like other gamebirds, flight is fast with rapid wingbeats followed by a glide on downcurved wings.
Found mainly on farmland in many parts of Britain and Ireland. (Map: page 202)

Quail

Much smaller than Grey Partridge – 17 cm. Very secretive, usually located by 'whip, whip-whip' call (said to sound like 'wet my lips') heard particularly at dawn and dusk. Sandy-brown plumage with buff streaks, no barring on flanks, cream stripe on top of head and over eye. Male (**4**) has dark streaks on throat.
Rather rare summer visitor to corn- and hay-fields mainly on the chalk downlands of southern England.
(Map: page 202)

Grey Partridges

Red-legged
Partridges

Quails

4 ♂

1 Red-legged
Partridges

♂

2 ♂

Grey Partridges

3 ♀

Hilary Burn.

(Common) Pheasant *Phasianus colchicus*

The original home of the Pheasant was between the Black Sea and China, but it was first introduced into England by the Normans in the 11th century and later was introduced into Scotland, Wales and Ireland. Pheasant numbers are unnaturally high in areas where they are hunted as they are still bred in captivity and released; Pheasants are fewer away from gamekeepers or shooting interests and may even be declining.

In the past, the protection of Pheasants meant the destruction of birds of prey, but now the law protects these predators. There are other benefits from shooting, as woods and covers which are preserved for Pheasants are also often oases for wildlife that would have difficulty in surviving in otherwise bleak farmland.

Pheasants' food includes grain, seeds, berries, roots, shoots and insect larvae. Most food is found on the ground where Pheasants spend most of the day, but at night they generally roost in trees, away from ground predators such as foxes.

Golden Pheasant *Chrysolophus pictus*

The natural home of this colourful pheasant is the mountains of central China. The first ones were brought to Britain in the 18th century, but Golden Pheasants were not encouraged to breed wild until the end of the last century and, even now, despite many attempted introductions, they are firmly established in only a few areas.

In spite of the male's colourful plumage, Golden Pheasants are difficult to observe. They are long-legged and agile, slipping easily through dense vegetation.

Lady Amherst's Pheasant *Chrysolophus amherstiae*

There are probably fewer than 200 of these incredibly beautiful pheasants wild in Britain.

Named after the wife of a Governor General of India, who sent specimens to London from which the species was first identified, Lady Amherst's Pheasants are native to the high mountain slopes of southwest China and Tibet. The species was introduced into Britain in about 1900 and has successfully colonised a few young conifer plantations, and mixed and deciduous woodlands, especially where there is dense undergrowth.

Lady Amherst's Pheasants are extremely secretive, and observation in the wild in Britain is very difficult; if disturbed, they run or skulk rather than fly.

Common Pheasant
Male – 75 cm. Female – 60 cm. Plump, with small head, long neck and long tail. Typical male (**1**) is large and colourful with white collar and long pointed tail. Interbreeds with other races, resulting in a variety of plumages. Female (**2**) is sandy-brown with darker marks and long tail (but shorter than male's). Flies with rapid wingbeats followed by a glide. Runs with tail cocked. Male's crowing call is 'korrk-kok' followed by loud rustling wings.
Resident in farmland, parkland and woods in most parts of British Isles.
(Map: page 203)

Golden Pheasant
Male – 100 cm. Female – 70 cm. Smaller bodied than Pheasant, but with longer tail. Male (**3**) is very brightly coloured. Female (**4**) is like female Pheasant, with domed head and longer, downcurved tail. Rarely flies. Crowing call is more high pitched than Pheasant's.
Secretive, living in coniferous woods, mainly in East Anglia, and a few other places.
(Map: page 203)

Lady Amherst's Pheasant
Male – 110 cm. Female – 80 cm. Exotic-looking male (**5**) has very long black-and-white tail. Female (**6**) is like female Golden Pheasant, but less golden and has horn-coloured bill and blue-grey feet. Call is similar to Golden Pheasant's.
Found in dense woods mainly in Bedfordshire.
(Map: page 203)

6 Lady Amherst's Pheasant ♀

3 Golden Pheasant ♂

4 Golden Pheasant ♀

Common Pheasant ♂

Common Pheasant ♂

2 Common Pheasant ♀

5 Lady Amherst's Pheasant ♂

1 Common Pheasant ♂

Hilary Burn.

Water Rail *Rallus aquaticus*

The Water Rail is one of the birds likely to be skulking in a reedbed and its strange calls may be heard by day or by night.

Our Water Rails do not migrate, but those living farther north and east migrate here in the autumn and return in spring. Britain and Ireland, therefore, receive an additional winter population.

Water Rails are extremely slim birds and move through dense vegetation with ease, leaving no obvious paths. In winter, they may be forced out of their normal habitat by floods or by ice.

Although Water Rails swim frequently, they usually feed in shallow water. Their food is mainly animal matter such as insects or small fish, although shoots, roots and fruits are also eaten.

The **Spotted Crake** *Porzana porzana* is rare and extremely secretive; it breeds in only a few lowland swamps and fens. It is most often noted here on passage in autumn. It is small, the dark body is flecked with white spots and the bill is yellow with a reddish base. Its persistent 'h'wit, h'wit' call sounds rather like a whiplash and is most likely to be heard after dark.

Corncrake *Crex crex*

Once, the grating call of the Corncrake would have been a familiar summer sound in farmland throughout both Britain and Ireland, but the species has steadily declined since the middle of the 19th century. Changes in farming techniques, especially the earlier cutting by machine of grass for hay and silage, are blamed for its decline, not only here, but also in much of northern and western Europe. Climatic change in Africa may have played a part in the decline.

Corncrakes are extremely secretive and it is often only their distinctive call which betrays their presence. The call, from which both the common and scientific names are derived, can be imitated by drawing a wooden ruler across the teeth of a comb, and is heard mostly at night but also by day.

Corncrakes in flight appear weak, but this is far from the truth, as they are long-distance migrants. Migrating at night, they are capable of long journeys with little or no rest and they spend the winter in Africa, probably south of the Equator. Flying from southern Africa to northern Europe is very risky, but Corncrakes face an extra hazard; because they fly low they frequently collide with overhead wires and cables which cover so much of western Europe.

Water Rail

Smaller than Moorhen – 25 cm. Secretive, with long, red bill, long legs and large feet. Upperparts of adult (**1**) are brown with black streaks. Face, neck and underparts blue-grey. Whitish feathers under tail. Flanks are barred black-and-white. Flight is weak, with legs trailing. Juvenile (**2**) has pale stripe over eye, pale throat and dark bill which may appear short. Variety of calls including grunts and a pig-like squeal.
Water Rails live in reedbeds and other dense waterside vegetation in many parts of the British Isles.
(Map: page 203)

Corncrake (3)

Smaller than Moorhen – 28 cm. Yellowish-buff with darker marks on back and chestnut wings. Appears short-necked; bill is short. Greyish on head and breast. Very secretive. Song is a loud repetitive 'crek, crek'.
Summer visitor to hayfields and other areas with tall vegetation mainly in western Scotland and Ireland.
(Map: page 203)

Corncrake

3 Corncrakes

Moorhen
juvenile

1 *adult*

Water Rails

2 *juvenile*

Hilary Burn

(Common) Moorhen *Gallinula chloropus*

Wherever there is fresh water there will probably be a Moorhen (a corruption of 'Merehen') nearby. Reedbeds, farm ponds, muddy ditches and edges of large reservoirs are home for this familiar species. Only northwest Scotland and a few other upland areas have not been colonised because Moorhens usually avoid fast-flowing water or pools with little or no cover.

Moorhens will often skulk and may be difficult to see, yet where they become accustomed to people they can become quite tame. They will sometimes nest, roost and feed in trees and bushes, but most of their time is spent among waterside plants and on land searching for food, which includes pondweed and other plants, snails, insects, small fish and even the eggs of other birds.

In early spring, Moorhens often build display platforms, where much of the courtship takes place, and later one of these is converted into a nest in which the eggs are laid. Once the young have hatched, they move to one or more specially constructed 'brood nests' as an alternative to their true nest. Two or three broods may be reared in a summer and juveniles of early broods may help to feed the young of the later ones.

(Common) Coot *Fulica atra*

A first glance might show little difference between Coot and Moorhen: both may be found on the same lake and one might wonder if these two related species compete for the same food. In fact, they could hardly be more different.

While the solitary Moorhen searches for food among waterside vegetation, flocks of Coots gather on open water and find most food by diving one or two metres below the surface. Moorhens' toes are long and thin for climbing; Coots' toes are partly webbed for swimming and diving efficiently.

Coots feed on plants, seeds and insects and also take eggs of other birds. Although most food is found in water, flocks of Coots sometimes feed on land, especially in winter. They are highly territorial and very aggressive. Fights are easy to spot as the quarrelling birds appear to sit on their tails and strike at each other with wings, feet and bills.

When breeding, Coots usually choose lakes with waterside vegetation from which they build a nest. In winter, flocks visit reservoirs, even those with concrete banks, where they may be joined by Coots from northern and eastern Europe.

Moorhen
33 cm. Adults (**1**) look black with red-and-yellow bill, white line along flanks and white under the tail. The tail is constantly flicked when swimming or walking. Head jerks backwards and forwards when swimming. The long legs and large feet are yellow-green. Juveniles (**2**) are browner than adults, with white throat and chin and less distinct line along flanks. Has a variety of throaty calls including the familiar 'crorrk'.
Lives near fresh water, from small ponds to large lakes, in most parts of the British Isles. (Map: page 203)

Coot
Larger than Moorhen – 37 cm. Adult (**3**) is all-black waterbird with white bill and forehead. Rounded head and rounded back. Tail sits flat on water, not flicked like Moorhen's. Large grey-green feet are lobed. Juvenile (**4**) is dark grey with whitish throat, neck and belly. Most common call is a hollow-sounding 'kwok' (said to resemble 'coot', hence its name). Patters along water surface to get airborne and flies with legs trailing.
Found mainly on large areas of fresh water in most parts of the British Isles except northwest Scotland. (Map: page 203)

Moorhen

Coots *fighting*

Moorhens *displaying*

4 Coot *juvenile*

2 Moorhen *juvenile*

3 Coots

1 Moorhens

Hilary Burn

(Eurasian) Oystercatcher *Haematopus ostralegus*

These birds may not feed on oysters, but they do eat shellfish, especially mussels, cockles and limpets. The powerful bill is used to stab or prise open shells; individuals specialise in these two different feeding techniques, which are imitated by their young. The Oystercatcher differs from most other waders in that it feeds its young instead of letting them feed themselves.

Breeding all around our coast, Oystercatchers are absent only where feeding is difficult or where there are too many holidaymakers. Nesting inland is a recent development; at first they spread up some large Scottish rivers, but soon moved to nearby farmland. This change was possible because Oystercatchers feed on earthworms. More recently, some inland gravel workings in southern Britain have also been colonised.

Large flocks of migrant Oystercatchers from northwest Europe winter on our estuaries. Some individuals are long-lived: one bird survived for 35 years.

(Pied) Avocet *Recurvirostra avosetta*

There can be few more attractive sights than a pair of Avocets with young. For many years, this could only be seen abroad, as the species became extinct in Britain in the middle of the 19th century. Fortunately, Avocets returned in 1947 and, as a result of RSPB protection, they now nest at many coastal sites. So successful was this protection and habitat management that the bird was chosen as the RSPB emblem. There are several RSPB reserves where one can watch these beautiful waders.

Avocets do not probe the mud with their beaks as do most other waders; instead, they sweep their bills from side to side and filter tiny shrimps or insect larvae from the water, or delicately snap up a small creature. Feeding usually takes place in shallow water, but Avocets can wade through deep water and will sometimes swim or even up-end, like ducks, to reach food.

Stone-curlew *Burhinus oedicnemus*

Fewer grazing animals, including rabbits reduced by myxomatosis, and the ploughing of chalk-grassland for agriculture, have contributed to the decline of Stone-curlews so that only about 200 pairs breed each year.

During daylight, Stone-curlews are hard to see as they sit or stand and rely on camouflage for protection. They become more active at dusk and continue to feed through the night. One of the best times for hearing their eerie call is at 3 o'clock on a spring morning.

Oystercatcher
Larger than Lapwing – 43 cm. Adult in summer (**1**) is a distinctive black-and-white wader with long orange-red bill and pink legs. Broad white wing-bar shows in flight. Juvenile and adult in winter (**2**) have white collar. Call is loud 'kleep-kleep'.
Seen around the coasts of Britain and Ireland in summer and winter. Also, nests inland in Scotland and northern England. (Map: page 203)

Avocet
Size of Oystercatcher – 43 cm. Adults (**3**) are black-and-white, with slim, black, upswept bill and long, blue-grey legs. The feet are webbed. Fully grown juvenile (**4**) resembles adult, but is browner. Call is a fluty 'kleep'.
Rare breeding species needing shallow pools near the coast in order to breed. Winters on sheltered estuaries in southern Britain. (Map: page 204)

Stone-curlew (5)
Larger than Lapwing – 41 cm. Sandy brown with darker streaks, rounded head with large yellow eyes, long thick legs and short bill. Ungainly bird, often standing hunched up. In flight, two bold whitish wing-bars are very noticeable. Call is Curlew-like 'coo-ree', mainly heard at night.
Rare summer visitor to sandy heaths and chalk downland mainly in southeastern England. Seen elsewhere on migration. (Map: page 204)

Avocet

Oystercatchers

4 *juvenile*

5 Stone-curlews

Avocets

3 *adult*

2 *winter*

1 *summer*

Oystercatchers

Hilary Burn

Ringed Plover *Charadrius hiaticula*

This familiar species is also found in the High Arctic. Ringed Plovers which nest in Britain and Ireland are the most southerly population, except for a few in France. Ours are mainly resident, but those breeding farther north are long-distance migrants, and some of these pass through our islands en route to winter quarters in southern Africa.

In recent years, more Ringed Plovers have started to nest away from their traditional coastal sites; at first farmland near the coast was used, and then gravel workings and shingle areas far from the sea. Those which still nest on coastal beaches are nowadays often disturbed by holiday-makers.

When feeding, Ringed Plovers, like several other species, have developed a special technique known as foot-pattering: the bird rapidly vibrating wet mud with its foot. This habit appears to encourage prey, such as worms, to come to the surface, perhaps in the mistaken belief that it is raining.

Little Ringed Plover (Little Plover) *Charadrius dubius*

There are few better examples of a species taking advantage of a newly created habitat than the Little Ringed Plover and its colonisation of gravel workings.

This attractive, small plover generally nests farther south than the Ringed Plover and its traditional habitat is inland shingle banks near rivers. New gravel diggings offer a similar habitat. The increasing numbers of Ringed Plovers breeding inland often brings the two into competition for the best nest-sites; where this occurs the larger Ringed Plover usually dominates.

Soon after they return to their breeding grounds in March or April, their display flight may be seen: the long, slow wingbeats as the bird zig-zags to and fro. As with other small plovers, this species benefits from 'disruptive' camouflage, the bold pattern helping to break up the outline against a background of shingle.

Kentish Plover *Charadrius alexandrinus*

Although Kentish Plovers were first discovered breeding in Kent, the name is misleading as they ceased nesting there many years ago. Indeed, since 1956, this attractive species has ceased to breed regularly anywhere in Britain, although a few sometimes visit the south and east coasts of England (mainly in May and August). Kentish Plovers are still reasonably common in many parts of the Continent.

Little Ringed Plover

Smaller and more delicate than Ringed Plover – 15 cm. Adult (**1**) has white line above black forehead and yellow eye-ring. No wing-bar shows in flight. Legs are yellowish-green. Call is fluty 'peeoo'. Juvenile (**2**) has scaly back and incomplete breast band. *Summer visitor, mainly to sand and gravel workings in many parts of England.* (Map: page 202)

Ringed Plover

Smaller than Redshank – 19 cm. Adult (**3**) has black-and-white head pattern and black breast band. Legs are orange. White wing-bar shows in flight. Juvenile (**4**) has scaly back, lacks the head pattern of adult and has an incomplete breast band. Feeding birds run swiftly, stop suddenly and whole body tilts forward when food is sighted. Call is an attractive 'too-li'. *Found mainly on shingle and sandy seashores, but nests inland in some places.* (Map: page 202)

Kentish Plover

Smaller than Ringed Plover – 16 cm. Adult has black bill and usually black legs, narrow black eye-patch, dark patches on sides of breast and white wing-bar in flight. Male (**5**) has rusty crown. Female (**6**) is paler. Juvenile (**7**) resembles female and usually has dark legs. Beware confusion with young Ringed Plovers with muddy legs! *Rare visitor, mostly in spring and autumn, to shingle or sandy beaches.* (No map)

Kentish Plover

Ringed Plovers

Ringed Plovers

Little Ringed Plover

6 Kentish Plover ♀

7 Kentish Plover *juvenile*

5 Kentish Plover ♂

2 *Little Ringed Plover juvenile*

1 Little Ringed Plover

4 Ringed Plover *juvenile*

3 Ringed Plover

Hilary Burn

(Northern) Lapwing *Vanellus vanellus*

The small flocks of Lapwings which are to be seen in the countryside in June or July are migrants from Europe and often the first indication that, for some species, the breeding season is over and autumn migration has begun.

Numbers of Lapwings continue to build up during late summer and autumn as more arrive from the Continent and join those which nested here. A sudden cold spell, however, will cause many of them to fly south or west, where often the weather is milder and feeding easier. If the cold weather is prolonged, Lapwings will move even farther, to Ireland, France or even Spain. In Spain, the Lapwing is called '*Ave fria*', the bird from the cold.

Lapwings breed in a variety of habitats, from ploughed fields to lake edges, but 96% depend on farmland. In southern Britain, the number breeding has declined dramatically in recent years. This change may be mainly due to changes in farming practice and draining of wet meadows. Northern populations appear more stable.

The Lapwing is such a familiar bird that it has several widely used names, including 'Peewit', which describes its call, and 'Green Plover', which describes the colour of its plumage and its relationship.

In February, many Lapwings begin to display over their territories and it is then that their wheezy, 'peewit' call is most often heard. The male flies slowly over his territory but soon speeds up, until suddenly he climbs steeply, pauses, and then tumbles downwards, straightening out only a metre or so above the ground, and sweeps low over the field before rising and tumbling yet again. During these spectacular manoeuvres, the displaying bird's wings make a far-carrying humming, from which the species' official name, Lapwing, is derived. On the ground, courtship continues, with the orange undertail-coverts playing an important part in the highly ritualised display.

The eggs are laid in a hollow on the ground and are beautifully camouflaged. The chicks also merge with their surroundings. Like other wader chicks, they leave their nest soon after hatching, and, if danger threatens, the conspicuous adult will attempt to distract the predator while the chicks lie still, flat on the ground.

Lapwings feed on insects, grubs, worms, snails, slugs and some seeds. They are, therefore, no threat to any crops and are an attractive addition to many farmers' fields. In winter, they often form large flocks together with Golden Plovers on ploughed land, stubble or old pasture.

Lapwing
30 cm. Black, white and dark metallic green with orange under the tail. At a distance, appears black-and-white. Crest is obvious on adults (**1**) on the ground. Juveniles (**2**) have a scaly back and shorter crest. Usual flight is lazy, wings are broad and rounded with an obvious black-and-white underwing pattern. In display, twists, turns and dives. Call is a wheezy, drawn-out 'peewit'. *Breeds on farmland and other open ground in most parts of the British Isles. Migrants arrive from Europe for the winter.*
(Map: page 202)

Lapwing *display*

Golden Plover

Golden Plover

2 Lapwing *juvenile*

1 Lapwing *adult*

Hilary Burn

(Eurasian) Dotterel *Charadrius morinellus*

The summer home of Dotterels is the rounded tops of the highest mountain chains, where there is little vegetation and snow lies longest. To avoid snow, Dotterels nest on wind-swept plateaux, usually 850 m or more above sea level. Strangely, it is the female Dotterel that has the brightest plumage and, once the eggs are laid, it is usually the male which incubates and tends the young while the females gather together in groups.

Unfortunately, some of the best breeding areas are now regularly visited by tourists and nesting Dotterels are often disturbed. Perhaps the best place to see them is at a traditional stopping area, where small groups, known as 'trips', may be seen on the same lowland fields each year while on their spring migration from North Africa. In the Netherlands, breeding has occurred on reclaimed land, below sea level.

(European) Golden Plover *Pluvialis apricaria*

There are few more beautiful sights or sounds than Golden Plovers displaying over moorland in spring, when they chase each other excitedly or 'switch-back' over their territories and reach a great height while giving their simple but lonely-sounding song. A typical territory contains one or more hummocks or stones which are used by them as lookouts. If danger threatens, adults try to lead the intruder away from the nest or young by first running towards the danger, then running away, sometimes dragging a wing and pretending that they are injured.

In favoured areas, where possible nesting territories are fewer than the number of pairs, some Golden Plovers wait their turn to nest until another pair has finished breeding.

Up to 300,000, or 30% of the European population, winter in Britain. Some visit coastal marshes, but many join flocks of Lapwings inland, on farmland.

Grey Plover *Pluvialis squatarola*

These birds nest on Arctic tundra, but small numbers may be seen on British and Irish estuaries at most seasons of the year, especially in September when migration is at its height. When feeding they are usually well spaced out, but high tide forces them off their feeding grounds and then they may gather at regular high-tide roosts.

Their diet includes shellfish, insects, and crustacea such as crabs. Their bills are short, so most food is picked up from the surface of wet mud.

Dotterel
Smaller than Lapwing – 22 cm. Colourful at close range, with chestnut belly. White stripes over eyes which meet at back of head, and a pale breast band. Female (**1**) is brighter than male (**2**). Autumn plumage is browner and marks fainter. Juvenile (**3**) is buff with faint marks and streaked back.
Summer visitor to the tops of our highest hills. Seen in lowland Britain only on migration. (Map: page 204)

Golden Plover
Smaller than Lapwing – 28 cm. Round-headed with yellow spangled back. In summer has black belly, black breast and face pattern which is more clear-cut on those breeding in northern Europe (**4**) than on those nesting in the British Isles (**5**). Underwing is white. In winter (**6**) belly is pale. Call is a lonely 'pee-ye-wee-oo'.
Nests on upland moors. Winters on lowland farmland or coastal marshes.
(Map: page 204)

Grey Plover
Smaller than Lapwing – 28 cm. Plumper than Golden Plover. Often hunched up and looks 'neck-less'. Breeding plumage (**7**) is black-and-white spotted back, separated from black face and underparts by white line. In winter (**8**), face and underparts are pale, back of adult is brownish-grey. Juvenile is spotted white. Black 'arm-pit' (axillaries) shows in flight. Call is a sad 'tee-oo-ee'.
Visits estuaries and seashores, mainly in autumn and winter; rare inland.
(Map: page 204)

Grey Plover

Dotterel

Golden Plover
southern race

Golden Plovers
winter

Golden Plover
northern race

6 Golden Plover *winter*

Grey Plovers *winter*

8 Grey Plover
winter

3 Dotterel
juvenile

7 Grey Plover
summer

5 Golden Plover
southern race

4 Golden Plover
northern race

1 Dotterel ♀

2 Dotterel ♂

Hilary Burn.

(Red) Knot *Calidris canutus*

About 300,000 Knots, two-thirds of the western European winter population, feed on British or Irish estuaries between September and March. Thousands may be seen twisting and turning together over their feeding grounds or high-tide roosts and looking, from a distance, like clouds of smoke. Closer to, however, their white bellies contrast with their grey backs and flocks flash grey-and-white in winter sunlight.

Most of the Knots which visit Britain and Ireland breed in Greenland, although some come to us from Siberia. Our estuaries are rich in food, and Knots probe in wet sand and mud for small crabs, insects and shellfish.

Sanderling *Calidris alba*

On a sandy beach, Sanderlings can often appear like clockwork toys as they run amazingly fast along the edge of the sea, snatching sand-hoppers and other small food items from the tide's edge and, at the same time, dodging the wash from the waves. Sanderlings also probe with their bills in wet sand, often around pools left by an outgoing tide. They are frequently seen in small groups and are quite tame; sometimes they mix with other species such as Dunlin and Knot.

The breeding grounds are north of the Arctic Circle and many birds travel through Europe to winter in Africa as far south as South Africa.

Little Stint *Calidris minuta*

The plumage of this delicate wader is very variable and can often be confusing. Little Stints are passage migrants which breed in Europe north of the Arctic Circle and winter as far south as South Africa. Those which visit the British Isles are usually seen between August and October and most are juveniles.

All birds moult most of their feathers at least once a year; the main moult usually takes place after breeding. Because the northern summer is so short, Little Stints, like some other Arctic breeders, suspend their moult until they have reached winter quarters. In the tropics both adults and juveniles can slowly grow new feathers in readiness for their return journey.

Temminck's Stint *Calidris temminckii*

This species winters in Africa and those birds which visit the British Isles on migration are often seen near inland pools. They breed in northern Europe and a few nest in Scotland.

Knot
Larger than Ringed Plover – 25 cm. Plump with straight bill and rather short legs. Usually in flocks, often in very large numbers. Has faint wing-bar. Grey-and-white in autumn and winter (**1**). Brick-red underparts in summer (**2**). Call is low 'knut'.
Mainly on estuaries in autumn and winter.
(Map: page 202)

Sanderling
Larger than Ringed Plover – 20 cm. Plump and active. Rather short, straight bill. In autumn and winter (**3**), has pale grey back, white underparts and sometimes shows black mark on front of wing. Broad white wing-bar. In breeding plumage (**4**), has reddish-brown back, head and breast.
Seen on sandy beaches in autumn and winter. (Map: page 205)

Little Stint
Smaller than Ringed Plover – 13 cm. Very small with short, fine, black bill. In winter (**5**) has scaly brown back and white breast. 1st-year birds (**6**) have V pattern on their backs. Breeding plumage (**7**) reddish-brown.
Mainly seen in autumn around shallow water.
(Map: page 205)

Temminck's Stint
Smaller than Ringed Plover – 14 cm. Like Little Stint, but less lively when feeding and in autumn (**8**) is greyer, with less scaly back, paler legs and darker breast. Outer tail is white. General appearance when breeding (**9**) rather like small Common Sandpiper.
Small numbers occur on passage, especially May and August. (No map)

Knot

Dunlin

Sanderling

Temminck's Stint

Little Stint

Knots

1 Knot *winter*

2 Knot *summer*

Dunlin

3 Sanderling *winter*

4 Sanderling *summer*

9 Temminck's Stint *summer*

5 Little Stint *winter*

8 Temminck's Stint *autumn*

6 Little Stint *1st-winter*

7 Little Stint *summer*

Hilary Burn.

Purple Sandpiper *Calidris maritima*

The name 'Purple' is rather misleading as this colour may be seen only at very close quarters, as a purplish sheen on some of the back feathers.

Purple Sandpipers breed mainly in the Arctic and winter farther north than other waders. Many move hardly any distance after breeding, and winter on northern ice-free coasts, while others move south or west, but only very few travel as far as southern Europe.

They search for food on rocky coasts, where they often prefer flat rocks projecting into the sea. They sometimes mix with Turnstones. Food is mainly small fish, insects, shrimps, shellfish and vegetable matter and is picked up as it is washed ashore. Small groups often feed on the very edge of the sea and somehow manage to dodge the larger waves while ignoring human observers.

Dunlin *Calidris alpina*

Dunlins are the most common wader of our estuaries. Usually they feed together in small groups, with heads down; looking round-shouldered as they probe the mud methodically in their search for food. They also form large flocks that twist and turn together in flight.

Dunlin plumage is very variable and so is their length of bill. Those with the shortest bills breed in Iceland. Because the unfeathered parts of a bird lose heat most quickly, bills and legs of populations which live in cold climates tend to be shorter than those of Dunlins living in warmer regions.

Like many other waders, Dunlins forsake estuaries and beaches when nesting and move to moorland. In Britain, they prefer poorly drained moors with scattered pools, although in Ireland they usually nest on lower, wet areas near lakes and marshes.

Common Sandpiper *Actitis hypoleucos*

The shrill 'willy-wicket' call, a glimpse of the typical bow-winged flight, with wings flicking below the level of the body, and then a distant view of the bird bobbing on a partly submerged stone, are usually the first clues that a Common Sandpiper is around.

Fast-flowing upland streams or lochs with stony edges are the normal summer home. Generally, Common Sandpipers are seen only in ones or twos.

Although most Common Sandpipers winter in Africa, a few remain in southern Britain. In spring and autumn, migrants are regularly to be seen near water in most areas, both inland and near the coast.

Purple Sandpiper

Larger than Ringed Plover – 21 cm. A dumpy, often tame, wader with rather short yellowish legs, yellow base to bill and a white wing-bar. In winter (**1**), the back is almost black, the head and breast dark brown and the underparts pale with dark marks. In breeding plumage (**2**), the back becomes more scaly and the face paler. *Visits rocky coasts in winter and feeds close to the edge of the sea.* (Map: page 205)

Dunlin

Smaller than Ringed Plover – 18 cm. Common, small wader with variable plumage. Medium length, black bill usually curved down towards tip. Rather short black legs. White wing-bar and white sides to rump and tail. Short-necked and round-shouldered. Reddish-brown back and pale underparts with black belly in breeding plumage (**3**). Greyer in winter (**4**), with white belly. Call, hoarse 'dzee'. *Breeds on damp upland moors. Winters on the coast, especially on mud-flats, but also visits inland lakes.* (Map: page 205)

Common Sandpiper (5)

Larger than Ringed Plover – 20 cm. Often bobs, rather like a wagtail. Brownish back, white belly, streaked breast or brown 'smudges' on either side of breast. White wing-bar and white sides to tail in flight. Flies with stiff, bowed wings and also briefly glides. Call is shrill 'tee-we-we'. *Summer visitor to upland lakes and rivers. Visits other areas on migration.* (Map: page 205)

Common Sandpiper

Dunlin

Purple
Sandpiper

3 *summer*

Dunlins

Dunlins

4 *winter*

Dunlins

2 Purple Sandpiper
summer

Turnstone

1 Purple Sandpiper
winter

Hilary Burn

5 Common Sandpiper

Pectoral Sandpiper *Calidris melanotos*

The small numbers of Pectoral Sandpipers which visit the British Isles are North American birds which breed in Alaska and northern Canada and normally winter in South America. Some, however, cross the Atlantic by accident during migration, particularly in autumn.

These sandpipers also breed in Siberia, and, while some migrate south to Australia for the winter, many more cross the Bering Strait and follow the route of the North American Pectoral Sandpipers to South America, a journey of at least 16,000 km.

Ruff *Philomachus pugnax*

Before so many of our wet meadows were drained for farming, Ruffs were much more numerous than they are today. As the wetlands disappeared, the numbers of breeding Ruffs also declined until the species became extinct as a British breeder early in the 20th century. In 1963, however, Ruffs were found nesting on the Ouse Washes on the Cambridgeshire–Norfolk border and a few pairs have nested there and at a few other sites since then.

Male Ruffs return to their breeding grounds from Africa in March and the females, known as 'reeves', return a few weeks later. They assemble at display areas, called 'leks', in the early morning: the males, sporting their exotic breeding plumage, display silently, sometimes fighting mock battles and often 'freezing' for short periods. It appears that males with darker neck feathers are more successful at attracting reeves than are those with white feathers.

Once mating has taken place, the reeves are left to incubate the eggs and look after the young, while the males moult out of their bright breeding plumage.

Outside the breeding season, Ruffs visit the margins of inland lakes and coastal marshes where they feed on insect larvae, small shellfish and seeds. A few stay with us for the winter.

Pectoral Sandpiper (1)
Size of Ringed Plover – 19 cm. Longer neck than many other small waders. Similar to Ruff, but smaller, with finer, slightly downcurved bill. Brown back with pale 'Snipe-like' stripes. Streaked breast which ends abruptly above white belly. Legs are greenish-yellow. In flight, tail has dark centre. 'Zig-zag' flight like Snipe when disturbed.
Rare visitor, mostly in autumn in western Britain. Visits shallow pools, both near the coast and inland. (No map)

Ruff
Larger than Ringed Plover – male 29 cm, female 23 cm. A confusing wader with a variety of plumages and a size difference between male and female. Shorter bill than Redshank. Appears 'round-shouldered' when feeding, but very upright when alert. Female (**2**) and male in winter (**3**) have grey-brown backs with buff-edged feathers and buff underparts. Leg colour very variable, from green to orange, but usually brownish. In flight there is slight wing-bar and also black centre to tail with white oval patches on each side. Male in breeding plumage (**4**) has warty face and colourful 'ruff'.
Rare breeding species of low-lying, wet grassy meadows. At other seasons visits wet marshy places. (Map: page 205)

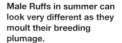

Male Ruffs in summer can look very different as they moult their breeding plumage.

4 Ruffs ♂
spring

♀

Ruffs

3 Ruff ♂
winter

2 Ruff ♀

1 Pectoral
Sandpiper

Hilary Burn

Jack Snipe *Lymnocryptes minimus*

While walking through a wet field in winter you may disturb feeding Snipes, which will fly off as you approach. Sometimes, after the Snipes have flown, a smaller Jack Snipe will also take to the air, almost from under your feet, and then land again not far away. So good is its camouflage, however, that, even if you see where it lands, it can be almost impossible to observe among dense vegetation.

Even when Jack Snipes feed undisturbed, they seldom move far from cover. They bob and sway which helps them to blend with their surroundings.

(Common) Snipe *Gallinago gallinago*

'Drumming' is the name given to the strange, bleating sound which Snipes make with their outer tail feathers as they 'switchback' over their territories in spring. The outer tail feathers are formed in such a way as to produce vibrations when air rushes past them; this noise may carry up to one kilometre.

A female Snipe incubates her own eggs without help from the male. After the eggs hatch, the young quickly leave the nest and the brood is split, with each parent taking care of a few chicks. Although young Snipes take seven weeks to grow fully, they are able to fly after two weeks and this gives them extra protection.

The Snipe feeds mainly on worms. It cannot see its prey, but the tip of the bill is sensitive and flexible, which enables the bird to locate its food in damp soil and grasp its prey. The draining of water meadows and the ploughing of grassland have contributed to a recent, rapid decline in the number of Snipes breeding in lowland Britain.

(Eurasian) Woodcock *Scolopax rusticola*

The best time to see Woodcocks is at dusk or dawn in spring and early summer when males perform their display flight known as 'roding', flying 10–15 m above the ground and following a regular route over one or more woods. This slow, deliberate, owl-like flight is not territorial; these are males searching for females.

Woodcocks' camouflage is superb and they are very difficult to observe in their woodland home. When feeding, Woodcocks walk slowly, bobbing and swaying. When disturbed they sometimes carry their young from danger between their legs.

In winter, Woodcocks in northern Britain move west to Ireland or south to southern England. Others from northern Europe cross the North Sea to winter in Britain.

Jack Snipe (1)
Size of Ringed Plover – 19 cm. Smaller than Snipe, with shorter bill and shorter legs. Walks with a bobbing action. Crown is dark with pale stripes on either side. Often reluctant to fly, but when disturbed usually takes off silently, without zig-zagging, and often lands again close by.
Visits marshy fields, ditches and edges of lakes in winter.
(Map: page 205)

Snipe (2)
Larger than Ringed Plover – 27 cm. Very long bill and rather short legs. Brownish plumage with paler stripes on back and pale stripe through centre of crown. Underparts are buff. When disturbed, it flies with a zig-zag flight and makes a distinctive 'scraap' call. In spring, it makes a bleating sound during its display flight, and also a 'chipa-chipa-chipa' call, given from the ground, perched on a post or tree stump, or in flight.
Breeds in wet places such as rushy fields and wet upland moors. Visits other wet places in winter.
(Map: page 205)

Woodcock (3)
Larger and plumper than Snipe – 34 cm. Has long bill, short legs and beautifully camouflaged plumage with dark bars across the crown. Rounded wings are obvious in the display flight at dusk when the most common calls may also be heard: a loud, short 'tsiwick' and a soft croak.
Lives in woods with dense ground cover. Will feed in more open places at night.
(Map: page 205)

Woodcock

Common Snipe *drumming*

Common Snipe

Jack Snipe

2 Common Snipes

1 Jack Snipe

3 Woodcock

Hilary Burn

Black-tailed Godwit *Limosa limosa*

This large wader, with long bill and long legs, has become more common as a winter visitor to our coasts and especially to estuaries in the south of the British Isles in recent years: these migrants have come from Iceland.

The Black-tailed Godwit is also increasing as a breeding species here: once widespread, it became extinct as a British breeding bird, but in the 1930s it returned, and from 1952 it has regularly nested at the Ouse Washes on the Cambridgeshire/Norfolk border. Since then it has also nested successfully at several other sites.

When feeding, godwits either wade in deep water or probe in soft mud for insects, worms or shellfish.

Bar-tailed Godwit *Limosa lapponica*

Like many of the waders which do not breed in the British Isles, Bar-tailed Godwits may be seen throughout the year. Most are passage migrants which visit our estuaries to feed in spring and again in late summer. A few non-breeders may remain around our coasts during the summer, and some winter here while the rest migrate to southern Europe or Africa.

While both Black-tailed and Bar-tailed Godwits visit our coasts, they seldom mix. Bar-tails prefer sandy areas, but Black-tails like muddier areas or pools near the sea. Nest-sites are also separate: Black-tails breed in central Europe and Iceland, Bar-tails in northern Scandinavia and Russia.

(Eurasian) Curlew *Numenius arquata*

Its lonely-sounding, bubbling call, which gives the Curlew its name, is usually heard as the bird rises steeply and hangs on trembling wings before sailing downwards again. Curlews nest mostly in the uplands. They started to expand to lowland farms, but like other farmland waders they are in decline.

Outside the breeding season, they live on the coast where they feed mainly on shellfish, small crabs, shrimps and lug-worms. The long bill is used either to pick up food from the surface or for probing in wet mud or sand. Like other waders, Curlews eat most of their prey whole, and indigestible parts are regurgitated in the form of pellets.

Whimbrel *Numenius phaeopus*

This small 'curlew' declined as a breeding bird in the late 19th and early 20th centuries, but has increased again, especially in Orkney and Shetland. It is a passage migrant around our coasts and occasionally migrates overland.

Black-tailed Godwit
Smaller than Oystercatcher – 41 cm. Large wader with long legs which project beyond tail in flight. White tail ends with black band. White wing-bar is obvious in flight. Back and breast reddish in breeding plumage (**1**); grey in winter (**2**).
Rare breeding bird of damp meadows or moors. Visits coasts and estuaries at other times. (Map: page 206)

Bar-tailed Godwit
Smaller than Black-tailed Godwit – 38 cm. No wing-bar and bill often noticeably upswept. Feet project only slightly beyond tail in flight. Tail is barred and rump is pale. In winter (**3**) is similar colour to Curlew. In breeding plumage (**4**) breast and underparts are chestnut-red.
Mainly seen on coasts between August and March. (Map: page 206)

Curlew (5)
Largest wader – 55 cm. Streaky brown with very long, downcurved bill and no obvious head markings. Very pale rump shows in flight. Call: 'croow-wee' and a loud bubbling song.
Breeds on moors and wet meadows; at other times found around coasts. (Map: page 206)

Whimbrel (6)
Similar to Curlew, but smaller – 41 cm with shorter bill. Has two dark bands divided by pale streak on crown. Call is a series of seven high-pitched whistles.
Breeds on moors in the north of Scotland. Visits coasts on migration. (Map: page 206)

Black-tailed Godwits

Bar-tailed Godwits

Whimbrels

Curlew

Redshank

5 Curlew

4 Bar-tailed Godwit *summer*

Redshank

3 Bar-tailed Godwits *winter*

1 Black-tailed Godwits *summer*

6 Whimbrel

2 Black-tailed Godwit *winter*

Hilary Burn.

Spotted Redshank *Tringa erythropus*

On its Arctic breeding grounds, it is the male which mostly incubates the eggs and looks after the young. In Britain and Ireland, however, it is mainly a passage migrant, although a few winter in the south. Some of the migrants passing through in summer show the amazingly beautiful velvety, black plumage.

When feeding, this species resembles a graceful Redshank, but sometimes it will chase after its prey or swim or up-end like a duck.

(Common) Redshank *Tringa totanus*

This active, noisy wader is found around shallow water where it feeds on insects, shellfish, worms and some vegetation. Its nest may be some way from water and the newly hatched chicks are taken on the often dangerous journey to water. A brood was seen to travel 2 kilometres in 24 hours, negotiating walls, roads, fences and a ditch, the adult carrying the young over a wall between its legs.

In spring, salt marshes often ring with the calls of displaying Redshanks, flying with fast, shallow wing-beats. When landing they often settle with wings raised for a few moments, displaying vivid white underwings.

The species' old name, 'watchdog of the marshes', is well deserved as it is usually the first wader to fly when humans approach and its alarm is a warning to other birds. Although often seen singly or in small numbers, they sometimes nest in small colonies and may be seen in flocks near the coast in winter. Like other waders, Redshanks often swim when feeding or when crossing deep dykes or channels.

It nests near the coast and also inland. In recent years, inland nesting has declined as a result of drainage of wet meadows. In winter, it is vulnerable to freezing weather conditions.

(Common) Greenshank *Tringa nebularia*

The Greenshank breeds in wild country: from rough, boggy, moorland slopes with occasional clumps of trees, to forest edges and even, sometimes, within woodlands.

The chief breeding areas in Scotland are threatened by forestry schemes, and egg-collectors still raid nests.

In much of Britain and Ireland it is only a passage migrant: stopping to feed and to partly moult before completing its journey to the Mediterranean or Africa.

The long, slightly upcurved, bill is not only used for probing in wet areas and for picking up food from the surface, but is also often swept from side to side as the bird catches insects and other small creatures.

Spotted Redshank
Larger than Redshank – 30 cm, but more slender and with longer red legs and longer bill. Breeding plumage (**1**) is black with white spots. In winter (**2**) has mottled grey back and paler underparts. Pale V-shaped rump extends up back. Unlike Redshank, it has no white on wings. Call is loud 'chew-it'.
A passage migrant which visits wet places, often near coasts, mainly between July and October but also seen in spring. A few winter here.
(Map: page 206)

Redshank
Smaller than Oystercatcher – 28 cm. Medium-sized wader (**3**) with long red legs, slender bill with red base, brown back with darker marks and pale underparts. In flight shows large white stripe along hind edge of wings, and white rump. Call is a loud, ringing 'tew' or 'teuk' or 'teup' often repeated and slurred.
Breeds on damp marshes or grassy fields. Common around the coast.
(Map: page 206)

Greenshank
Larger than Redshank – 30 cm. Slim, long-necked wader with long greenish legs and long, thick, slightly upturned bill. Back is very dark in spring (**4**), but is greyer at other times. In flight there is no wing-bar, but long V-shaped pale rump extends up its back. Call is loud 'tew, tew tew'.
Nests inland in the north of Scotland. Visits edges of lakes and coastal marshes elsewhere in spring and autumn. A few winter in the south. (Map: page 206)

Greenshank

Spotted Redshank

Spotted Redshank

Common Redshank

2 Spotted Redshank *winter*

3 Common Redshank *summer*

Common Redshank *winter*

1 Spotted Redshank *summer*

Common Redshank *juvenile*

4 Greenshank *summer*

Greenshank *juvenile*

Hilary Burn.

Curlew Sandpiper *Calidris ferruginea*

These birds are long-distance migrants. They breed in the north and northeast of Russia and many migrate to southeast Asia or Australia, while others travel southwest and winter around the Mediterranean or in Africa. The numbers occurring in Britain and Ireland vary greatly from year to year, but most are seen in September.

On migration these birds fly at about 65 kph and travel hundreds of kilometres non-stop. In order to make these amazing journeys they must put on extra reserves of fat which gives them the energy required. One study has shown that Curlew Sandpipers wintering in South Africa increase their weight from 53 grams to 80 grams in about eight weeks, which should enable them to fly more than 3,000 km before stopping and feeding again.

Wood Sandpiper *Tringa glareola*

The Wood Sandpiper is most often seen as a passage migrant between July and September, with some arriving in the British Isles in spring. They are usually seen singly or in small groups. Wood Sandpipers breed in northern Europe and winter in Africa.

The Wood Sandpiper is common in northern Europe, especially in Scandinavia. It nests in marshes, boggy moorland and clearings in forests, usually on the ground but sometimes in old nests of birds such as thrushes. After two breeding attempts in Britain in the 19th century, regular breeding started in Scotland in 1959 and several sites are now used most years. The main threat to the species in Britain is forestry operations in its breeding areas.

Green Sandpiper *Tringa ochropus*

A shy wader which may sometimes be flushed accidentally from the edge of a lake or river, when all that is usually seen are the long, blackish wings and upperparts and a glowing white rump as the bird flies erratically away, looking like a large House Martin.

On the ground, Green Sandpipers often feed in shallow water with vegetation nearby or where they are sheltered by banks. Like Common Sandpipers, they often bob.

The Green Sandpiper has been found nesting in northern Britain, and may do so again. Instead of nesting on the ground like most other waders, it regularly uses the old nests of other birds, especially thrushes.

Curlew Sandpiper
Size of large Dunlin – 19 cm. Longer legs and longer neck than Dunlin. Downcurved bill and white rump. Breeding plumage (**1**) is brick-red with mottled back. In autumn (**2**) is similar to Dunlin. Juvenile (**3**) has brownish-grey back with rounded pale edges to feathers giving 'scallop pattern', buff breast and white underparts. Wing-bar shows in flight. Flight call is soft 'chirrup'.
Passage migrant to coastal marshes especially in late summer. (No map)

Wood Sandpiper (4)
Smaller than Redshank – 20 cm. Pale stripe over eye and yellowish legs. In flight no wing-bar, but white rump is obvious; underwing paler and legs longer and extend farther beyond tail than Green Sandpiper's. Back is brownish with white spots. Flight call is 'chiff-if-if'.
Passage migrant to coasts and marshes, mainly in eastern Britain in late summer. (Map: page 206)

Green Sandpiper (5)
Smaller than Redshank – 23 cm. Medium-length bill, dark greenish-brown upperparts and no wing-bar. In flight bold white rump contrasts with darker back; underwing darker than Wood Sandpiper's. Adult has spotted back in summer (**6**). Flight when disturbed is Snipe-like and the call is a shrill 'weet-a-weet'.
Mainly a passage migrant visiting freshwater margins from July to September. Some winter in the south. (Map: page 206)

Green Sandpiper

Wood Sandpiper

Dunlin

Dunlin

Curlew Sandpipers

Green Sandpiper

Wood Sandpiper

1 Curlew Sandpiper, *summer*

3 Curlew Sandpiper *juvenile*

2 Curlew Sandpiper *winter*

Dunlin

4 Wood Sandpipers

Green Sandpiper *winter*

6 Green Sandpiper *summer*

Hilary Burn

(Ruddy) Turnstone *Arenaria interpres*

Turnstones feed on insects and other invertebrates, many of which live under stones or seaweed. Its habit of using its stout bill to probe under stones, often pushing them aside in its search for food, has given the Turnstone its name. By hunting in this way, these birds find food which other waders do not reach.

Turnstones are usually seen in small groups, but larger flocks sometimes form at high tide. They often perch on man-made objects projecting from the water.

Turnstones have never been proved to breed in Britain. Those which are seen here breed either in northern Europe or in Greenland. Most of the northern European ones winter on the west coast of Africa and are passage migrants in Britain; those which spend the winter here are mainly from Greenland.

Red-necked Phalarope *Phalaropus lobatus*

As with the Dotterel, the roles of the male and female phalarope are largely reversed: the female is more brightly coloured and performs the courtship display; the male incubates the eggs and looks after the young.

The scientific family name, *Phalaropus*, means 'coot-footed' and the specific name, *lobatus*, also refers to the bird's partly webbed feet which help it when swimming. Phalaropes often spin round rapidly on the water, which helps to stir up food, which they then pick from the surface.

Only a few pairs nest in Britain each year, mostly in Shetland and on a few other islands off northern Scotland. They are remarkably tame and often allow observers to approach very close. The migration of Red-necked Phalaropes is still shrouded in mystery, but most winter in the southern Atlantic, off the African coast.

Grey Phalarope *Phalaropus fulicarius*

Known in North America as the Red Phalarope, this attractive wader is rarely seen in Britain in its colourful breeding plumage. It breeds mainly north of the Arctic Circle in North America and Siberia, with a few nesting in Iceland. Like the Red-necked Phalarope, it spends the winter at sea. It also frequently swims in the phalarope's typical, buoyant manner, often 'spinning' and quickly snatching prey from the surface of the water.

Usually, Grey Phalaropes are seen in ones and twos, but sometimes, when there are storms at sea, hundreds appear, having been blown into inshore waters during migration.

Turnstone
Larger than Ringed Plover – 23 cm. Short, stout bill and short, orange legs. Has broad breast band. In summer (**1**) back is black-and-chestnut and the head white with dark marks. In winter (**2**) head and back are blackish. In flight has white marks on wings, back and tail. Call is twittering 'kitititit'. *Usually seen on rocky seashores or mussel-beds, throughout the year.* (Map: page 207)

Red-necked Phalarope
Smaller than Dunlin – 17 cm. Long, fine, black bill. Usually seen swimming. In summer female (**3**) is brighter than male (**4**); both have grey head, white chin, chestnut neck and a dark back with bold stripes. In winter (**5**) back is grey with paler marks. The head is white with a dark crown and dark cheeks. Juvenile (**6**) has brownish back with buff stripes and buff breast. *A few pairs breed in damp grassy places with scattered pools in northern Scotland.* (Map: page 207)

Grey Phalarope
Larger than Dunlin – 20 cm. Larger than Red-necked with shorter, stouter bill. In summer (**7**) has chestnut underparts, white cheeks and stripy back. In winter (**8**) is like Red-necked but with plain grey back and less black on crown. 1st-winter (**9**) is like winter adult, but has stronger pattern on back. *Unusual passage migrant found both inland and on coast, especially after westerly gales, particularly in autumn.* (No map)

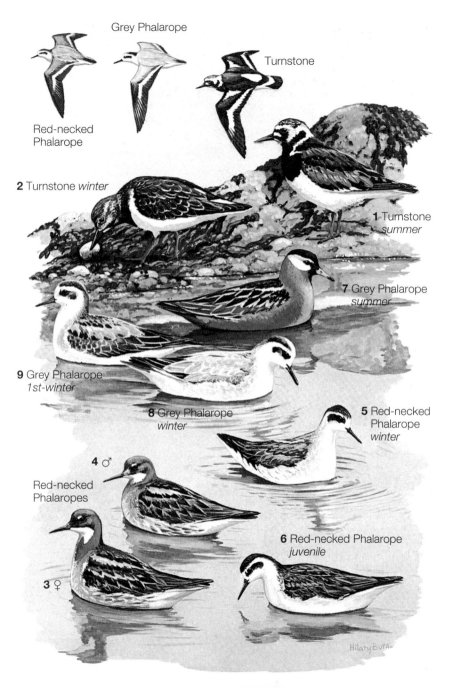

Grey Phalarope

Turnstone

Red-necked
Phalarope

2 Turnstone *winter*

1 Turnstone
summer

7 Grey Phalarope
summer

9 Grey Phalarope
1st-winter

8 Grey Phalarope
winter

5 Red-necked
Phalarope
winter

4 ♂

Red-necked
Phalaropes

6 Red-necked Phalarope
juvenile

3 ♀

Hilary Burn

Pomarine Skua *Stercorarius pomarinus*

An aerial pirate which is regularly seen off our coasts in autumn. 'Poms' breed in the Arctic, and winter in the open ocean.

Long periods of 'sea watching' are usually necessary to see these birds. The best time is when strong winds off the sea force them into inshore waters, but even then identification (especially of juveniles) is difficult and only with practice can one pick out differences from the other skuas, such as the broader, more rounded wings and powerful flight of a typical 'Pom'.

Arctic Skua *Stercorarius parasiticus*

Skuas are the pirates of our coasts, often chasing other seabirds in the air in order to make them drop their food. The chief victims are terns and the smaller gulls. This behaviour is known as kleptoparasitism. When not harrying seabirds, Arctic Skuas feed on carrion, berries, insects and eggs or young of other birds; they also chase and kill small birds and mammals.

Arctic Skuas breed in colonies on northern moorland, usually close to the sea. Animals such as sheep or dogs and even human beings are likely to receive a vicious attack if they enter the territory of an Arctic Skua.

Colour phases of these skuas vary from pale to very dark. In Britain, most of the breeding birds have dark plumage, the paler phases becoming more common in northern and eastern Europe.

Long-tailed Skua *Stercorarius longicaudus*

The Long-tailed Skua is the smallest and most graceful skua. It breeds in the Arctic and is a rather rare visitor to British and Irish coasts. It is seen mainly off western Scotland and Ireland and the east coast of England on migration to and from West Africa or even South America.

Like other skuas, the Long-tailed will harry other birds in flight, but on its northern European breeding grounds it feeds mainly on lemmings.

Great Skua *Catharacta skua*

The old Shetland name of 'Bonxie' is still widely used for this species. Numbers have increased since 1960 and it has spread from Shetland to other Scottish islands and also to the mainland. Over 8,000 pairs now nest, which is more than 50% of the world population.

Bonxies force large gulls and Gannets to disgorge their food; they will also attack and kill other birds. Observers on headlands in late summer may see Bonxies flying south to winter along Iberian or African coasts.

Pomarine Skua
Smaller than Herring Gull – 51 cm. Larger and more bulky than Arctic Skua with a heavier bill. Adult has 'spoon-like' central tail feathers and usually a dusky breast band. Both light (**1**) and dark (**2**) phases may be seen. Chases other seabirds. *Seen here on their way north in May and again on their return in autumn.* (No map)

Arctic Skua
Smaller than Herring Gull – 46 cm. Colour phases vary from pale (**3**) to very dark (**4**). Adults have long central tail feathers. Flight is graceful and hawk-like. Wings have white flashes near tips. Juvenile (**5**) is rich brown with pale barring. *Summer visitor to northern and western Scotland. Seen in other coastal areas on migration.* (Map: page 207)

Long-tailed Skua
Smaller and more graceful than Arctic Skua, but adult (**6**) has longer central tail feathers – 55 cm. Juveniles (**7**) have grey-brown back, neatly barred with cream or white, and longish, blunt-tipped central tail feathers. *Passage migrant to coasts, especially in May and September.* (No map)

Great Skua (8)
Size of Herring Gull – 58 cm. Like large, heavy, short-tailed gull. Often looks uniform dark brown with white wing-flashes. Flight looks slow and heavy, but is fast when attacking. *Breeds in northern Scotland. Seen around coasts on migration.* (Map: page 207)

6 Long-tailed Skua

Arctic Skua

1 Pomarine Skuas
light phase

7 Long-tailed
Skua
juvenile

Great Skua

2 Pomarine Skua
dark phase

3 *light phase*

5 *juvenile*

Arctic Skuas

Pomarine Skua
juvenile

4 *dark phase*

8 Great Skua

Hilary Burn

Black-headed Gull *Larus ridibundus*

The name 'sea-gull' should never be used to describe a Black-headed Gull as this species, more than any other gull, is more at home in a town park than flying over the open sea. The history of Black-headed Gulls in London provides fascinating evidence of how a successful species can adapt to a new environment.

Before 1880, Black-headed Gulls were seen only around the Thames estuary, but from that year they started to move up river, and by the end of the century they were seen regularly along the Thames and its tributaries. The species became more widespread in the early 1900s and by 1917 Black-headed Gulls were catching bread thrown to them from a hotel window! Large winter roosts grew up on some of the reservoirs and in 1940 a breeding colony was discovered on a large London sewage-farm. The invasion of London has been repeated in towns and cities throughout the British Isles.

'Black-headed' is hardly a fair description of a bird which has a mainly white head for almost half the year, and during the other half a dark brown one. The brown head is the breeding plumage and is used in display: when lowered and thrust forward, it is a sign of aggression; when held upright and turned away it is a sign of surrender.

Colonies vary in size from under ten to over 20,000. Within the colonies, pairs occupy small territories, which are defended by ritualised displays. Colonies give protection to nests and all the gulls in the colony are able to take advantage of local food supplies.

Most of the Black-headed Gulls which breed in Britain and Ireland are resident, although they may move around the country in winter. Our birds are joined by migrants from northern and eastern Europe and from Russia which arrive from early August onwards.

Black-headed Gulls feed on a wide range of food, including fish, worms, carrion and seeds. When ants are swarming, these gulls, and other birds, may be seen flying erratically as they catch 'flying ants' in the air. Often they will watch other feeding birds and then move in and rob them of their food. A regular victim is the Great Crested Grebe; Black-headed Gulls hover above a diving grebe and if it surfaces with a fish they swoop down and try to steal it.

Many Black-headed Gulls visit refuse tips, especially in winter when other food is scarce. Because they are so adaptable and exploit so many sources of food, it is not surprising their numbers have grown.

Black-headed Gull
The smallest of our common gulls – 36 cm. A slim bird with white stripe along front edge of its pointed wings. Adult has dark brown head in summer (**1**) and a dark smudge behind the eye in winter (**2**). Bill and legs are red. Juvenile (**3**) has ginger-brown on head, back and sides of breast. 1st-winter birds (**4**) have dark bar on wing, dark flight feathers and dark band on tail.
Breeds in colonies around inland lakes and on coastal marshes. Common throughout British Isles at all times of the year.
(Map: page 207)

1st-winter

adult *winter*

Common Gull

Lesser Black-backed Gull

Black-headed Gulls

3 *juvenile*

4 *1st-winter*

1 *summer*

2 *winter*

Hilary Burn.

Black-headed Gulls

Mediterranean Gull *Larus melanocephalus*

The number of Mediterranean Gulls seen in southern Britain has increased since the 1950s. In 1968 a pair was found nesting successfully within a Black-headed Gull colony and since then numbers have increased to about 60 pairs.

The main breeding colonies are around the Mediterranean and the Black Sea, but it has also nested in western and central Europe.

Little Gull *Larus minutus*

This, the smallest of the World's gulls, is a much more frequent visitor to both Britain and Ireland than in the past, and has attempted to breed here several times. The species also started to nest in North America in 1962. Until this recent expansion most nested in Siberia and northern and south-eastern Europe.

The migration and movement of Little Gulls still puzzle ornithologists. They may turn up anywhere and at any time of year, although the greatest numbers are seen in spring and autumn. In winter, flocks may suddenly appear near our coasts during severe weather conditions, which suggests that many must winter at sea.

Common Gull (Mew Gull) *Larus canus*

The Common Gull is another gull which does not deserve the title 'sea-gull'. Many of the 70,000 or so breeding pairs in Britain and Ireland nest far from the sea, and, when breeding is over for the year, these gulls, together with others which migrate here from northern Europe, are just as likely to be seen on a playing-field in the heart of a built-up area as they are standing on a windswept beach.

Although some Common Gulls nest among colonies of Herring Gulls around our coast, many more nest singly or in small groups on northern moorland, sometimes close to a pool or on shingle near a river. Occasionally they nest off the ground in trees or bushes.

Common Gulls are frequently to be seen feeding on rubbish tips in winter. They will also feed on carrion, even animals which have been killed on roads. Their natural food also includes insects, worms, small mammals and eggs.

Sabine's Gull *Larus sabini*

A graceful small gull which sometimes occurs on our coasts in autumn when en route from its North American breeding grounds to its wintering area of southern Africa. The adult has a dark head in summer and at all ages has a bold white triangular patch on its upperwings and a forked tail. (No map)

Mediterranean Gull

Size of large Black-headed Gull – 39 cm. More like Common Gull in shape, but looks heavier, with a thicker neck and stouter bill. Adult (**1**) has grey wings with white tips and a black head in summer. In winter (**2**) the head is mainly white with a dark streak behind the eye. 1st-winter (**3**) has more contrasting wing pattern than Common Gull.
Has sometimes nested in southern England and small numbers may be seen occasionally elsewhere outside the breeding season.
(Map: page 207)

Little Gull

Smaller than Black-headed Gull – 28 cm. Rather tern-like. Often picks food from the surface of the water in flight. Adult (**4**) has blackish underwing, grey upperwing and black head, but loses most black head-feathers in winter (**5**). 1st-year (**6**) has dark W pattern on back and underwing is pale.
Seen throughout the year mainly in coastal areas, especially in autumn.
(Map: page 207)

Common Gull

Smaller than Herring Gull – 41 cm, with smaller bill, thinner wings and lighter flight. Upperwings of adult (**7**) are uniform grey with white spots on the black wing-tips. On the ground it is rather elegant, with dark eyes and gentle look. Head is dusky in winter (**8**). 1st-winter birds (**9**) have dusky heads, grey backs, dark outer flight feathers and dark tail-band.
Breeds mainly in Scotland and Ireland. Regular visitor elsewhere. (Map: page 207)

Kittiwake

9 Common Gull
1st-winter

Sabine's
Gull
juvenile

5 Little Gull
winter

8 Common
Gull
winter

Little Gull
juvenile

2
Mediterranean
Gull
winter

Black-headed
Gull
winter

3
Mediterranean
Gull
1st-winter

6 Little Gull
1st-winter

Black-headed Gull

7 Common
Gull

4 Little
Gull

1 Mediterranean Gull

Hilary Burn

Lesser Black-backed Gull *Larus fuscus*

Several thousand years ago, a successful species of gull which nested in the Northern Hemisphere started to expand its range both eastwards and westwards. As it colonised new areas, so new races developed and eventually different species evolved. Two of these species nest in the British Isles: the Herring Gull which is descended from birds which spread from the west, and the Lesser Black-back whose ancestors came from the east. These species are, therefore, closely related, and their behaviour is similar; but they rarely inter-breed.

Many Lesser Black-backs nest on or near the coast, but they also nest inland, often on high moorland.

Traditionally, Lesser Black-backs have been regarded as summer migrants, but in recent years many, especially adults, have wintered in the British Isles.

Lesser Black-backs from Scandinavia also winter here and may be recognised by their much darker backs.

Herring Gull *Larus argentatus*

Most Herring Gulls do not look like adults until their fourth year. Although it takes a long time to become fully adult, a Herring Gull may have a long life: one individual is known to have lived 31 years.

Herring Gull colonies are mainly on cliffs, but they will also nest on rocky islands, dunes or shingle beaches and inland; recently some have started nesting on roofs of houses and other buildings.

Herring Gulls feed on a wide range of food: they will follow fishing boats to pick up scraps, they eat eggs, small mammals, carrion and visit rubbish tips. They have learned to drop shellfish on to rocks in order to get at the contents.

When feeding young, the red spot on the adult's bill is important as chicks peck at red by instinct and this pecking prompts the parents to regurgitate food.

The closely related **Yellow-legged Gull** *L. cachinnans* is similar to a Herring Gull, but with yellow legs. It breeds around the Mediterranean and occurs mainly in southern England in autumn, winter and spring. The first pair nested in Britain in 1995.

Glaucous Gull *Larus hyperboreus*

An increasing number of Glaucous Gulls are being seen in the British Isles. They are great scavengers and regularly visit harbours used by fishing boats and also rubbish tips. Some now summer in northern Scotland and have inter-bred with Herring Gulls in Shetland.

The rarer **Iceland Gull** *Larus glaucoides* is also sometimes seen in winter.

Lesser Black-backed Gull
Smaller than Herring Gull – 55 cm. Also lighter build with longer legs. Wings are longer than Herring Gull's and appear narrower. Smaller than Great Black-backed with smaller head and bill. Adult (**1**) has dark grey or black back and yellow legs. Immature (**2**) similar to immature Herring Gulls but have generally darker backs. *Breeds in colonies, usually near the coast. Some winter here.* (Map: page 207)

Herring Gull (3)
A large gull – 60 cm. Larger than Common Gull; has heavy, yellow bill with a red spot, and a fierce look. Back and upperwings are grey with white spots on the black tips. Legs are flesh-coloured or yellow. Immatures (**4**) generally have paler backs than Lesser Black-backs. *Nests all around our shores. Seen inland in winter.* (Map: page 208)

Glaucous Gull
Varies between Herring and Great Black-backed in size – 65–80 cm. Large head and bill. Adult (**5**) has pale grey back and white wing-tips. Immatures (**6**) are paler brown than other immature gulls with even paler wing-tips and no dark band on tail. *Mainly a winter visitor to east coast of Britain. Some summer in Shetland.* (Map: page 208)

Iceland Gull
Size of Herring Gull – 60 cm. Both adult (**7**) and juvenile are very similar to Glaucous, but smaller with a shorter, less heavy bill. *Winter visitor to east coast of Britain.* (Map: page 208)

4 Herring Gull *immature*

6 Glaucous Gull *immature*

Herring Gull immature

2 Lesser Black-backed Gull *immature*

2 Lesser Black-backed Gull *immature*

3 Herring Gull

Herring Gulls

Great Black-backed Gull

5 Glaucous Gull

7 Iceland Gull

Lesser Black-backed Gull *Scandinavian race*

1 Lesser Black-backed Gull

Hilary Burn

Great Black-backed Gull *Larus marinus*

The Great Black-backed Gull increased in Britain and Ireland during the 20th century. Between 1930 and 1956, the number of breeding pairs trebled and the species continues to increase in some areas.

This fierce and predatory gull often feeds on other seabirds: Puffins and Manx Shearwaters are frequent victims. Great Black-backs also feed on carrion, fish, other birds' eggs, shellfish, and also rabbits which they catch and kill. They are often to be seen around fishing ports, where they feed on scraps; although less tame than Herring Gulls, away from man they will dominate other species in their efforts to get food.

Most pairs of Great Black-backs nest on or near the coast, but this species is often seen inland and, in recent years, greater numbers have roosted regularly on inland lakes and reservoirs in winter.

(Black-legged) Kittiwake *Rissa tridactyla*

A truly coastal gull. No other member of this family is so dependent on the sea or spends so much time in the open ocean as the Kittiwake. They are at home far out to sea, where they find sufficient food, drink sea water and survive the fiercest winter gales. Kittiwakes often live for 20 years or more.

Nests, mainly consisting of seaweed, are built on small ledges on the steepest cliffs where eggs and young are safe from predators. Mammals cannot reach them and even larger gulls and skuas find it difficult to approach. These gulls always nest in colonies; the oldest ones usually return first in spring and generally nest on the best ledges in the centre of the colony; youngest birds return last and nest on the edges.

Juveniles leave their colonies in autumn and cross the Atlantic to the coast of Greenland where they join immatures from northern Europe and more local birds from Newfoundland and Greenland. Our young Kittiwakes remain on the other side of the Atlantic for one or two years before returning to the colony of their birth. They will not breed until at least four years old.

The number of Kittiwakes has greatly increased during this century. One fascinating result of this increase has been the growth of colonies on buildings near the sea: ruined castles, warehouses and even seafront hotels now have Kittiwakes nesting on their window-sills and other convenient ledges. Another recent development is the presence of Kittiwakes around harbours and fish docks in the middle of winter.

Great Black-backed Gull
Larger than Lesser Black-back – 64–79 cm. A gull with large head and bill. Looks heavy in flight, wings appear broad and the body bulky. Adult (**1**) has black upperparts and pink legs. Immatures (**2**) are streaky grey-brown with bold 'chequered' pattern. *Breeds on rocky coasts and seen elsewhere outside the breeding season. Rarely in large numbers away from the coast.* (Map: page 208)

Kittiwake
Smaller than Herring Gull – 39 cm. Rather like small Common Gull with slim, yellow bill, short black legs, dark eye and slightly forked tail. Adult (**3**) has grey back and wings with jet black wing-tips. In winter (**4**) adults have smoky grey back to head. Juvenile (**5**) has black mark behind eye, black half-collar, black band on tail and black W pattern on wings. 1st-summer birds (**6**) are like juveniles, but dark marks are much faded. Name comes from the call: a noisy 'kitti-wa-ak'. *Nests on tiny ledges on steep sea cliffs or, occasionally, on buildings. Commonly seen around our coast in summer, but rather unusual inland.* (Map: page 208)

1 Great Black-backed Gulls

Great Black-backed Gulls

2 *immature*

3 *adult summer*

5 *juveniles*
Kittiwakes

4 *adult winter*

5 *juvenile*

6 *1st-summer*

Hilary Burn.

Common Tern *Sterna hirundo*

It is not surprising that these graceful birds, with their long wings and forked tails, have been called 'sea-swallows'. Yet many nest well away from the sea, on inland shingle banks near rivers and around lakes or newly dug gravel or sand pits. Others are seen near inland lakes and rivers on their spring and autumn migration.

Common Terns may be seen in the British Isles between April and October. They fly south in autumn and most winter off the western African coast, as far south as South Africa.

Common Terns catch fish, insects and other prey by diving into the water. In coastal areas, the most commonly caught fish is the sand-eel. In spring birds fly over their territories carrying a fish and calling loudly. Later the fish may be presented by the male to the female.

Some colonies of Common Terns have become smaller in recent years because the best nest-sites have been taken over by gulls.

Arctic Tern *Sterna paradisaea*

No bird sees as much daylight in the course of a year as an Arctic Tern. It is truly a long-distance migrant, which breeds mainly north of the Arctic Circle and migrates in autumn to the very edge of Antarctica.

In the British Isles, the Arctic Tern is at the southern edge of its breeding range. Few pairs breed in southern England and Wales, but in Scotland Arctic Terns are numerous, especially around the coast, and greatly out-number Common Terns.

As with other terns, most of the food is caught below the water surface, by diving. When feeding, they will frequently hover. On their breeding grounds they will drive away intruders by swooping at them and pecking with the tip of their bill.

Identification of Common and Arctic Terns may be difficult, especially when mixed flocks of juveniles move along coasts in autumn; when not specifically identified, birdwatchers call them 'Commic Terns'!

Roseate Tern *Sterna dougallii*

The British and Irish population of Roseate Terns fell from 3,500 pairs in 1960 to fewer than 100 pairs in the early 1990s. The closest stronghold is in the Azores.

More Herring Gulls at tern colonies is one problem; the predation of adults by Peregrines, rats and foxes is another. Also the trapping of terns by children in West Africa may be a contributory factor to the decline.

Common Tern
Smaller than Black-headed Gull – 35 cm. Long, narrow, pointed wings and deeply forked tail. Adult in summer (**1**) has black cap and red bill with black tip. Best field mark is the dark outer primary feathers which appear as a dark wedge and contrast with the pale, translucent inner primaries. Adult in autumn (**2**) has white forehead, browner back and black bill. Call is a drawn-out 'kee-aarr'.
Summer visitor to coasts and inland lakes. (Map: page 208)

Arctic Tern
Size of Common Tern – 35 cm and very similar, but with slightly shorter legs, and rounder, smaller head. Adult (**3**) has all-red bill, white (not grey) rump, darker underparts, and lacks dark 'wedge' on wings. Juveniles (**4**) have pink base to black bill and more brown on back than juvenile Common Tern. Call 'kee-ar'.
Summer visitor nesting around the coast mainly in the north. A few colonies inland. (Map: page 208)

Roseate Tern
Larger than Common Tern – 38 cm. Slender body and longer legs than Common. Adults (**5**) are whiter than Common or Arctic. Bill is black, often with a red base. In spring, breast is a rosy pink. Long tail streamers project beyond wings when perched. Call is rough 'aac aach'. Juvenile (**6**) has black legs, dark head and white edge to underside of wings.
Summer visitor nesting mainly on rocky or sandy islands. (Map: page 208)

2 Common Tern *autumn*

Arctic Tern *autumn*

4 Arctic Tern *juvenile*

Common Tern *juvenile*

Roseate Tern *autumn*

6 Roseate Tern *juvenile*

3 Arctic Tern

5 Roseate Tern

1 Common Tern

Hilary Burn

Sandwich Tern *Sterna sandvicensis*

This, the largest of Britain's breeding terns, no longer nests at Sandwich Bay in Kent, where it was first identified and named. These birds are, however, still regularly seen there on migration, and there are colonies in other parts of the British Isles, mostly on sand or shingle bars, or grass-covered islands. These colonies are easily disturbed and sometimes all the birds will leave if suddenly alarmed and not return again.

Some Sandwich Terns seem to prefer to nest near Black-headed Gulls. Although they sometimes lose their food to the more aggressive gulls they probably benefit from the protection given by the Black-headed Gulls, which chase away the larger predatory gulls.

Food is mainly small fish, which may be caught up to 20 km from the breeding colonies. While the adults are away fishing, the chicks often gather together in crèches which may help to protect the young, but just how the parents find their chicks again in a large moving flock is a real mystery.

Little Tern *Sterna albifrons*

Unfortunately for the Little Tern, it has a liking for many of the beaches which are used by holiday-makers, and each year many pairs fail to nest successfully because they are disturbed by humans. Protection schemes now operate in several parts of the country, and some colonies are fenced. Foxes and crows continue to raid nests, egg-collectors still take some eggs, and this tern's habit of nesting low down on beaches results in many nests being lost during storms or at high tides.

In other parts of the world, even as close as France, Little Terns nest inland along rivers, but in the British Isles they are found only around sea coasts, where they usually fish close to the shore.

Black Tern *Chlidonias niger*

Although Black Terns are regular visitors in spring and autumn, they ceased to breed here regularly in the middle of the 19th century.

Belonging to a family known as marsh terns, the Black Tern breeds mainly near fresh water. In the British Isles, it is most likely to be seen on migration, hunting over inland lakes and reservoirs, although it is frequently seen near the coasts as well. Its typical flight is rather buoyant, but it often dips down to pick insects or other food from the surface of the water.

Sandwich Tern
Larger than Black-headed Gull – 41 cm. Longer, narrower wings and less deeply forked tail than Common Tern. Bill is black with yellow tip. Adult (**1**) in summer has pale upperparts, black cap and untidy crest. Forehead is white in winter, but often starts to whiten during the summer. Juvenile (**2**) is like adult in winter, but browner with brown, spotted crown. Call is harsh 'kirrick'. *Summer visitor to sea coasts. Rare inland.* (Map: page 208)

Little Tern
Smaller than Black-headed Gull – 24 cm. Smallest sea-tern. Adult in summer (**3**) has yellow bill with black tip, yellow legs, black cap with white forehead, dark line through eye and dark outer flight feathers. Juvenile (**4**) has darker bill and brown marks on back and head. Flight is hurried and bird often hovers. Call is 'kik-kik'. *Summer visitor to sandy or shingle beaches.* (Map: page 209)

Black Tern
Smaller than Black-headed Gull – 24 cm. Slightly forked tail and graceful flight. Adult in summer (**5**) has black head and body with grey wings and white under the tail. In autumn (**6**) has white head, neck and body with dark crown and white neck-collar with dark mark on shoulders. Juvenile is like autumn adult. Call 'kik, kik'. Often dips down to pick food from the water surface. *Very rare breeding bird, seen mainly in May and August–September.* (No map)

Sandwich Tern

Little Tern

2 Sandwich Tern *juvenile*

4 Little Tern *juvenile*

5 Black Tern

Black Tern

6 Black Tern *autumn*

1 Sandwich Terns

3 Little Terns

Hilary Burn

(Common) Guillemot *Uria aalge*

This is our most numerous seabird and the drama of its large, noisy, and often smelly northern colonies must be seen to be appreciated. The birds breed where the sea cliffs are steepest, and crowd together on tiny ledges or on flat-topped stacks. The single egg, which is incubated between the bird's feet, is pear-shaped and spins if knocked, so it is therefore less likely to roll off a cliff-edge.

This auk catches fish by diving and chasing its prey underwater. It regularly travels up to 16 km to find food and some have travelled as far as 200 km to food-rich waters.

The form of Guillemot known as 'bridled', because of its 'spectacle-like' markings, becomes more numerous towards the Arctic; in the south of Britain, only 1% of Guillemots are bridled compared with about 26% in Shetland.

Guillemots leave their colonies when the young are only half grown and all disappear out to sea, safe from the large, predatory gulls. Most adults will winter in British or Irish waters, although the young may travel farther afield. Many become victims of oil pollution incidents and are frequently washed ashore dead or dying.

Razorbill *Alca torda*

The British Isles are important as the breeding ground for many seabirds, especially the Razorbill: about 20% of its world population breeds here. Although not so numerous as Guillemots, Razorbills are rather more widespread. They nest among fallen boulders or in crevices and prefer sites where a rock roof gives their eggs and chicks some protection from gulls.

Razorbills' eggs are not pear-shaped like those of the Guillemot, but a more oval shape, as they are not normally laid on narrow ledges and are less likely to be knocked into the sea.

Young leave the cliffs when half grown. First- and second-year birds are migratory and may winter in the Bay of Biscay, while some even reach the Mediterranean. Older birds remain closer to the British Isles and, like Guillemots, suffer from oil pollution incidents.

Little Auk *Alle alle*

This, our smallest auk, winters far out to sea and is seen here only when strong winds force it near our coasts or, occasionally, blow it inland.

Little Auks feed on plankton. They nest in the Arctic and some of their breeding colonies, on inaccessible cliffs, contain more than a million pairs. Their droppings below the colony help lush vegetation to grow, which is grazed by geese and reindeer.

Guillemot (1)

Larger than Jackdaw – 42 cm. Dark brown-and-white penguin-like bird with black pointed bill. Some, known as bridled guillemots (**2**), have white 'spectacle' markings. Flight is fast with rapid wingbeats. In winter (**3**) neck and sides of head are white. Call is a growling 'arr'. *Breeds on rocky coasts. In winter it lives mainly out to sea.* (Map: page 209)

Razorbill (4)

Slightly smaller than Guillemot – 41 cm. Head and upperparts are black. Bill is black, deep and has white marks. When swimming, appears more plump than Guillemot, and its longer, more pointed tail is raised. In winter (**5**) has white neck and cheeks. 1st-winter birds have smaller bills. *Breeds on remote cliffs, stacks and rocky islands.* (Map: page 209)

Little Auk

Size of Starling – 21 cm. Dumpy and short-necked. Black-and-white in summer with a short, stubby bill. In winter (**6**) has white sides to neck and white throat and cheeks. Flies with fast wingbeats, and wings hardly raised above the level of the body. Underwing pattern is variable, but often appears dark. *Mainly a winter visitor, usually seen when storms at sea force it close to the shore.* (Map: page 209)

4 Razorbills

Razorbill

Guillemot

6 Little Auks
winter

3 Guillemots
winter

1
Guillemots

5 Razorbill
winter

2
Guillemot
bridled

Hilary Burn

Black Guillemot *Cepphus grylle*

Known also by its old Viking name of 'Tystie', the Black Guillemot is by far the rarest of our breeding auks. Like other members of the family, it needs rocky coasts for nesting, but not open cliff ledges like the Guillemot; instead, it nests in holes, crevices, under boulders and, often, in caves. Occasionally, young are reared in man-made structures such as holes in harbour walls or ruined buildings.

Before the breeding season gets under way, adults may be seen displaying: chasing, diving and calling with beaks open, showing their bright red mouths.

The chief food is fish, which is caught during dives lasting a minute or more and often taking place closer to the shore than those of other auks. They do not migrate far from their breeding grounds in winter and even those which breed in the Arctic may move only to the nearest ice-free water, where their pale winter plumage gives them the advantage of camouflage.

(Atlantic) Puffin *Fratercula arctica*

The Puffin is familiar to most people, yet it nests mainly on remote islands and can be very difficult to observe. It winters at sea, returning to its breeding colonies in March or April and leaving again in August. The population fluctuates; recently the numbers breeding at some northern colonies have increased dramatically while others farther south have declined.

Some Puffins breed in holes in cliff-faces or among boulders, but most nest in burrows on the grassy cliff-tops. The burrows are either dug out by the Puffins themselves or taken over from rabbits. The main enemies of nesting Puffins are rats and the large gulls; the safest colonies are on 'rat-free' islands or on steep slopes where gulls have more difficulty in attacking.

When feeding young, Puffins may be seen carrying ten or more fish in their bill. They can open their bills so that the two halves are parallel, and this, together with a series of hooks inside the bill, helps them to hold one fish while catching another. Fishing Puffins probably zig-zag through shoals of fish which helps to explain why their prey is often arranged alternately head-to-tail when carried in the bill.

Only one egg is laid, and the solitary chick remains in the burrow for six weeks, until fully grown. The parents reduce the number of feeds until it leaves the burrow and makes its way to the sea. This first journey usually takes place at night, but gulls and skuas still kill many young Puffins before they reach the sea.

Black Guillemot

Size of Jackdaw – 34 cm. In summer (**1**) is black with large white wing-patches. Legs and feet are bright red. In winter (**2**) is largely white with mottled back. Juveniles are like adults in winter, but browner. Frequently dives. *Breeds on rocky coasts mainly in northern and western Britain and all around the coast of Ireland.* (Map: page 209)

Puffin

Smaller than feral Rock Dove – 30 cm. Black-and-white with colourful, triangular bill in summer (**3**), clown-like face and red feet. In winter (**4**) face of adult is dusky and bill is less colourful. Juvenile (**5**) has small dark bill and dusky cheeks. Call is a growling 'arrr'. *Breeds in burrows on cliff-tops, mostly on islands. Winters at sea.* (Map: page 209)

Puffins

1 Black Guillemots

Black Guillemots

Guillemot *winter*

Razorbill *winter*

2 Black Guillemot *winter*

4 Puffin *winter*

5 Puffin *juvenile*

3 Puffin

Hilary Burn

Rock Dove (Rock Pigeon) *Columba livia*

Truly wild Rock Doves are at home only on the rocky, windswept coasts of western Scotland and Ireland. They feed mainly on seeds, and nest and roost on cliff ledges or in caves. It is from these birds that our familiar 'town pigeon' is descended.

For thousands of years, these birds have been domesticated. Special dovecotes have been built to provide safe roosts and nest-sites so that the young pigeons could be killed to provide fresh meat, especially in winter.

Many pigeons ignored their specially built homes and moved into towns and city centres where they were safe from predators and found suitable nest-sites on the surrounding buildings. To these urban flocks came colourful 'fancy' pigeons which had escaped, and also lost 'homing pigeons'. Now the variety of plumage colours is bewildering, but many still retain very similar colours to their Rock Dove ancestors.

So widespread are feral Rock Doves that it is possible that there are only a few pure Rock Doves left wild in the British Isles. Some of the feral birds have also returned to their original nest-sites on cliff ledges around our coasts.

Like other pigeons, Rock Doves or their feral descendants may be seen 'rain-bathing'. This involves lying on the ground with ruffled feathers, then leaning to one side and raising a wing so that rain falls on the underside. This behaviour may disconcert an observer, giving the false impression that the bird is injured.

Stock Dove (Stock Pigeon) *Columba oenas*

These birds are the only pigeons or doves in the British Isles which regularly nest in holes in trees. They may be found in a wide range of different habitats from large gardens to rocky cliffs. They nest wherever there are old trees, but will also nest in holes in buildings or on cliffs, under bushes or even in burrows.

Early in the last century, Stock Doves were found only in southeastern England, but then they spread to many new areas. In the 1950s, they declined because of the effect of toxic seed-dressings. The population later recovered, but, like many farmland birds, is now declining again.

In spite of liking town parks, Stock Doves rarely feed with feral Rock Doves; instead, they feed mainly on grain and other seeds. Flocks of Stock Doves may often be seen feeding together, sometimes with Wood Pigeons.

Breeding Stock Doves display in spring or summer. In their aerial display, they fly in large circles with wings held in a shallow V. On the ground, the male puffs out his neck feathers and calls while bowing to the female.

Rock Dove

33 cm. Blue-grey, with paler grey back, white rump, two black wing-bars and white underwing. The familiar feral Rock Dove (**1**) has a variety of plumages, including dark grey, reddish-brown and white. Some resemble true wild Rock Doves.
True Rock Doves are only found on remote, rocky, western coasts of Scotland and Ireland. Feral Rock Doves are common in towns throughout the British Isles.
(Map: page 209)

Stock Dove (2)

Size of Rock Dove – 33 cm. Smaller and darker than Wood Pigeon without white patches on wings or neck. Has two short black wing-bars and black rear edge to wings. Differs from Rock Dove by having grey rump. Call is deep, quiet but far-carrying 'ooo-wah'.
Nests in woods, parks and farmland where there are old trees. Resident, found in most parts of the British Isles except the far north.
(Map: page 209)

Stock Dove

Rock Doves
feral

1 Rock Doves
feral

2 Stock Dove

Wood Pigeon

(Common) Wood Pigeon *Columba palumbus*

Once, Wood Pigeons were numerous only in deciduous woods, but times have changed, and now they nest in town centres, in small copses, in hedges or even on the ground. In many areas, they are serious farmland pests.

One reason for their success is their long breeding season, which lasts from April to October, with some nesting even in winter. Generally, Wood Pigeons in towns nest earlier than those in farmland, many of which are rearing young at harvest time when there is a plentiful supply of grain. Apart from man, Wood Pigeons have few enemies, which may also account for their success.

In summer their aerial display-flights may be seen, as they rise slowly, make a clapping sound with their wings and then glide down again. When alarmed, they crash out of a tree or bush and clap their wings loudly.

Wood Pigeons eat mainly vegetable matter and they feed their young (called squabs) on a special fluid known as pigeon's milk which is made in the adult's crop.

(Eurasian) Collared Dove *Streptopelia decaocto*

The Collared Dove is a relative newcomer to Britain and Ireland. Its spread across Europe is a remarkable story. At the start of the 20th century, it was found only in Asia and southeast Europe. Then, in about 1930, it began to spread northwestwards, reaching Austria in 1938 and the Netherlands in 1947.

The first Collared Doves to breed in Britain nested in Norfolk in 1955, and the species has now spread to the west coast of Ireland and Shetland, and has even reached Iceland.

Although Collared Doves lay a clutch of only two eggs, their breeding season may last from March to September and up to five broods may be reared in one year. This fast breeding and lack of competition with other species has helped their extraordinary increase in numbers.

(European) Turtle Dove *Streptopelia turtur*

The Turtle Dove is the only pigeon or dove which is a summer visitor. It returns from its winter quarters in West Africa in late April or May, and its soothing, purring song is to be heard in the English countryside for most of the summer, but recently numbers have declined.

Like other pigeons, Turtle Doves are largely vegetarian, feeding on seeds of many plants. Their flimsy nests are built in tall bushes or hedges and two eggs are laid. Two broods are usually reared before the doves leave again in late summer.

Wood Pigeon (1)

Larger than Rock Dove – 41 cm. Largest dove or pigeon. Plump, with rather small head. White patch on side of neck and white bars across wings. Pinkish breast and dark band on tail. Juvenile (**2**) lacks white on sides of neck. Song is a soothing 'co-coo-coo, coo-co'. Often seen in large flocks, especially in winter.
Found in woods, farmland and town parks, throughout the British Isles except some northern islands.
(Map: page 209)

Collared Dove (3)

Slightly smaller than Rock Dove – 32 cm. Rather long tail, dark wing-tips and black half-collar. Plumage is pinkish-grey. White outer tail feathers when seen from above, distinct black-and-white tail pattern when seen from below. Song is monotonous 'co-cooo-cok'.
Widespread in the British Isles, usually near towns, villages or farms.
(Map: page 210)

Turtle Dove (4)

Slightly smaller than Rock Dove – 32 cm. Small, slim dove. Generally darker than Collared Dove with 'scaly' back and black-and-white patch on neck. Tail is black with white border. Call is a loud purring noise. Flight is often very rapid.
Summer migrant to woods and farmland in south and east Britain. Rare in Scotland and Ireland. (Map: page 210)

Turtle Dove

Wood Pigeons
display

Collared
Dove

Wood Pigeon

Stock Dove

Turtle Dove

3 Collared
Dove

Collared Dove

2 Wood Pigeon
juvenile

4 Turtle
Dove

1 Wood Pigeon

Rose-ringed Parakeet *Psittacula krameri*

The Rose-ringed Parakeet (formerly called the Ring-necked Parakeet) is common in India and parts of Africa and many have been brought to Britain as cage birds. Some have escaped or been deliberately released and are now breeding wild in parts of southeast England and around London. They have survived cold winters and are showing signs of increasing and spreading to new areas.

They nest in holes in trees and feed on buds and fruit. They will also visit bird tables in winter. If numbers continue to increase, this species may become a serious nuisance to fruit farmers.

(Common) Cuckoo *Cuculus canorus*

There are few life histories so strange as that of the Cuckoo. It spends the winter in central or even southern Africa and returns to the British Isles in April, when its familiar song is usually welcomed as a sign of spring. It feeds mainly on insects and their larvae, especially hairy caterpillars which are not usually eaten by birds.

While Cuckoos are pairing and claiming territories, noisy chases take place as males pursue females. Later, the male's display may be seen as he bobs and sways on a perch with wings drooped and tail raised and spread.

A female will usually return to the area where she was reared and there she will search out nests of small insectivorous birds, such as Dunnock, Meadow Pipit or Reed Warbler. She will wait until a nest contains some eggs and then lays her own eggs in it. After laying, she will remove one of the other eggs and then leave the host species to incubate her egg. The young Cuckoo generally hatches first and, although blind and unfeathered, instinctively sets about the task of pushing out the other eggs so that it will have the sole attention of its foster parents.

Eggs of Cuckoos may resemble those of the host species. The female cannot change the colour of her eggs, but she usually chooses one particular species, often the one by which she was reared and which her eggs sometimes, but not always, match.

Adult Cuckoos leave the British Isles in July and early August, but the young birds do not leave until late August or September, and thus have to navigate their own way to their African winter quarters, unaided by their parents.

Rose-ringed Parakeet
Size of Wood Pigeon – 41 cm. Bright green with very long tail and red bill. Male (**1**) has thin black line running from bill around his neck. Regularly makes loud screech in flight.
Resident in parts of England and is spreading to new areas, often on the edge of towns. (Map: page 210)

Cuckoo (2)
Slightly smaller than Kestrel – 33 cm. Rather like male Sparrowhawk with long tail, grey upperparts and barred underparts, but wings are pointed and the tail is graduated and spotted with white. Juvenile (**3**) is generally reddish-brown and rather Kestrel-like; it has a white spot on the back of its head. Flight is hawk-like with shallow wingbeats. Song is well-known 'cuckoo', but other sounds are made, including a bubbling call by the female.
Summer visitor to most parts of the British Isles.
(Map: page 210)

The newly hatched young Cuckoo pushes the host's eggs out of the nest.

Rose-ringed
Parakeets

♀

1 ♂

2 Cuckoo

Cuckoos

3 Cuckoo
juvenile

Dunnock

Hilary Burn.

Barn Owl *Tyto alba*

This species hunts mainly at night, but may occasionally be seen hunting in daylight in winter, when food is in short supply, or in summer when feeding young.

Although many Barn Owls nest in barns, others use holes in old trees. Unfortunately, modern barns are not as suitable for nesting Barn Owls as old ones, some of which even had special holes to allow owls easy access.

Their population is now half that of 50 years ago. The decline has largely been caused by the loss of feeding areas, especially rough grassland and field margins.

They should be welcomed on farms as small mammals make up 90% of their prey. They have superb hearing and can locate their prey in total darkness. When hunting, they fly close to the ground with a slow wavering flight and frequently hover before dropping on to their prey.

The **Snowy Owl** *Nyctea scandiaca* is a very large, mainly white owl which sometimes visits northern Britain from the Arctic. It has nested in Shetland.

Tawny Owl *Strix aluco*

This is the commonest owl in Britain (but is absent from Ireland). It may be found even in towns, provided that there are old trees in which it can roost and nest. Usually it nests in a hole in a tree, but will also use old buildings, holes in cliffs or even disused nests of larger birds such as crows.

Tawnys usually hunt at night. By day, they roost in holes or in trees, close to the trunk, where they may be 'mobbed' by small birds which give alarm calls to draw attention to the predator.

When hunting, they often use a perch from which they drop on to their prey. They feed mainly on small mammals and birds, but insects and worms are also taken.

Little Owl *Athene noctua*

This owl is widespread throughout Europe, but did not breed in Britain until the end of the 19th century, when there were several attempts to introduce it into various parts of England. Some of these attempts were successful and now the Little Owl is quite common on lowland farms and in many other habitats, including some towns. It does not, however, breed in Ireland.

Little Owls may often be seen in daylight, sitting on roadside walls or posts. Much of their hunting takes place at dawn or dusk. The chief prey consists of insects and worms. It also takes mammals and small birds.

A hole in a deciduous tree is the most common nest-site; some have been in use for at least 25 years.

Barn Owl (1)

Smaller than Wood Pigeon – 34 cm. White underparts and honey-coloured back with dark marks. White face is rather monkey-like. Makes a long, eerie shriek as well as other 'hissing' or 'snoring' calls.

Found mainly on farmland in most parts of Britain and Ireland. Rarer in northern Scotland. (Map: page 210)

Tawny Owl (2)

Smaller than Wood Pigeon – 38 cm. Large brown owl with darker marks and white flecks on its back. Underparts are pale with dark streaks. Wings are broad and rounded. Tail is short. Song is the familiar 'hoohoo-oo-oooo' and a loud, sharp 'kewick'.

Lives in woods throughout Britain. Not found in Ireland. (Map: page 210)

Little Owl (3)

Size of Starling – 22 cm. Small and flat-headed. Brown back is spotted with white. Underparts are pale with brown streaks. Bobs when alarmed. Flight is undulating, usually close to the ground. Has repetitive 'kiew-kiew' call, rather like a mewing kitten.

Found mainly on farmland and in parkland in England and Wales. (Map: page 210)

2 Tawny Owl

Barn Owl

Barn Owl

3 Little Owls

Hilary Burn

Long-eared Owl *Asio otus*

In Britain, the Long-eared Owl breeds mainly in conifer woodland or in pine trees in isolated plantations. In Ireland, where it is the commonest owl, it is as likely to be found in deciduous as in coniferous woods. It often breeds in old nests of other species, especially those of Magpie or Carrion Crow, or a squirrel's drey.

Long-eared Owls hunt mainly at night and feed on small mammals, birds and insects. Although most are resident, others arrive here from northern Europe for the winter, and communal roosts of 12 or more of these owls may sometimes be found. In some winters, exceptionally high numbers are seen.

The tufts of feathers on the head are, of course, not ears, but probably used by the owls to communicate. They are raised when nervous, but always lie flat in flight.

Short-eared Owl *Asio flammeus*

A hunting Short-eared Owl flies one or two metres from the ground, flapping, gliding and sometimes hovering as it searches for short-tailed voles which make up 65% of its diet. Other small mammals and birds are also caught. Much of the hunting takes place during daylight.

As with many birds of prey, incubation begins as soon as the first egg is laid, so the young hatch at intervals. When food is scarce, only the eldest and strongest will live, but, when food is plentiful, the whole brood may survive. The population of these owls depends, therefore, on the population of voles.

In winter, these owls may visit farmland, rough ground and coastal marshes. There have been local increases in the breeding numbers, often associated with places with young conifer plantations.

(European) Nightjar *Caprimulgus europaeus*

At dusk, most insect-eating birds go to roost, but it is then that the Nightjar becomes active: twisting and turning in flight as it catches night-flying insects, especially moths, in its large mouth. On summer evenings, the strange, continuous, almost mechanical song may be heard, the pitch altering as the bird turns its head.

Nightjars winter in Africa and are one of the last migrants to return here in spring. During the day, they perch lengthways on a branch and are beautifully camouflaged. They nest on the ground where, again, they blend with their surroundings.

During the last 50 years, Nightjars have declined. Climate change may have reduced insect food in the north while the loss of heathland reduced the southern population.

Long-eared Owl (1)
Slightly smaller than Tawny Owl – 36 cm, with longer wings and tail. Rather slender, with delicately streaked body, cat-like face and orange eyes. Ear-tufts show only when perched. In flight, it has deep wingbeats followed by a glide with wings held in line with the body, the underparts showing up as uniformly dark. Song is a low, drawn-out hoot. Young give high-pitched squeaks, like an unoiled hinge.
A secretive owl of woods in many parts of Britain and Ireland. (Map: page 210)

Short-eared Owl (2)
Size of Tawny Owl – 38 cm. Long wings and short tail. Mottled brown upperparts. Streaked breast, but pale belly and flanks. Round face and fierce yellow eyes. Often perches on the ground. When hunting, flies low with a few wingbeats followed by a glide with wings held in a shallow V. Call a hoarse bark. Song a hollow 'boo-boo-boo-boo'.
Breeds in open country, especially moorland and young plantations in northern Britain. More widespread in winter. (Map: page 210)

Nightjar
Smaller than Kestrel – 27 cm. Long tail and long wings. Silent, hawk-like flight. Delicately marked grey-and-brown plumage. Male (**3**) has white spots on wings and tail. Loud churring song is heard after dark. Flight call is sharp 'coo-ik'. Wings are clapped in display.
Summer visitor to heaths, moors and plantations, mainly in the south.
(Map: page 211)

Long-eared Owl

Short-eared Owl

3 Nightjar ♂

Nightjar

1 Long-eared Owl

2 Short-eared Owls

Hilary Burn.

(Common) Swift *Apus apus*

When a young Swift leaves its nest, it may not land again for months or even years! Swifts are perfectly adapted to life on the wing: they sleep, eat, drink, gather nest material and even mate without landing.

Within a few days of leaving its nest in a hole in a building, or a crack in a cliff-face, the young Swift will be heading for central or southeastern Africa, where it will spend the winter before returning the following spring. Not until its fourth year will it be able to breed successfully. Some immature Swifts may remain in Africa for a whole summer; others will travel north, but roam over Europe.

Swifts have all four of their toes pointing forwards which helps them to cling to vertical surfaces. They do not usually land on the ground deliberately and, if they do so, they may have difficulty in becoming airborne again.

Hoopoe *Upupa epops*

This exotic bird is a rather rare visitor to the British Isles, but each spring a few appear to overshoot their normal breeding areas in central and southern Europe and arrive in Britain or Ireland, mainly near the south or east coasts. Very occasionally a pair will stay and breed.

The bird's name comes from its curious whooping call, made with its head between its legs. It feeds mainly on insect larvae and often hunts on areas of short grass, where it probes with its long bill.

(Common) Kingfisher *Alcedo atthis*

A Kingfisher usually hunts from a branch, or some other perch, overhanging a stream or river, but will also sometimes hover before plunging into the water to seize an unsuspecting fish. A variety of small fish are caught, including sticklebacks and bullheads which have to be beaten against a branch before being swallowed, head first.

Kingfishers lay their eggs in a chamber at the end of a tunnel, dug into a river bank or some other soft cliff. Nests become very smelly and unpleasant while in use.

The iridescent blue of the Kingfisher is not a true colour, but is caused by light being reflected off the microscopic parts of the feathers; this is known as 'structural colour'.

Kingfishers are usually found near slow-flowing rivers or lakes. Some remain all winter, so long as waters remain unfrozen, but others move downstream and visit coastal waters. In cold winters, many die. Water pollution also seriously affects Kingfisher populations and may have eliminated this species from some industrial areas.

Swift (1)

16.5 cm. Shorter body, but longer wings than Swallow. Dark brown, with pale throat, short forked tail and narrow crescent-shaped wings. Never perches on wires and rarely lands. Flight is fast and call is a shrill screech. Often seen in flocks. Juveniles have a 'scaly' appearance.
Summer visitor from May to August. Seen in town and country in most of the British Isles. (Map: page 211)

Hoopoe (2)

Smaller than Rock Dove – 28 cm. Long, downcurved bill, pinkish-brown body; broad, rounded, black-and-white wings and a large crest which may be raised or lowered. Has curious bouncing flight. Song is quiet but far-carrying 'oop-oop-oop'.
Unusual spring migrant and summer visitor, seen mainly in southern England. Most occur in March–April.

Kingfisher

A little larger than House Sparrow – 16.5 cm. Large head and bill, short tail. Bright blue-green upperparts with vivid blue streak on back. Underparts are chestnut. White throat and white patch on neck. Female (3) has red base to lower mandible. Call is a shrill whistle. Flight is fast, straight and, usually, low over water or nearby fields.
Found near lakes and rivers in England, Wales and Ireland, but only in a few places in southern Scotland. (Map: page 211)

1 Swifts

House
Martin

Swallow

2 Hoopoes

3 Kingfisher ♀

Hilary Burn.

Wryneck *Jynx torquilla*

Formerly, the Wryneck commonly nested in holes in old trees, especially in orchards, in southeast England, but no longer does so. A few pairs occasionally breed in Scotland.

The name Wryneck comes from the way the bird twists and turns its head.

Green Woodpecker *Picus viridis*

The Green Woodpecker often feeds on the ground, where it hunts for ants and may, sometimes, be found a long way from the trees. On the ground, it appears clumsy and moves with a series of hops. If disturbed, the bright yellow rump is the most obvious feature as it flies away. Sometimes its distinctive droppings may be found: they resemble ash from a cigarette and contain the remains of hundreds of ants.

This woodpecker seldom 'drums', so its laughing call (given by both sexes and from which it derives its name 'yaffle') is often the first clue that the species is present.

The nest-hole is excavated by both sexes and has an entrance 6.5 cm across. As with other woodpeckers, no nest material is used except for a few wood chips.

Great Spotted Woodpecker *Dendrocopos major*

As with other woodpeckers, its flight is deeply undulating with wings almost closing at regular intervals. All woodpeckers climb trees in a series of hops with the stiff tail feathers pressed against the trunk for support.

A Great Spotted Woodpecker is seldom seen on the ground. It feeds on insects, nuts, seeds and berries. When feeding, the tongue can extend 4 cm beyond the tip of the bill.

Unique adaptations to muscles and bones in the head and neck allow woodpeckers to use their bills to 'drum' and to chisel out nest-holes without the impacts harming the bird.

Lesser Spotted Woodpecker *Dendrocopos minor*

This, our smallest woodpecker, is secretive and generally hard to observe. In early spring, its call and drumming reveal its whereabouts. Drumming involves as many as 14–15 blows per second with the bill and its purpose is to declare territory, not to drill a nest-hole. The male has a wonderful moth-like display, but luck as well as patience are needed to observe it.

The nest-hole is excavated slowly in decaying wood, from one to as much as 20 m above ground, often on the underside of a branch.

The chief food of this woodpecker is wood-boring insects which are caught with its long tongue.

Wryneck (1)
Slightly larger than House Sparrow – 16.5 cm. Delicately marked brown plumage with darker brown, arrow-shaped mark on back. Rather short, pointed bill. *Rare breeding species. More likely to be seen on migration, especially on the British east coast in autumn.*

Green Woodpecker (2)
Size of feral Rock Dove – 32 cm. Dark green back, paler green below. Bright yellowish rump. Flight is undulating. Red crown. Juvenile (3) is heavily streaked. Loud laughing call. *Prefers grassy areas with plenty of old trees. Widespread in the south and increasing in Scotland. Absent from Ireland.* (Map: page 211)

Great Spotted Woodpecker
Smaller than Blackbird – 23 cm. Large white patches on shoulders show well in flight. Male (4) has red nape: both sexes have red under the tail. Juvenile (5) has red crown. Call is loud 'tchick'. Flight is undulating. Loud drumming made in spring. *Found in most British woods, but not in Ireland.* (Map: page 211)

Lesser Spotted Woodpecker
Size of House Sparrow – 14 cm. Barred back and wings. Male (6) has red crown. Female (7) pale crown. Flight is undulating. Call is quiet 'tchick'. Song is high, fast 'pee-pee-pee'. Drumming is higher-pitched and longer than Great Spotted's. *Found in parkland in southern England and Wales.* (Map: page 211)

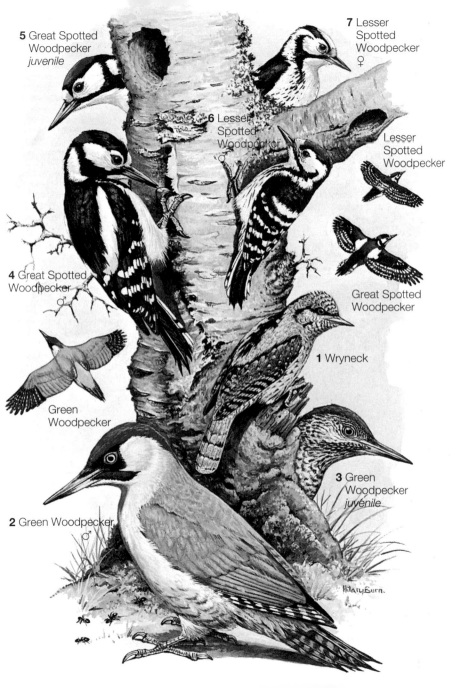

5 Great Spotted
Woodpecker
juvenile

7 Lesser
Spotted
Woodpecker
♀

6 Lesser
Spotted
Woodpecker
♂

Lesser
Spotted
Woodpecker

Great Spotted
Woodpecker

4 Great Spotted
Woodpecker
♂

1 Wryneck

Green
Woodpecker

3 Green
Woodpecker
juvenile

2 Green Woodpecker
♂

Hilary Burn.

Woodlark *Lullula arborea*

In summer, Woodlarks are usually found on dry heathland or downland where there are scattered trees which can be used as song-posts, long grass for nesting, and short grass for feeding. They also nest in recently cleared areas of woodland.

They are less likely to be seen in large flocks than are Skylarks, and they roam away from their breeding areas in winter. Although some of our breeding population is resident, most probably migrate for the winter.

The number breeding in Britain has increased during the last one hundred years: about 600 pairs now nest annually.

Skylark *Alauda arvensis*

The Skylark is one of the most widespread of any bird breeding in Britain or Ireland. Not only is it found on all types of farmland, but also on salt marshes, dunes and rough ground, and even in built-up areas. It is missing only from the tops of the highest mountains. Recent changes in farming practice may have affected breeding success as the breeding population has fallen by more than a half in the last twenty years.

It announces its territory by singing, and, as it often nests in treeless country, it has overcome the lack of songposts by singing in the sky, often at a great height, where it hangs – almost invisible to our eyes.

Our Skylarks are mostly resident, but in winter, especially in cold weather, flocks fly in from Europe. In long cold spells, many die.

Skylarks feed on seeds, leaves, worms and insects and their larvae, as well as a variety of other animal and vegetable foods.

In the past, many were trapped and killed for food, their tongues being considered a great delicacy. Although trapping has now died out in Britain, it continues in some European countries, where vast numbers of Skylarks are killed each year.

Shore Lark (Horned Lark) *Eremophila alpestris*

Shore Larks are scarce rare winter visitors, mainly on the British east coast .

They normally nest on dry Arctic tundra, but also on more southerly short grassland in North America, in mountain ranges in North Africa and the Middle East and on upland steppes in central Asia.

Shore Larks nest on the ground, amongst vegetation. The young leave the nest before being able to fly; they split up and lie still when danger threatens, behaviour which helps to protect them from predators.

Woodlark (1)
Slightly larger than House Sparrow – 15 cm. Like Skylark, but smaller, with stripes over eyes which meet on back of head. Short tail has white corners. Black-and-white patch on leading edge of wing. Flight is rather jerky. Song is sweet and musical, given from a perch or in a circling song flight. Call is a pleasant 'kit-loo-eet'. *Breeds mainly on heathland in southern England and parts of Wales.*
(Map: page 211)

Skylark (2)
Smaller than Starling – 18 cm. Brown streaked back, pale underparts and streaked breast. Short crest. Broad wings with pale hind edge. White outer tail feathers. Often seen in flocks in winter. Loud, clear, rapid, warbling song is usually given in a song flight as the bird rises, circles, hovers and then drifts downwards; also from posts or the ground. *Widespread throughout the British Isles.*
(Map: page 212)

Shore Lark
Smaller than Skylark – 16.5 cm. Pale brown upperparts, whitish below. Male (**3**) has yellow face with black on forehead, cheeks and breast, and also has two small black horns. Female, juvenile (**4**) and male in winter (**5**) have less distinct face markings. *Rare visitor mainly seen on east coast of England. Has nested in Scotland.*
(Map: page 212)

Woodlark

Skylarks

3 Shore
Larks

5 Shore Lark
♂ winter

Meadow
Pipit

2 Skylarks

4 Shore Lark
juvenile

Woodlark
juvenile

1 Woodlark

Hilary Burn

Sand Martin *Riparia riparia*
This species returns to the British Isles in March, usually a few days, or even weeks, before the first Swallow. It winters in Africa, south of the Sahara, and most return to the same colony as the previous year.

Sand Martins nest in burrows which they usually dig for themselves in banks. Although some may tunnel in river banks or sea cliffs, many use man-made cliffs in sand or gravel quarries.

Although Sand Martins are widespread, numbers declined by 90% after 1969 as a result of a drought in the Sahel region of West Africa, the area where they winter. Since 1986, there has been a partial recovery.

(Barn) Swallow *Hirundo rustica*
Once, long ago, it was thought that when Swallows disappeared in winter they hid at the bottom of lakes or flew to the moon. We know now that most of our Swallows fly to South Africa. We also know that since 1980 the population of British Swallows has been slowly declining.

Most Swallows return here in April and rear two, and sometimes three, broods. In the past, they must have nested in hollow trees or in caves; now, most nest inside buildings, especially barns, where their mud cup is built on a rafter or some other support.

Swallows hunt insects in the air. Their short, wide bills make it easier for them to catch their flying prey. Often they hunt over lakes and rivers where flying insects are more plentiful. Since they can feed while flying, martins and swallows can migrate in the daytime, whereas most other small birds feed during the hours of daylight and migrate at night. Flocks of migrating swallows and martins often roost overnight in reedbeds.

House Martin *Delichon urbica*
Although House Martins are familiar summer visitors, their winter quarters are still relatively unknown. We know they reach Africa, but exactly where remains a mystery.

House Martins once nested mainly on cliffs and some still do so; most, however, build cup-shaped nests under the eaves of houses. Nests may take 12–14 days to build and contain about 2,500 tiny pellets of mud. The birds prefer to nest in colonies and each pair may raise two or three broods each year. Young birds from early broods help to feed those in later broods.

Recently, House Martins have recolonised some city centres because more insects are now available as a result of cleaner air.

Sand Martin (1)
Smaller than Swallow – 12 cm. Brown back, white underparts and brown breast band. Fluttering flight is less graceful than Swallow's. Wings are pointed and tail slightly forked. Has chattering song and call. Often seen in small flocks. *Summer visitor. May be seen feeding over water in most parts of the British Isles.* (Map: page 212)

Swallow
19 cm. Long, pointed wings, and forked tail with long streamers. Upperparts blue-black, underparts whitish, and face dark red. Juvenile (**2**) has slightly forked tail and no streamers. Male (**3**) usually has longer tail-streamers than female (**4**). Flight is graceful, often close to the ground. Call is rather sharp 'tswit'; also has twittering song. *Summer visitor to most of Britain and Ireland except for town centres, rugged mountains and remote islands.* (Map: page 212)

House Martin (5)
Smaller than Swallow – 12.5 cm. Dark blue-black back, white underparts and white rump. Tail is forked. Rather fluttering flight on stiff, almost triangular wings. Call is 'cirrup'. *Summer visitor. Nests on buildings throughout Britain and Ireland. Rather scarce in northern Scotland.* (Map: page 212)

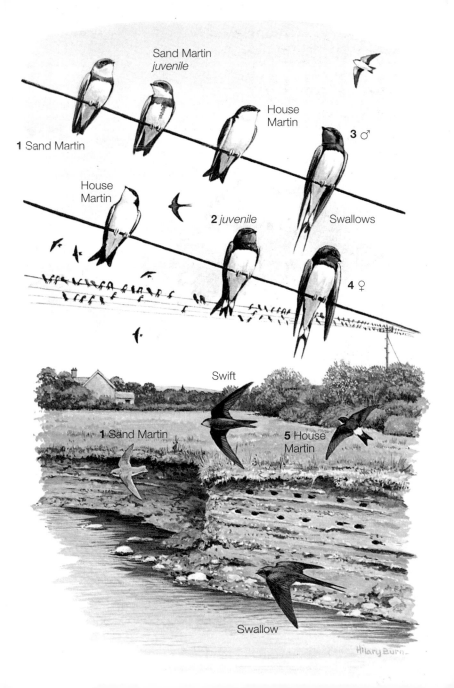

Sand Martin *juvenile*

House Martin

1 Sand Martin

3 ♂

House Martin

2 *juvenile*

Swallows

4 ♀

Swift

1 Sand Martin

5 House Martin

Swallow

Hilary Burn

Tree Pipit *Anthus trivialis*

Usually it is the song or call which first attracts one's attention to this small brown bird. Although a short version of the song may be given from a perch, the full song is heard only during the Tree Pipit's distinctive display flight, as the bird flutters steeply upwards, starts singing before it reaches maximum height and continues as it parachutes down, with wings raised and tail spread, to land on the perch from which it started, or at least close by. They nest on the ground.

Meadow Pipit *Anthus pratensis*

Walk across a moorland in summer and it is quite possible that the only birds you will see will be Meadow Pipits; certainly they will outnumber any other species. Between March and July, their song flight may easily be seen as they rise from the ground with rather feeble notes gathering speed, followed by a succession of sweeter notes as they parachute down again. The advantages of this method of stating territory are obvious on moorland where there are few natural perches: an aerial display is by far the best.

The Meadow Pipit is only a winter visitor to many lowland areas. Most will leave their upland territories after breeding and may be seen in small flocks travelling around the countryside. Some Meadow Pipits will leave this country in autumn and migrate southwards, while others arrive here from farther north.

Research has shown that Meadow Pipits which nest on higher land lay smaller clutches of eggs, but the young survive better. Cuckoos regularly search out Meadow Pipits' nests in which to lay their eggs.

Rock Pipit *Anthus petrosus*

This pipit is to be found on rocky coasts throughout the year. Like other pipits, it has an aerial song flight, but uses rocks for take-off and landing.

Nests are built in rock crevices or on ledges, and are seldom more than 500 m from the sea. Rock Pipits feed on grassy areas near the sea or on rocky beaches where they hunt for insects, other small creatures and seeds.

Water Pipit *Anthus spinoletta* (4)

Closely related to the Rock Pipit, this species breeds in mountain areas on the Continent, and some overwinter in Britain, especially on watercress beds. It has a browner back, white outer tail feathers, a white stripe over the eye and, in spring, a pinkish breast. (Map: page 212)

Tree Pipit (1)

Sparrow-sized – 15 cm. Similar to Meadow Pipit, but slightly larger, with rather longer tail, and more stocky. May also be more yellow on breast and have more obvious, rather regular spots. Legs are pinkish. Call is hoarse 'teez'. Musical song ending with '. . . seea, seea, seea' as bird parachutes down to a perch.
Summer visitor to various habitats where there are trees and shrubs throughout Britain. (Map: page 212)

Meadow Pipit (2)

Sparrow-sized – 14.5 cm. Variable brown plumage with darker streaks, white outer tail feathers and, on some individuals, obvious white wing-bars. Tail is often wagged like a wagtail's. Slightly smaller than Tree Pipit, with tail a little shorter. Call is a thin 'seep'. Repetitive song given in flight.
Breeds in open country, especially upland areas. Widespread in winter.
(Map: page 212)

Rock Pipit (3)

Larger than House Sparrow – 16.5 cm. Larger, darker and greyer than Meadow Pipit, with grey, not white, outer tail feathers, dark legs and longer bill. Call is 'phist', and is less squeaky than that of Meadow Pipit. Song is loud, with obvious trill at end, and is given during song flight.
Found all around British and Irish coasts except in southeast England.
(Map: page 212)

Meadow Pipits

Tree Pipit

Meadow Pipits

4 Water Pipit

Meadow Pipit

3 Rock Pipit

1 Tree
Pipit

Hilary Burn.

2 Meadow Pipit

Yellow Wagtail *Motacilla flava*

The first Yellow Wagtails usually return to Britain from West Africa in late March or early April. From then on, they may be seen in wet meadows, where they often catch insects around the feet of grazing animals. In recent years, the number breeding in Britain has fallen.

The species is found throughout Europe, but the plumage varies, especially the colour of the head of the male, which ranges from black to yellow. Sometimes in spring, blue-headed Yellow Wagtails from nearby western Europe are seen in Britain.

Although Yellow Wagtails nest on the ground, they regularly perch in trees and bushes. Their distinctive call and bounding flight help to distinguish the species when in the air.

Grey Wagtail *Motacilla cinerea*

The Grey Wagtail is seldom seen far from water. In spring and summer, it is usually to be found near fast-flowing streams and rivers in upland districts. Some pairs nest in lower areas, but nearly always near waterfalls, mill races or weirs.

Outside the breeding season, Grey Wagtails move away from the upland territories and visit slower-flowing rivers and even appear on the coast. Some – especially those from Scotland and northern England – leave the British Isles and migrate southwards into Europe. Those which remain are at risk in severe winter weather.

Pied Wagtail *Motacilla alba*

The Pied Wagtails which breed in the British Isles and nearby parts of Europe have dark grey backs and black rumps. The paler race, common throughout Europe, sometimes called the 'White Wagtail', visits Britain and Ireland on passage and sometimes breeds in Shetland.

Although Pied Wagtails are often seen near water, they are also found in dry places, running about on short grass or even flat areas such as car parks or school playgrounds. In winter, many visit farmland to feed. When feeding, they chase insects on or near the ground, dashing erratically, changing course suddenly and wagging their tails all the time.

In summer, they defend their breeding territories, but in winter only some males hold territories, the others flocking together. Night-time roosts may involve 1,000 or more individuals; they are often in reedbeds, but may be in bushes or trees, and some are in towns: on buildings, in greenhouses or at sewage-works. Before roosting, they gather together in open spaces.

Yellow Wagtail
Smaller than Pied Wagtail – 16.5 cm. Slim, with a long tail. Male (**1**) has bright yellow underparts, greenish back and yellow head. Female (**2**) is duller. Both sexes lose most of their yellow plumage by autumn. Juvenile (**3**) looks 'washed out' and has suggestion of black bib. Male of nearby Continental race (**4**) has bluish crown and cheeks and white stripe over eye. Call is 'tsweep'.
Summer visitor to wet meadows, some arable fields and marshes near the sea. Found mainly in central and southeastern England.
(Map: page 213)

Grey Wagtail
Size of Pied Wagtail – 18 cm. Slim, with very long tail. Blue-grey head and back, yellow under tail, and greenish rump. Male (**5**) has black throat and yellow belly in summer. Call is shorter and more metallic than Pied Wagtail's: a sharp 'zit'.
Breeds near fast-flowing rivers, usually in upland areas. Moves to lowland areas in winter.
(Map: page 213)

Pied Wagtail
18 cm. Slim, neat, black-and-white, with a long tail which is constantly wagged up and down. Female (**6**) has greyer back than male (**7**). Juvenile (**8**) is browner with dusky underparts and dark V on breast. Continental race (**9**) has pale grey back and grey rump. Flight is bounding. Call is 'chis-ick' or 'chee-wee'.
Found throughout British Isles. Usually, but not always, near water. (Map: page 213)

5 Grey Wagtail ♂

Grey Wagtail ♀

Grey Wagtail *juvenile*

8 Pied Wagtail *juvenile*

7 Pied Wagtail ♂

6 Pied Wagtail ♀

3 Yellow Wagtail *juvenile*

9 Pied Wagtail Continental race ♂

Yellow Wagtail blue-headed race ♂

1 Yellow Wagtail ♂

2 Yellow Wagtail ♀

Hilary Burn.

(Bohemian) Waxwing *Bombycilla garrulus*

This exotic-looking winter visitor gets its name from curiously shaped secondary feathers on its wings which look like pieces of red wax. It breeds in the far north of Europe, North America and Russia. A few reach Britain in most years and are first seen on the east coast before they move inland in their search for berries.

In some autumns there are invasions of Waxwings and vast numbers are seen, which is typical of species that rely on a food supply which varies from year to year. When the population is high and food supplies become depleted, they move in huge numbers into western Europe, including Britain and, more rarely, Ireland.

(White-throated) Dipper *Cinclus cinclus*

Fast-flowing upland rivers and streams contain a great many invertebrates which are fed on by fish and also by the Dipper.

This species has evolved unique hunting methods: when searching for food, it wades into water and submerges, or will swim or dive. When underwater, it moves along the river bed, head into the current and wings spread to prevent it from bobbing straight up to the surface. Food is located by sight and the eye is protected by a third, white eye-lid which can often be seen when a Dipper is perched, as it is flicked over the eye and gives the appearance that the bird is winking.

Nests are built close to the water, often in a crevice in a rock or under a bridge. Sometimes, several Dippers will roost together under a bridge, which protects them from strong winds. The fast-flowing rivers hardly ever freeze and Dippers survive cold winters better than many other small birds.

(Winter) Wren *Troglodytes troglodytes*

These birds are found in such totally different habitats as woodland, moorland, rocky islands and dense reed-beds. After a series of mild winters, when the Wren population is high, this is our most numerous breeding species. During a harsh winter, however, the number of Wrens may be reduced to only one-fifth or so, although a total recovery may take only three or four years.

Wrens sing throughout the year in order to maintain their territories. Only on winter nights do they flock together in communal roosts. Some roosts are in nest-boxes: on one occasion 63 Wrens were seen to enter one box. Another roost, in an attic, attracted 98 Wrens, all of which entered by the same small hole.

Waxwing (1)

Smaller than Starling – 18 cm. Pinkish-brown with pink crest. In flight, looks rather like Starling. Call is a trilling 'sirrr'. Often seen in flocks. *Scarce winter migrant. A few visit eastern Britain most years with many more during 'invasions'.* (Map: page 213)

Dipper (2)

Smaller than Starling – 18 cm. Dumpy, with short tail. Adult appears black with chestnut belly and white 'bib'. Juveniles are greyer. Flight is fast, direct and often close to the water. Perches on rocks where it 'bobs'. Call is a short 'zit'. Song is a sweet warbling. *Found near fast-flowing water, mainly in upland areas. Visits lower rivers in winter, when it may even be seen on the coast.* (Map: page 213)

Wren (3)

Tiny – 9.5 cm. Dumpy, with short tail which is often cocked up. Dark brown with paler underparts and pale stripe over eye. Call is a hard 'tic-tic' or forceful trill. Song is a loud, fast warbling, usually with a trill near the end, the tiny bird appearing to tremble with emotion. *Found throughout the British Isles; especially common where there is dense vegetation.* (Map: page 213)

Starlings

Waxwings

1 Waxwings

3 Wrens

2 Dipper

Hilary Burn

Dunnock (Hedge Accentor) *Prunella modularis*

The Dunnock is often overlooked by non-birdwatchers, yet it is common in parks and gardens as well as in woods, and even on moorland or rocky islands. On farmland, it is one of the most numerous breeding birds.

Despite one of its old names – 'Hedge Sparrow' – the Dunnock is not related to sparrows: it has the thin bill typical of species which feed mainly on insects. One old country name for the Dunnock was 'Shuffle-wing' which referred to its habit of flicking open one wing above its back in display. As with most song birds, territories are established during the breeding season, though in many cases Dunnock territories are occupied not only by a male and a female, but also by one or more other adults. Winter territories are also established and sometimes occupied by small groups of Dunnocks.

(European) Robin *Erithacus rubecula*

This is Britain's national bird. It is common in parks and gardens and often becomes tame; elsewhere in Europe, however, it is rather shy and difficult to observe. It defends a territory in both summer and winter and may be heard singing in most months of the year. After the breeding season, until about January, the Robin's song is different – slower and rather sad. Males and females occupy separate territories in winter. While males seldom move far from their breeding areas, the females may move farther afield, and some even leave the country. Robins from northern Europe migrate, and some winter in eastern Britain.

Robins have elaborate displays in which their red breast plays an important part as a visual danger signal to other Robins which enter an occupied territory.

Robins usually nest in a hollow on a bank or in a hedge, but they will also nest in odd places such as garden sheds or in old tin cans which are lodged in hedges. They feed mainly on insects, although they also eat berries and worms. On average, Robins live only a little more than a year, but at least one survived 11 years.

Bluethroat *Luscinia svecica*

These birds breed in continental Europe and winter in Africa. Bluethroats have nested in Britain on at least two occasions; others occur on migration, especially in May or September; they usually belong to the red-spotted race, from northern Europe, in which the male in spring has red in the centre of his blue throat. Bluethroats of the white-spotted race from central Europe are seen less often. They are usually very secretive and difficult to observe.

Dunnock (1)
Sparrow-sized – 14.5 cm. Rather secretive. Brown streaky plumage with grey head and breast. The bill is thin. Feeds with body held close to the ground and moves with mouse-like jerks. Frequently flicks its wings. Call is a loud piping 'tseep' and song is a Wren-like warble, but slower, less forceful and with no trills. *Widespread throughout British Isles. Usually found near trees or bushes.* (Map: page 213)

Robin (2)
Sparrow-sized – 14 cm. Upright, and often appearing plump, with red face and breast and white belly. Male and female look alike. Juvenile (**3**) lacks any red and is speckled. Call is a loud 'tic, tic'. Attractive warbling song is heard in spring, but it also has a different, slower, sadder song in autumn and winter. *Common throughout the British Isles, except in far north. Usually found near trees or bushes.* (Map: page 213)

Bluethroat
Size of Robin – 14 cm. Slim with white stripe over eye and reddish patches at base of dark brown tail. In spring, the male (**4**) has a brilliant blue throat with, depending upon its race, either a red spot or a white spot in the centre. Females have a pale throat. In autumn, juveniles (**5**) have a variety of different throat patterns. Call is a sharp 'tacc, tacc'. *Seen mainly on the British east coast in autumn.* (No map)

1 Dunnock

3 Robin
juvenile

2 Robins

5 Bluethroat
juvenile

4 Bluethroat
red-spotted race ♂

Dunnock

Hilary Burn

(Common) Nightingale *Luscinia megarhynchos*

These birds may sing at any time of day or night, but it is after dusk or before dawn, when most other birds are silent, that their magnificent song can best be heard. On a calm night, it can carry for up to a mile. In Britain, Nightingales are highly secretive and spend much of their time in dense bushes or on the ground where they hunt for worms, spiders and insects. They generally sing from dense cover, although elsewhere in Europe they are often rather easier to see.

Nightingales winter in central Africa and usually return to Britain in mid-April. Males return first and their song may be heard until late May or early June when the young hatch. The favourite habitat is deciduous woodland with dense ground cover.

In some parts of Britain Nightingales have declined during this century, but in southeast England, where numbers are largest, the population seems to be stable in spite of great fluctuations from year to year.

Black Redstart *Phoenicurus ochruros*

The Second World War left many ugly bomb-sites and derelict buildings in London which were quickly colonised by the Black Redstart which had, until then, been a very rare breeding species. The number of Black Redstarts breeding in Britain is still not large, but has continued to grow slowly. Buildings in central and southeastern Britain continue to be used, but some nests are built in natural holes in cliffs.

Adult male Black Redstarts are unmistakable, but some start to breed before they have fully adult plumage. Black Redstarts are seen at all seasons of the year, but especially in spring and autumn when some on passage from continental Europe are also seen.

(Common) Redstart *Phoenicurus phoenicurus*

In parts of Europe the Redstart is very common around towns and villages and will occupy sites similar to those used by the Black Redstart. In Britain, however, Redstarts nest mainly in holes in trees or walls.

Redstarts feed mainly on insects. The male catches much of his prey in flight while the female feeds more often on the ground. The red tail, which gives the species its name, is used in display.

Redstarts became rarer after 1969 when several British species which winter in Africa were affected by a prolonged drought in the Sahel region, on the southern fringe of the Sahara. Since 1976 numbers have increased again, but many former nesting sites remain unoccupied.

Nightingale (1)

Larger than Robin – 16.5 cm. Rich brown upperparts, reddish tail and large eyes. Very secretive. Juveniles are spotted. Loud, rich song is repetitive with long pauses and may be heard by day as well as by night.
Summer visitor to woods and dense thickets in southeastern England.
(Map: page 213)

Black Redstart

Size of Robin – 14 cm. Robin-like and rather active. Often perches on ground or on rocks or walls. Adult male (**2**) has dark grey body, pale patch on wings and rusty red tail. Female (**3**) and juvenile have paler bodies and lack pale patch on wings. Alarm call is a hard 'tucc, tucc'. Song is fast warble followed by a rattle.
Present throughout the year. Breeds in ruined buildings, power-stations, and also on sea cliffs. Usually seen near the coast in winter.
(Map: page 214)

Redstart

Size of Robin – 14 cm. Very active, regularly quivering its rusty red tail. Male (**4**) has reddish underparts, grey crown and white forehead. Female (**5**) and juvenile have greyish-brown backs and buff underparts. Call is 'hooveet'; has warbling song with a strange jangle.
Summer visitor. Nests in holes in trees or walls. Found in woods, parks, heaths and moors mainly in northern and western Britain.
(Map: page 214)

4 Common Redstart ♂

5 Common Redstart ♀

2 Black Redstart ♂

3 Black Redstart ♀

1 Nightingales

Hilary Burn

Whinchat *Saxicola rubetra*

The Whinchat and Stonechat are closely related, yet Stonechats are mainly resident in the British Isles whereas the Whinchats are summer migrants which winter in tropical Africa. Whinchats will feed on spiders or worms, but most of their food is insects, many of which are caught as they visit flowers.

Whinchats have declined in numbers this century, especially in southeast England, and are most common in upland areas where many pairs have taken to breeding in young conifer plantations.

(Common) Stonechat *Saxicola torquata*

The Stonechat gets its name from its sharp call which sounds like two pebbles being knocked together. The call is often given from the top of a gorse bush.

While some Stonechats migrate, most remain in Britain for the winter; they may move away from their breeding areas, especially to the coast, where it is milder, since they are vulnerable in icy conditions. In the past, Stonechat populations have recovered quickly after severe winters, but in recent years numbers have continued to decline.

Like most species, Stonechats moult their feathers after breeding. The male's new head feathers are black, but they have buff tips which give a dull mottled appearance. During the winter the buff tips wear away, leaving a smart black head by the next breeding season.

(Northern) Wheatear *Oenanthe oenanthe*

This is often the first migrant to be seen in the British Isles in spring. In some years, the first Wheatears appear before the end of February, but most arrive in late March or early April, with a second rush in May. These later Wheatears often belong to a larger and brighter race which stop off *en route* for their breeding grounds in Greenland.

Wheatears make amazing migratory journeys. They all winter in Africa, south of the Sahara, and as well as some migrating northwest to Greenland, others migrate northeast across Asia to nest in Alaska. Those from Greenland fly direct to Morocco on their autumn migration: a non-stop journey of 4,100 km across the Atlantic.

Wheatears nest in burrows, among stones or in stone walls. In Britain they nest mainly in the north and west, in grassy areas that have been closely grazed at sea level, and it is common in upland areas. Their song is attractive and often given during a fluttering song flight. They also sometimes hover like tiny Kestrels when on the lookout for food or predators.

Whinchat
Smaller than Robin – 12.5 cm. Short-tailed. Often perches upright on fences or low bushes. Male (**1**) has white stripe over eye, white patches on wings and at base of tail. Female (**2**) is similar, but paler. Juvenile has a faint stripe over eye. Call is a sharp 'tic, tic'. *Summer visitor to open areas with some bushes, especially in north and west of Britain and parts of Ireland. Seen elsewhere on migration.* (Map: page 214)

Stonechat
Smaller than Robin – 12.5 cm. Short-tailed and plump. Often perches on tops of bushes or on wires. Male in summer (**3**) has black head, white on neck and orangish breast. Female (**4**) and juvenile are less colourful. Call is sharp 'tac, tac'. *Usually seen in open areas with some bushes, especially gorse. Most common in heathland and especially coastal localities (where it is relatively mild in winter).* (Map: page 214)

Wheatear
Larger than Robin – 15 cm. White rump and short black tail. Often perches on the ground where it stands very upright. Male in spring (**5**) has black cheeks, blue-grey back and sandy breast. Female (**6**), juvenile (**7**) and male in autumn look paler and 'washed out'. Call is a hard 'chack, chack'. *Summer visitor to uplands and some coastal localities. Seen elsewhere on migration.* (Map: page 214)

Whinchat

Stonechat

Wheatear

Wheatear
*Greenland
race* ♂

Whinchats 1 ♂

2 ♀

7 *juvenile*

6 ♀

Wheatears

5 ♂

3 ♂

winter ♂

4 ♀

Hilary Burn

Stonechats

Ring Ouzel *Turdus torquatus*

This is the blackbird of mountain areas. It breeds in wild, hilly country where there are crags and rocky gullies. Its loud, sweet, simple song is repeated from a prominent perch, and echoes amongst the rocks. In autumn, it flies south to winter in southern Europe or North Africa.

Migrants bound for British or Irish breeding sites start to arrive in March and are more likely to be seen in western areas. Ring Ouzels are generally more numerous on the British east coast in late April and May: these are mostly *en route* to northern European breeding grounds.

Ring Ouzels have declined during this century while Blackbirds have become more numerous and spread northwards. It is possible that there is some competition between them, and Blackbirds have taken over some of the territories once occupied by Ring Ouzels.

(Common) Blackbird *Turdus merula*

This familiar bird is recognisable, even at a distance, by the way it moves and especially by the way it raises its tail on landing.

Originally, Blackbirds probably lived on the edge of woodland, but they have adapted to living on farmland as well as in parks and gardens. Now, Blackbirds which nest on farms and in gardens are more successful at producing young than those in woodland. Juveniles in towns, however, are commonly caught by domestic cats.

A Blackbird may often be seen (or heard) turning over dead leaves under trees or bushes as it searches for worms, insects, millipedes or small snails. Many kinds of fruit, especially berries, are also eaten. Like many other species, it does not digest the hard parts of its food, but ejects them through its beak in the form of pellets. Over the years, many unusual foods of Blackbirds have been recorded, including newts, tadpoles, fox droppings, putty, elvers, a shrew and even a dead Blackbird.

In some parts of northern Britain, Blackbirds leave their breeding grounds for the winter, but elsewhere they are resident and may be joined by others from Europe. They seem to be able to survive cold weather quite well: after the very cold winter of 1962–63, the Blackbird population fell by 18% whereas that of the Song Thrush fell by 57%. Recently, despite mild winters, the population has fallen, and conservationists are concerned that agricultural changes may be affecting Blackbirds.

During a mild spell in winter, Blackbirds may start to nest, but young hatched at that time seldom survive. By April, the first clutch of eggs has usually been laid and this will be followed by two, or occasionally three more.

Ring Ouzel

Slightly smaller than Blackbird – 23 cm. Male (**1**) is sooty black with white crescent on breast and pale patch on wing. Female (**2**) is scaly brown with pale crescent on breast. Juvenile often lacks mark on breast, but is greyer than a juvenile Blackbird. Song is clear piping; call is loud, hard 'tac, tac'.
Summer visitor to mountains and moorland. Sometimes near coasts in spring and autumn. (Map: page 214)

Blackbird

25 cm. Male (**3**) is all black with yellow bill and eye-ring. Female (**4**) is dark brown, often with pale chin and rather spotted brown breast. Juvenile (**5**) is reddish-brown with speckled brown breast. Immature male (**6**) has dark bill and browner plumage than adult. Has chinking alarm call or scolding 'tuc, tuc'. Song is clear and fluty, but tails off at end.
Found throughout the British Isles, except in very mountainous country.
(Map: page 214)

Ring Ouzel ♂

6 Blackbird *immature* ♂

2 Ring Ouzel ♀

1 Ring Ouzel ♂

4 Blackbird ♀

5 Blackbird *juvenile*

3 Blackbird ♂

Hilary Burn.

Song Thrush *Turdus philomelos*

Until about 1940 Song Thrushes outnumbered Blackbirds, but then the situation was reversed, and the decline of the Song Thrush has continued. There is now less than half the number that there were 30 years ago.

On a summer evening, it is still the Song Thrush's song which resounds through much of our countryside and is often the last song to be heard before the woods become dark and the only sounds are those of truly nocturnal creatures. The song is simple, but attractive: a short phrase is repeated several times, then apparently discarded in favour of another which is, in turn, repeated and discarded and so on until the first phrase returns again. During mild spells in autumn and winter, when food is plentiful, Song Thrushes may be heard singing, proclaiming their territories as in spring and summer.

Song Thrushes feed on worms, insects, fruits and, of course, snails. Snails are usually eaten in summer or late winter when other food is scarce. When a Song Thrush finds a snail it takes it to a stone, a dead branch, a tin can or a bottle, and then hits it against this 'anvil' until the shell breaks.

In autumn, our Song Thrushes are joined by migrants from Europe, which share the harvest of berries until it runs out and worms become an important food again.

Redwing *Turdus iliacus*

Listen carefully on a calm autumn night and you may hear the thin 'tseep' of migrating Redwings. Redwings migrate by day and by night, but it is after dark that their flight-calls are especially valuable in helping to keep flocks together. Morning will often find parties of newly arrived Redwings stripping the berries from our hedges, often in the company of Song Thrushes, Fieldfares and Blackbirds. In the evenings, Redwings gather together in large communal roosts.

Flocks of Redwings move around the British Isles in winter, especially in very cold weather. Then they may be seen in town gardens, on playing fields or on other areas of short grass. During prolonged frosts, many fail to find sufficient food and die, others move west or south in search of warmer areas.

Two races of Redwings visit the British Isles in winter: many cross the North Sea from Scandinavia while another, slightly larger, race migrates here from Iceland. A few Redwings breed regularly in Scotland: the first pair was found in Scotland in 1925, then large numbers were discovered in the 1950s and 1960s; despite a recent decrease some pairs still nest each year.

Song Thrush (1)

Smaller than Blackbird – 23 cm. Brown above, pale below with many small spots on breast. Orange underwing shows in flight. Call is a sharp 'sipp'. Song is loud and sweetly repetitive. Juvenile has buff streaks on back.
Breeds almost anywhere if there are trees or bushes.
(Map: page 214)

Redwing (2)

Smaller than Blackbird – 21 cm. Like rather dark Song Thrush with white stripe over eye, reddish flanks and dark red (not orange) under the wing. Flight call is a high-pitched 'tseep'.
Mainly a winter visitor. A few pairs nest in Scotland.
(Map: page 214)

Redwing

Song Thrush

Redwings

Blackbird ♀

Fieldfare

Song Thrush

Mistle Thrush

2 Redwing

1 Song Thrush

Hilary Burn

Fieldfare *Turdus pilaris*

As winter approaches, flocks of thrushes leave Scandinavia, cross the North Sea, and arrive in the British Isles. Fieldfares are one of these migrants, and their noisy, rather ragged-looking flocks can be seen moving around farmland between October and April. On winter evenings they often gather in large, communal roosts and spend the night in dense bushes.

These migrants from the north join other, resident thrushes and take advantage of the supply of berries and other fruits which are usually found in plenty in our countryside in autumn. Fieldfares also find food in orchards where they feed on windfalls. Later in winter, when the fruits have gone, they turn to worms and any insect food they can find.

In Scandinavia, colonies of Fieldfares nest in town parks and gardens as well as in birch woods and other habitats. During the last hundred years the Fieldfare has been spreading to new areas in Europe, and recently it has colonised Iceland and Greenland. In 1967, it nested in Britain for the first time and a few pairs have nested regularly since then.

Mistle Thrush *Turdus viscivorus*

As storm clouds gather and the wind strengthens, many species stop singing and take cover. Not the Mistle Thrush: in these conditions, it can often be heard singing strongly, while perched at the top of a tall tree. Not surprisingly, this habit has earned the Mistle Thrush the old country name of 'Stormcock'.

In autumn, Mistle Thrushes travel around the country-side in noisy, chattering flocks as they gradually strip the ripe berries from the trees and bushes. In many areas, they start with the rowan, or mountain ash, and flocks may often be seen on remote moorland in search of this food supply. In towns and villages, they may gorge themselves on berries from churchyard yew trees or hunt for worms in parks or on playing fields.

Later in autumn, many first-year Mistle Thrushes leave their family flocks, move south and may fly to the conti-nent. Adults which remain will often defend a particular fruit-bearing tree, such as a holly, which will ensure a substantial supply of food throughout the winter.

Mistle Thrushes have not always been so widespread. Until about 1800, they were found only in southern England or Wales, but then they spread into Ireland and northwards in Britain until, now, they are common everywhere but the far north of Scotland.

Fieldfare (1)
Slightly larger than Blackbird – 25.5 cm. Chestnut back, dark tail, grey head and grey rump. Call is a noisy, laughing chuckle: 'chack-chack-chack'. Usually seen in flocks. Flight often appears lazy, and white underwing is obvious.
Winter visitor to the British Isles. A few remain in summer and nest.
(Map: page 215)

Mistle Thrush (2)
Larger than Blackbird – 27 cm. Larger, greyer and more upright than Song Thrush, and also appears to have a smaller head. Outer tail feathers show white in flight. Breast is pale, with large spots. Flight looks leisurely, with wings closing at regular intervals. Underwing is white. Juvenile (**3**) has pale, spotted head and streaky back. Call is a chattering rattle. Song is loud, clear and rather like that of Blackbird.
Found throughout the British Isles, except in the far north.
(Map: page 215)

Mistle Thrush

Mistle Thrush

Fieldfares

Mistle Thrush

Blackbird ♀

Fieldfares

Song Thrush

3 Mistle Thrush *juvenile*

2 Mistle Thrush

1 Fieldfare

Hilary Burn

Cetti's Warbler *Cettia cetti*

The arrival of the Cetti's Warbler in Britain and its colonisation are quite remarkable. At the beginning of the 20th century, it was found mainly around the Mediterranean, but more northerly areas were gradually colonised and in 1972 it was found nesting in Britain for the first time. At first colonisation was rapid, but had slowed down by the early 1980s, and severe winter weather in 1985 dramatically reduced numbers. Since then, the population has returned to around 400 pairs, but the centre of population has shifted from the southeast to the, usually milder, southwest of England.

Unlike most of our warblers, Cetti's does not migrate for the winter: yet it does feed on insects, which explains why prolonged periods of cold weather are likely to affect the population.

A male Cetti's Warbler may have two or more females, but he takes no part in nest-building or incubating the eggs, and helps only a little with rearing the young. Song is heard mostly during the day but unpaired males may sing after dark.

Grasshopper Warbler *Locustella naevia*

The amazing, reeling song of this secretive warbler is usually the only clue to its presence. Since human hearing deteriorates with age, this bird's high-pitched trill, which may continue for a minute or more without a break, becomes increasingly hard to hear as one becomes older.

Grasshopper Warblers usually sing from dense cover, and move through vegetation rather like mice. They have surprisingly long middle toes, which apparently help them to grip several stems at once and give them extra support when moving around in dense undergrowth. Much of their time is spent on or near the ground.

Although their amazing song may frequently be heard in daylight, dawn and dusk are probably the best times to hear it. Song may also be heard after dark, and some individuals will sing all through the night.

Savi's Warbler *Locustella luscinioides*

Although closely related to the Grasshopper Warbler, the Savi's Warbler looks rather like a Reed Warbler and lives in dense reedbeds with scattered bushes, which it may use as song-posts.

In the past, Savi's Warblers regularly nested in the Fens of East Anglia, but became extinct by 1856. A few are now nesting again in southeast England.

Cetti's Warbler (1)

Size of Great Tit – 14 cm. Secretive. Rather dumpy, like large Wren. Reddish-brown back, paler underparts and pale stripe over eye. Tail is very rounded and often cocked up. Call is a short 'twick' or loud 'chee'. Song starts suddenly and is fast and loud.
Scarce resident of wet, densely vegetated places, largely in southwest England. (Map: page 215)

Grasshopper Warbler (2)

Smaller than Great Tit – 13 cm. Rather secretive. Brown, streaked upperparts, paler underparts and rounded tail. Song is a long, high-pitched, drawn-out, insect-like trill, often heard at dusk or even after dark.
A summer visitor to most parts of the British Isles where there is thick, low vegetation. Often found in damp places or in young plantations. (Map: page 215)

Savi's Warbler (3)

Size of Great Tit – 14 cm. Rather like large Reed Warbler. Buff-coloured plumage, paler breast and whitish chin. Tail is rounded. Call is a sharp 'spitz'. Song is a buzz, rather like Grasshopper Warbler's trill, but faster and lower-pitched. *Summer visitor to a few large reedbeds, mainly in southern England.* (Map: page 215)

Marsh Harrier ♀

Cetti's Warbler

2 Grasshopper Warbler

3 Savi's Warbler

Hilary Burn

1 Cetti's Warbler

Sedge Warbler *Acrocephalus schoenobaenus*

Dense waterside vegetation is the normal breeding site for the Sedge Warbler. In some places, it even nests in reedbeds, close to Reed Warblers, but in other places it chooses drier sites, such as damp ditches and even young conifer plantations.

Sedge Warblers arrive in April or early May; they rear one or two broods before feeding up in readiness for their return flight to Africa. Most British Sedge Warblers make the journey across Europe, the Mediterranean and the Sahara Desert in one single flight. To make this amazing journey, they store body-fat from which they get the necessary energy. Many birds store fat and increase their weight by about 30%, but the Sedge Warbler almost doubles its weight just before it migrates.

The British population reflected climatic change in the Sahel zone of North Africa. Numbers fell dramatically in 1969 with the onset of drought, remained low during the 1970s, and then fell farther. Since rain returned to the Sahel, our population has started to recover.

Marsh Warbler *Acrocephalus palustris*

Widespread over much of Europe and closely related to both Reed and Sedge Warblers, Marsh Warblers nest in only a very few places in southern Britain.

Marsh Warblers are superb mimics, and have been heard to copy the songs or calls of over 50 other species.

(Eurasian) Reed Warbler *Acrocephalus scirpaceus*

These birds prefer to nest in dense, wet reedbeds, where they generally breed in colonies, but they will sometimes nest in drier areas. Reedbeds give the nests protection from ground predators, but they are more likely to be raided from the air, especially by Cuckoos, which regularly lay their eggs in Reed Warblers' nests.

Rough weather also causes problems for Reed Warblers, as many nests are beaten to the ground, and in wet or cold summers adults have difficulty in finding enough food for their young. To overcome these seasonal food shortages, Reed Warblers incubate their eggs before the clutch is complete, which results in the eggs hatching at different times. In poor seasons, only the eldest will survive, while in good years all will live. This arrangement, known as asynchronous hatching, is common among birds of prey, but unusual in smaller species.

Drainage and river management have reduced the number of natural reedbeds and many colonies of Reed Warblers have disappeared. Some, however, have benefited from new reedbeds in flooded sandpits or gravelpits.

Sedge Warbler (1)
Smaller than Great Tit – 13 cm. Streaked back, orange-brown rump and flanks, white stripe over eye and dark crown. Call is a loud 'tuc'. Warbling song has grating trills and sparrow-like chirrups. Sings from a perch, or in a short display flight. *Summer visitor to most lowland parts of Britain and Ireland and is usually found near water.* (Map: page 215)

Marsh Warbler (2)
Size of Reed Warbler – 12.5 cm. Very similar to Reed Warbler, but plumage appears less rufous, throat is paler and bill is a little stouter. Best distinction is song; musical and varied, with imitation of many songs and calls. Often sings from an exposed perch. *Small numbers of these summer visitors breed in southern England. Likes nettle beds or dense willows near water.* (Map: page 215)

Reed Warbler (3)
Smaller than Great Tit – 12.5 cm. Plain brown back, rich brown rump and pale underparts. Bill is long, and forehead steep. Hard churring call and long, fast, churring, repetitive, warbling song. *Summer visitor to dense reedbeds in England and Wales.* (Map: page 215)

Aquatic Warbler
***Acrocephalus paludicola* (4)**
Size of Sedge Warbler – 12.5 cm. Rather rare and secretive. Yellow streak on crown, bold black stripes on back, and streaked rump. *Passage migrant seen in reedbeds mainly in autumn.* (No map)

1 Sedge Warbler

4 Aquatic Warbler

Sedge Warbler *juvenile*

3 Reed Warbler

2 Marsh Warbler

Cuckoo *juvenile*

Hilary Burn.

Dartford Warbler *Sylvia undata*

The Dartford Warbler takes its English name from Dartford Heath in Kent, where the species was first identified. It no longer breeds at Dartford. Lowland heaths with large expanses of gorse and heather are its favourite habitat, but these have, for too long, been regarded as 'wasteland' and most have either been ploughed up or had houses built on them. The heaths of Surrey, Hampshire and Dorset are the last stronghold for this species.

Dartfords do not migrate and, being mainly insect-eaters, suffer in severe winters when their food is hard to find. After a series of mild winters, numbers often build up again and other heaths in southern England are colonised. Recently a few pairs have colonised parts of East Anglia.

Lesser Whitethroat *Sylvia curruca*

In many parts of England and Wales, this warbler is much more common than is generally realised. Unless one is familiar with its song the Lesser Whitethroat is easily overlooked. In addition, its song is usually heard for only a few weeks after its return in spring. Adults can, however, be noisy when their young have just fledged, in late summer.

The Lesser Whitethroats which breed in Britain probably winter in Ethiopia or the Sudan, in northeast Africa. Most of those which leave Britain in autumn fly to north Italy and from there fly southwards across the Mediterranean and straight to their winter quarters. In spring, they return by a different route, around the eastern end of the Mediterranean and then fly straight to Britain.

Common Whitethroat *Sylvia communis*

Until 1969, the Common Whitethroat was one of our most numerous summer visitors, but in that year observers all over western Europe noticed that only small numbers had returned and, later, research showed that the population had fallen by 77% in one year, thus presenting one of the most curious ornithological mysteries ever recorded.

Scientists have now deduced that the disappearance of the Common Whitethroat was caused by severe drought in the Sahel zone of Africa, the area in which western European Whitethroats wintered. Many must have died because of the sudden climatic change. Although numbers of Common Whitethroats have increased again, they are still well below the level of 1968.

Dartford Warbler
Smaller than Great Tit – 12.5 cm. Small and dark, with a long tail. Male (**1**) has dark brown upperparts, grey head and reddish underparts. Female (**2**) and juvenile are paler. Usually very secretive, but will sing from the top of bushes. Call is a grating 'tchirr'.
Resident on a few heaths in southern England.
(Map: page 215)

Lesser Whitethroat (3)
Smaller than Great Tit – 13.5 cm. Small, grey and secretive. Has white throat and dark cheeks. Back is greyer than that of Whitethroat, and lacks any reddish-brown in wing. Call is a sharp 'tacc'. The song starts with a quiet warble followed by a loud rattle of one note repeated several times, rather like the start of the song of Yellowhammer.
Summer visitor to places with thick cover or thick hedges, mainly in southern and eastern England and parts of Wales. Rare in Scotland and does not breed in Ireland. (Map: page 216)

Common Whitethroat
Size of Great Tit – 14 cm. Male (**4**) has grey head, white throat and reddish-brown wings. Female (**5**) and juvenile have brown heads. Call is a hard 'chack' or scolding 'tchurr'. Song is an unmusical jumble of phrases, often given during a short song flight (**6**).
Summer visitor to patches of scrub in most parts of lowland Britain and Ireland.
(Map: page 216)

4 Common Whitethroat ♂

6 Common Whitethroat *display*

1 Dartford Warbler ♂

5 Common Whitethroat ♀

2 Dartford Warbler ♀

3 Lesser Whitethroat

Hilary Burn

Icterine Warbler *Hippolais icterina*

This species is widespread over much of central and eastern Europe, but is a rather rare visitor to Britain. In autumn, the first-winter birds appear grey-green and washed out compared with juvenile Willow Warblers.

Melodious Warbler *Hippolais polyglotta*

The Melodious Warbler is most common in southwest Europe and usually visits Britain only in autumn. Most occur in southwest Britain and Ireland, mirroring the European breeding distribution.

Barred Warbler *Sylvia nisoria*

This regular autumn visitor from central and eastern Europe is more numerous in some years than in others. It spends much of the time moving clumsily around in dense cover, such as elder bushes and clumps of ivy, where it feeds on berries as well as insects. Almost all the Barred Warblers seen in Britain are juveniles.

Garden Warbler *Sylvia borin*

Despite its name, this warbler is not common in gardens. Like other warblers, the Garden Warbler is rather secretive and best located by its song. Although most warblers can be easily identified by their songs, the similarity between those of Blackcap and Garden Warbler is so great that even experienced ornithologists often need to see the bird to confirm its identity.

Garden Warblers are rare in northern Scotland and Ireland. They arrive in April or May after wintering in central or southern Africa.

Blackcap *Sylvia atricapilla*

In the opinion of some people, the song of the Blackcap is as good as, if not better than, that of any other British bird. In spring and early summer, its song can be heard in woods with thick undergrowth, especially brambles.

The Blackcap has significantly increased in numbers in recent years. Until recently, it was considered to be a summer migrant which left in autumn for western Mediterranean or West Africa. Now, however, it is seen regularly in midwinter, particularly in western and southwestern England and in Ireland, where it will visit gardens. These wintering Blackcaps are from northern Europe and appear to have learned to supplement their natural diet of insects and berries with food from bird-tables, where they are sometimes aggressive towards other garden birds.

Icterine Warbler (1)
Larger than Willow Warbler – 13.5 cm. Yellow-and-green, with bluish legs, long bill with wide base, peaked crown, pale eye-ring, long wings with, usually, a pale panel. Underparts paler, with almost no yellow in autumn. *Seen mainly on British east coast in autumn.* (No map)

Melodious Warbler (2)
Larger than Willow Warbler – 13 cm. Wide-based, long bill. Often has flatter head, browner paler legs, browner back and shorter wings than Icterine. *Rare visitor mainly to coastal areas in autumn.* (No map)

Barred Warbler
Larger than Great Tit – 15 cm. Large, clumsy greyish warbler with domed head and heavy bill. 1st-winter (3) is brown, with little barring, has dark eye and pale edges to wing feathers. Call is sharp 'tchack' or 'tcharr'. *Mainly seen in autumn on British east coast.* (No map)

Garden Warbler (4)
Size of Great Tit – 14 cm. Plain brown back with paler underparts and no obvious marks. Call is sharp 'check'. Song is a fast warble. *Summer visitor to woods, scrub or young plantations.* (Map: page 216)

Blackcap
Size of Great Tit – 14 cm. Rather grey. Male (5) has black cap. Female (6) and juvenile have brown caps. Call is hard 'tacc'. Shorter, richer and more varied song than Garden Warbler. *Mainly summer visitor.* (Map: page 216)

2 Melodious Warbler

1 Icterine Warbler

4 Garden Warbler

6 Blackcap ♀

3 Barred Warbler
1st-winter

5 Blackcap ♂

Hilary Burn

(Common) Chiffchaff *Phylloscopus collybita*

Willow Warblers and Chiffchaffs look so similar that, unless they are heard singing, it is often difficult to identify them with certainty – such birds are sometimes referred to as Willow/Chiffs. With care, one of the best ways of distinguishing these species is by wingshape. The Chiffchaff's wing is shorter and more rounded. At rest, the Willow Warbler's longer primaries extend farther beyond the secondaries.

Although a few Chiffchaffs are seen in southern Britain in winter, most winter in France or around the western Mediterranean and return in late March or early April. Their song, often heard from leafless branches of a tree, is usually the first clue that spring migration is underway.

Recent studies have shown that 'the Chiffchaff' is comprised of several very similar species. The **Iberian Chiffchaff** *P. brehmii* has occurred in Britain occasionally.

Willow Warbler *Phylloscopus trochilus*

The Willow Warbler is our most numerous summer visitor. About three million pairs arrive each April from their wintering areas in central and southern Africa. Some birds make this journey ten or more times.

Individuals differ in the amount of yellow in their plumage: some may appear brown-and-white, while others, especially young in autumn, may be very yellow.

Like other warblers, they feed chiefly on insects and spiders.

All birds have to renew their feathers in a process called moult. Most species replace all their feathers every year, but Willow Warblers undergo two complete moults, once in summer and again in their African winter quarters.

Wood Warbler *Phylloscopus sibilatrix*

A particularly attractive warbler which arrives in Britain in late April and leaves again in September. It spends the winter in central Africa.

Its song can be heard in mature woods with little ground cover. When singing from a perch, its whole body shakes, but sometimes the song is given as it flies from branch to branch. The male has a butterfly-like display and will spiral down to the woodland floor.

Unpaired males sing throughout the breeding season, but paired males also continue to sing in the hope of attracting a second female, resulting in polygyny.

Chiffchaff (1)
Smaller than Blue Tit – 11 cm. Best identified by song 'zip-zap, zap, zip-zap . . .'. Brown above, pale below, pale stripe over eye, some individuals slightly more yellow. Legs usually dark. *Mainly a summer visitor to woods with thick undergrowth and places with mixed bushes and trees. Rather scarce in northern Scotland and in upland areas.* (Map: page 216)

Willow Warbler (2)
Smaller than Blue Tit – 11 cm. Difficult to tell from Chiffchaff, but song is series of notes trickling down the scale. Some are more yellow than others. Legs and feet are pale. Juvenile in autumn (**3**) is more yellow than adult. *Summer visitor to most parts of Britain and Ireland. Found in woods, scrub and almost treeless areas.* (Map: page 216)

Wood Warbler
Slightly larger than Willow Warbler – 13 cm. Adult (**4**) has yellow-green back, bright yellow throat and breast, sharply divided from pure white belly, and yellow stripe over eye. Juvenile (**5**) is duller. Song is either a repetitive 'duu' or a single note repeated faster and faster and ending in a trill. *Summer visitor to mature woodland, especially oak and beech. Scarce in southeast England and northern Scotland. Rare in Ireland.* (Map: page 216)

4 Wood Warbler

5 Wood Warbler
juvenile

1 Chiffchaff

Chiffchaff
juvenile

3 Willow
Warbler
juvenile

2 Willow Warbler

Hilary Burn

Goldcrest *Regulus regulus*

These birds can be surprisingly difficult to see although they are relatively common. The best method of locating one is to sit quietly in a conifer wood and listen for its thin call or highpitched song. In autumn and winter, they will rove through all types of woodland and often join small flocks of tits. Once located, a Goldcrest may appear quite tame and come close.

While searching for their insect food, they frequently hang upside down or hover to pick insects from the undersides of leaves. Their beautiful nests are made from moss, woven together with spiders' webs, and often hang under dense foliage towards the end of a branch.

Goldcrests and Firecrests appear the same size, but Goldcrests generally have fractionally shorter tails and may be a little lighter, which makes them the smallest bird found wild in the British Isles. It is amazing to think of such a tiny bird making migratory flights across the open sea, but many do exactly that. Although most of our Goldcrests are resident, many in Europe are migrants and each autumn a large number cross the North Sea from northern Europe to winter in Britain.

Like many other small birds, Goldcrests suffer in cold winter weather, and after a particularly severe spell the population falls dramatically. In general, however, numbers appear to be increasing, and the species must have been helped by the many conifer plantations which have recently been established.

Firecrest *Regulus ignicapillus*

For many years, Firecrests were usually seen only in spring and autumn as they reached the British Isles while on migration, although a few were also seen in winter. On the Continent, Firecrests have been colonising new areas, and in 1962 this species was discovered breeding in southern England.

The number of pairs which nest here is still small and varies greatly from year to year, but it seems as if the Firecrest will colonise parts of Britain, especially places where there are mature conifers within mixed woodland plantations with open spaces.

Like Goldcrests, Firecrests are very active and often secretive; their songs or calls make it less difficult for the birdwatcher to locate them.

In late autumn, the very rare **Yellow-browed Warbler** *Phylloscopus inornatus* may be seen on the coast. It breeds in Siberia and normally winters in southeast Asia, but each year some migrate eastwards and reach Europe, with noticeable influxes in some years.

Goldcrest

Smaller than Wren – 9 cm. Tiny and very active. Greenish, rather dumpy with short tail. Eye is noticeably large at close range. Orange-and-yellow crown of male (**1**) and yellow crown of female (**2**) can be difficult to observe. Juvenile (**3**) lacks the yellow crown. Call is high-pitched 'zit'. Song is two high notes repeated rapidly, finishing with a short trill.
Resident in conifer woods in all parts of the British Isles, but also regularly visits deciduous woods. (Map: page 216)

Firecrest (4)

Size of Goldcrest – 9 cm. Similar to Goldcrest, but with dark line through eye and broad white stripe over eye. More contrast between greener back (often bronze tint on sides of nape) and whiter underparts. 'Zit, zit' call is lower in pitch than that of Goldcrest and the harsher song has no trill.
Rare breeding species mainly in southern England, but occurs on passage on south and east coasts in spring and autumn. (Map: page 216)

Yellow-browed Warbler (5)

Smaller than Willow Warbler – 10 cm. Rather Goldcrest-like. Greenish with pale underparts, obvious supercilium and two wing-bars, one longer than the other. Has high 'tsweet' call.
Rare autumn visitor mainly to the east coast. (No map)

4 Firecrest

Firecrest *juvenile*

Goldcrests

2 ♀

3 *juvenile*

1 Goldcrest ♂

Coal Tit

Hilary Burn

5 Yellow-browed Warbler

Spotted Flycatcher *Muscicapa striata*

This is one of the last summer visitors to arrive; the largest numbers not reaching the British Isles until the second or third week of May. Warm weather in May encourages early nesting, and more young are reared if June is warm and sunny. Sometimes, they have a second brood.

A Spotted Flycatcher feeds almost entirely on insects, which it generally catches in the air by fluttering out from a perch, twisting and turning, then seizing its prey and returning to the same or a nearby perch. It is often this hunting flight which first attracts one's attention to this small brown bird. Many other small birds will also fly up and catch insects in the air, but none do so as regularly or with such expertise as the flycatchers.

The most usual habitat for Spotted Flycatchers is the edge of woodland or glades in woods, but they will also visit gardens, especially large ones with mature trees. Their neat nest is often situated amongst vegetation against the trunk of a tree or a wall. They will, however, build in old nests of other species and, like Robins, sometimes use open-fronted nest-boxes or even old tin cans.

Red-breasted Flycatcher *Ficedula parva*

In autumn, many small passage migrants which should be moving south through Europe get off course and arrive tired on the east coast of Britain. Juveniles are especially involved. One such species that regularly arrives in tiny numbers is the Red-breasted Flycatcher, which breeds in central and northern Europe.

Pied Flycatcher *Ficedula hypoleuca*

This neat summer visitor breeds mainly in deciduous woods in upland valleys, especially in the food-rich sessile oak woods. The Pied Flycatcher nests in holes in trees, and readily uses nest boxes. The population in some woods has been greatly increased by the erection of such boxes.

Although very obvious while nesting, Pied Flycatchers seem to disappear after their young leave the nest because they become silent and feed high in the tree tops. Soon, they fly straight to the Iberian Peninsula, where our birds mix with Pied Flycatchers from other parts of Europe. At this stopping point, they rest and feed, quickly regaining lost fat which gives them the energy to complete their journey and cross the Mediterranean and the Sahara to their winter quarters in west central Africa. In spring, they return by a different route, farther to the east.

Spotted Flycatcher (1)
Slightly smaller than House Sparrow – 14 cm. Very upright when perched. Grey-brown back, whitish underparts and dark streaks on its rather flat head. Juvenile has more streaks on breast. Catches insects in flight and often returns to same perch. Call is a high-pitched 'see' or a sharp 'tsee, tuc, tuc'.
Summer visitor to open woodland throughout Britain and Ireland. (Map: page 217)

Red-breasted Flycatcher
Size of Blue Tit – 11.5 cm. Smaller than other flycatchers. Dumpy. Grey-brown above, pale underparts. White patches at base of tail and strikingly white undertail-coverts. Often droops wings and flicks tail, frequently cocked up like a Wren's. Female lacks orange throat of male (**2**). Juvenile like female, but buff spots on wings.
Regular passage migrant on south and east coasts in autumn. (No map)

Pied Flycatcher
Smaller than House Sparrow – 13 cm. Plumper than Spotted Flycatcher. Catches insects in the air. Male in spring (**3**) is black-and-white, but resembles female in autumn. Female (**4**) and juvenile are brown with white wing-bars. Call is a sharp 'tac', or 'wheet'. Song is two notes repeated with a short trill.
Summer visitor to deciduous woods in Wales, northern and western England and some parts of Scotland. Passes through other areas on migration. (Map: page 217)

3 Pied Flycatcher ♂

Swallow

4 Pied
Flycatcher
♀

Spotted
Flycatchers

2 Red-breasted
Flycatcher ♂

1 Spotted
Flycatcher

Hilary Burn.

Bearded Tit *Panurus biarmicus*

The old name of 'Bearded Reedling' was appropriate for this species, which is not closely related to the tits, but to the babblers, a family widespread in Africa and Asia.

Once, when there were many more reedbeds than there are today, the Bearded Tit must have been quite common; but, with the draining of so many wetlands and the collecting of eggs and skins in the 19th century, it became a rare species. Cold winters also greatly reduced its numbers and, after the particularly severe winter in 1947, only a few pairs survived in East Anglia. From then on, however, the population started to recover. In 1959, after a good breeding season, many started to erupt from their East Anglian reedbeds and move westwards; this movement occurred again in subsequent autumns, and new colonies were established, but it remains a rare bird with only about 400 pairs breeding each year, mainly in the large East Anglian reedbeds.

They can be hard to see in their reedbeds, especially when it is windy and their distinctive calls cannot be heard. Bearded Tits feed on insects, small snails and seeds, especially the seeds from the common reed *Phragmites*.

Long-tailed Tit *Aegithalos caudatus*

It is the calls of Long-tailed Tits that usually first alert a birdwatcher to this attractive species. Stand still and one of them may come very close.

Long-tailed Tits are only distantly related to the other British tits, from which they differ in a number of ways. For instance, they do not nest in holes, but build a superb spherical nest of moss, spiders' webs and lichens, lined with up to 2,000 feathers, almost always built in prickly shrubs to deter predators.

A brood of 8 to 12 young may be reared, and other Long-tailed Tits may help with the job of feeding the young. These helpers may have had their own nests destroyed by predators, or be inexperienced young birds in their first summer.

Like many other species, Long-tailed Tits die in large numbers in cold winters. During the short midwinter days, they have to spend 90% of the daylight hours feeding; otherwise, they will not survive the long cold nights. In the evenings, little groups huddle together in small roosts so as to conserve heat.

Outside the breeding season, they travel around in flocks, which vary in size between about 5 and 30 or more; sometimes other species such as Goldcrests, Blue Tits, Treecreepers or Chaffinches will mix with these flocks.

Bearded Tit
Larger than House Sparrow – 16.5 cm. Secretive, often flies low with weak, fluttering flight. Tail is very long. Orange-brown body. Male (**1**) has black 'moustache' and grey head. Juvenile (**2**) is like female (**3**), but with dark marks on back. Call is a sharp 'ping, ping'.
Resident in large, dense reedbeds, mainly in southeastern England. Visits smaller reedbeds elsewhere in winter. (Map: page 217)

Long-tailed Tit (4)
14 cm. Tiny round body and very long tail. Pink, black and white plumage. Juvenile (**5**) has brown on sides of head. Often travels around in small flocks. Call is a high-pitched 'see, see' and a low 'triupp'.
Resident in woods and hedges in most parts of the British Isles. (Map: page 217)

4 Long-tailed Tits

5 *juvenile*

2 Bearded Tit *juvenile*

Blue Tit

Reed Bunting ♂

3 ♀

Bearded Tits

Hilary Burn

1 ♂

Marsh Tit *Parus palustris*

Despite its name, the Marsh Tit tends to be found in drier woods than the closely related, and very similar, Willow Tit. It may sometimes be seen with flocks of other tits, but it seldom travels far from its own territory and pairs generally remain together until one of their rather short lives comes to an end; then, it is quickly replaced by another from a small floating population of unmated Marsh Tits.

Marsh Tits are not common visitors to gardens and are most likely to occur in large gardens with mature trees on the edge of towns. They nest in holes in trees and only rarely use nestboxes.

Like the Coal and Willow Tits, the Marsh Tit is subordinate to Blue and Great Tits when in competition for food. Marsh Tits will often hide food in the morning and retrieve it again later in the day. Their memory for where food has been stored is excellent.

Willow Tit *Parus montanus*

The Willow Tit is so similar to the Marsh Tit that it was recognised as a different species only as recently as 1897.

Although Willow Tits may live in the same deciduous woods as Marsh Tits, they are less specialised and may also be found in mixed woods, in conifer plantations and even on farmland with comparatively few trees as well as waterside habitats.

Willow Tits often breed in damp woods, perhaps because that is where there are most rotten tree stumps in which they can excavate their own nest-holes. The excavation is carried out by the female and a new hole is made each year. Like the Marsh and Coal Tits, the Willow is known to store food.

Coal Tit *Parus ater*

The Coal Tit, the smallest of the tits, is common in most parts of Britain and will sometimes visit gardens in winter. It is most numerous in coniferous woods and is one of the few species to benefit from the large number of new conifer plantations.

Coal Tits feed mainly on insects. Like the Crested Tits, which also live in coniferous woods, they have a finer bill than those tits which feed mainly in deciduous woods, this adaptation helping them when they probe amongst long conifer needles and cones. When food is plentiful, Coal Tits will often store some of it. An example of this can be seen in gardens where they sometimes hide peanuts in many different places.

Marsh Tit (1)
Size of Blue Tit – 11.5 cm. Small tit with brown back, pale underparts, even paler cheeks, glossy black cap and a small black bib. Juvenile (**2**) is indistinguishable from juvenile Willow Tit. Call is a loud 'pitchou' and a scolding 'chicka dee-dee-dee'. *Resident in deciduous woods in England, Wales and southern Scotland. Sometimes visits gardens.* (Map: page 217)

Willow Tit (3)
Size of Blue Tit – 11.5 cm. Very similar to Marsh Tit, but with larger, dull black crown, larger black bib, pale wing panel and buff flanks. Call is a buzzing 'eez eez eez' and a loud harsh 'chay' repeated several times. *Resident in both deciduous and coniferous woods in England, Wales and southern Scotland.* (Map: page 217)

Coal Tit (4)
Smaller than Blue Tit – 11 cm. Greenish-grey with pale underparts, a black cap and a white stripe on back of head. Two small wing-bars. Call is a piping 'tsuu'. Song is a fast, highly pitched 'teechu, teechu, teechu'. *Resident throughout the British Isles, mainly where there are conifer trees.* (Map: page 217)

Coal Tit
juvenile

Blackcap ♂

4 Coal Tit

1 Marsh Tit

2 Marsh Tit
juvenile

3 Willow Tits

Hilary Burn

Crested Tit *Parus cristatus*

The old pine forests of the Scottish Highland glens are the home of the Crested Tit in Britain. Once, when the forests were larger, they were probably more widespread, as they still are on the Continent.

Crested Tits usually excavate a nest-hole in the stump of an old pine, but they will also use nestboxes in forestry plantations. They often join roving flocks of other small birds in woods in autumn and winter.

Blue Tit *Parus caeruleus*

Anyone who feeds birds in a garden will be familiar with the Blue Tit. Like many of our garden birds, the Blue Tit is a woodland species and nests in holes; it visits gardens regularly, however, and may be encouraged to stay and nest if a suitable nestbox is provided.

Before and during nesting, the male may be seen feeding the female. This behaviour, known as 'courtship-feeding', is common in some other species as well; it not only helps to keep the pair together, but provides the female with extra food which is vitally important as she will produce more than her own weight of eggs.

Seven to fourteen eggs may be laid, but garden nests often have smaller clutches than those in woodland. Although gardens may be safe places for Blue Tits, there is often a shortage of suitable food. It is easier for them to rear large families in woodland, as a brood of young needs between 600 and 1,000 caterpillars each day.

Blue and Great Tits are well known for making holes in milk-bottle tops in order to reach the cream. This behaviour was first recorded in Southampton in 1929, but the habit quickly spread as tits watched and learned from successful individuals.

Great Tit *Parus major*

A Great Tit is more at home on the ground than are the other tits. With its powerful bill, it is able to open nuts and seeds. It regularly visits gardens.

In Britain, Great Tits are largely resident, but may join with other tits in winter. In some years, on the Continent, especially after a good breeding season, tit numbers become large and Great, Blue and Coal Tits move away from their breeding areas; some cross the sea and reach Britain. Great Tits are widespread in Europe, Asia and the Far East. There are many different races, some of which lack yellow on their underparts.

Like other members of its family the Great Tit nests in holes which give protection to eggs and young.

Crested Tit (1)
Size of Blue Tit – 11.5 cm. Rather plump, with black-and-white crest, brown back, pale underparts and black chin. Call is a distinctive soft, high-pitched purr or trill. *Resident in the mature pine woods of the Scottish Highlands.* (Map: page 217)

Blue Tit (2)
Smaller than Great Tit – 11.5 cm. Very active, often hanging upside down to reach food. Blue crown, white cheeks, yellowish-green back, blue wings and tail and yellow underparts. Juvenile is duller, with yellowish cheeks. Call is 'tsee, tsee, tsee'. Song includes similar notes and also a trill. *Resident throughout the British Isles where there are trees and bushes.* (Map: page 217)

Great Tit (3)
Slightly smaller than House Sparrow – 14 cm. Large tit with black crown, striking white cheeks and black band down the centre of yellow underparts. Male generally has broader black band than female. Young birds are duller and paler. Many different calls including a loud, sharp 'tink, tink'. Song is loud 'tee-chur, tee-chur'. *Resident throughout the British Isles, except in Highland areas and northern islands.* (Map: page 218)

1 Crested Tit

Greenfinches
♂
♀

Great Tit
♂

Blue Tits

Coal Tit

2 Blue Tit

3 Great Tit

Hilary Burn

(European) Nuthatch *Sitta europaea*

These birds nest in holes in trees or, sometimes, in holes in walls or in banks. To stop entry by larger species, the Nuthatch has evolved the habit of plastering mud around the entrance hole until nothing larger than a Nuthatch can get through. They will also use nest-boxes where the hole is the correct size, but the instinct to plaster is so strong that any cracks are filled with mud and more may be added to the roof, both inside and outside, and to the point where the box joins the tree. Inside, a nest is constructed which comprises large numbers of flakes of bark or dead leaves.

Nuthatches feed on insects or seeds, especially nuts. They will search for food on the ground or in trees. On finding a suitable nut, a Nuthatch will usually wedge it in a crevice in the bark and hammer it with its bill until it can get at the contents.

In Britain, a Nuthatch seldom travels far from its breeding territory and this probably explains why it is common in some places, yet absent from others which look just as suitable. Even where numerous, it can be hard to locate until one is familiar with its calls.

(Eurasian) Treecreeper *Certhia familiaris*

It is usually difficult to observe a Treecreeper for more than a few seconds because its normal method of feeding is to work its way around a tree trunk, moving upwards all the time, until it reaches the thinner branches, when it flies down to the bottom of another tree and starts to spiral upwards again.

It nests in cavities in tree trunks or behind loose bark. A foundation of small twigs forms the base of the nest and a more delicate cup is built on top. In winter, Treecreepers roost in crevices, but many have discovered the soft bark of the introduced wellingtonia tree, in which they can excavate hollows to fit their tiny bodies.

On the Continent, this species is usually found in coniferous forests in upland areas. In the lower deciduous woods there lives another, closely related species, the **Short-toed Treecreeper** *Certhia brachydactyla*, which breeds in the Channel Islands but not in Britain. It is likely that, after the last Ice Age, Treecreepers followed the spread of Scots pine into Britain, but, before the Short-toed could follow the advance of the deciduous trees, Britain had become separated from the Continent. Subsequently, our Treecreepers adapted to the food-rich, lowland deciduous woods.

Nuthatch (1)

Size of Great Tit – 14 cm. Climbs with short hops both up and down tree trunks or branches. Short tail and large head, with rather long, stout bill. Blue-grey back and buff underparts. Black stripe through eye. Call is a loud 'tuwit, tuwit'. Song is a repeated 'quee-quee-quee' recalling Kestrel's and Lesser Spotted Woodpecker's songs.
Resident in mature deciduous or mixed woodland in England and Wales. Rare in Scotland.
(Map: page 218)

Treecreeper (2)

Smaller than Great Tit – 12.5 cm. Mouse-like, as it climbs up tree trunks with jerky movements. Brown, streaked back and whitish underparts. Bill is long and downcurved. Pale wing-bar can sometimes be seen. Call is high-pitched 'tsee, tsee'. Song is 'see, see, see, sissi-see' getting faster towards the end.
Resident in woods throughout the British Isles.
(Map: page 218)

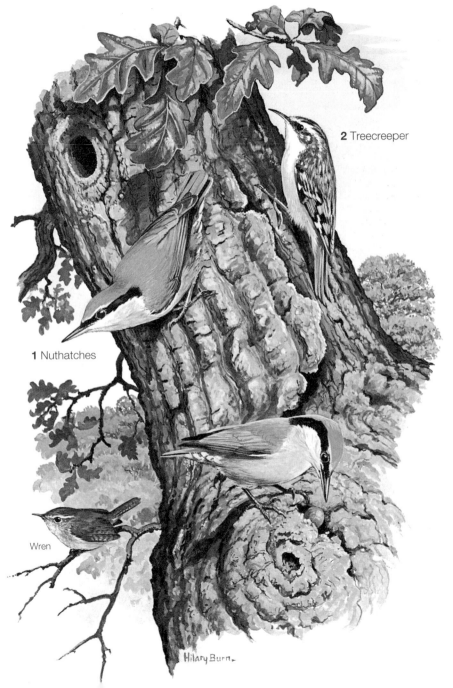

2 Treecreeper

1 Nuthatches

Wren

Hilary Burn

Golden Oriole *Oriolus oriolus*

This is a summer migrant to the deciduous forests of central and southern Europe. In spring, a few overshoot their traditional breeding areas and arrive in Britain. Some of these Golden Orioles then stay to nest, and in recent years the number of pairs has increased to more than 20. In England they prefer poplar plantations.

Green Woodpeckers can be mistaken for female and juvenile Golden Orioles as they also have a bounding flight and are similar in colour. Golden Orioles feed on insects, and, in autumn, fruit. They winter mainly in tropical and southern Africa.

Red-backed Shrike *Lanius callurio*

The Red-backed Shrike feeds on insects, including bees, worms, small birds and small mammals. It has evolved the gruesome habit of storing surplus prey by spiking it on thorns or even on the barbs of a barbed-wire fence, hence its old, country name of 'Butcher Bird'. Ornithologists call this store its 'larder'.

The Red-backed Shrike has been steadily declining in Britain during the last hundred years and has now ceased to breed regularly. The reason for this decline is not obvious. A gradual change in the climate may have reduced the amount of food available. Destruction of heathland has restricted the amount of suitable habitat available and it may be that while the shrike declines in western Europe it increases in the east; we do not know for certain.

Great Grey Shrike *Lanius excubitor*

A hunting Great Grey Shrike will perch on top of a tree or bush with only its tail moving up and down or from side to side. It resembles a small bird of prey and its habits are similar. Suddenly it will swoop down, grasp its prey and return to a perch. The prey may be eaten at once or stored in the shrike's larder.

Although not common winter visitors, a small number of Great Grey Shrikes have regular winter territories here and for that reason are quite easy to locate, and their hunting posts are quite predictable.

Great Grey Shrikes feed mainly on small birds, but will also take mammals and insects. They arrive here from October onwards and leave again in early spring for their breeding grounds, which can be anywhere from central France northwards to the Arctic Circle.

Golden Oriole

Smaller than Blackbird – 24 cm. Secretive, spending much time near tops of trees. Male (**1**) has vivid yellow body, black wings and black on tail. Female (**2**) and juvenile are yellowish-green with darker wings. Song is a fluty 'weela-weel'.
Rare summer visitor.
A few pairs breed, mainly in southern Britain.
(Map: page 218)

Red-backed Shrike

Smaller than Starling – 17 cm. Often perches on top of bush or fence. Longish tail which is frequently moved up and down or from side to side. Thick bill has hooked tip. Male in summer (**3**) has blue-grey head with black mask and chestnut back. Female (**4**) is duller, and juvenile is like female, but more 'scaly'. Call is a sharp 'chack'.
Rare visitor to southern Britain as migrants, mostly in May and September.

Great Grey Shrike (5)

Smaller than Blackbird – 24 cm. Regularly perches on top of bushes or on wires. Grey upperparts, black mask, pale underparts, and black wings with a white bar. Flight is undulating, and it often hovers.
Winter visitor mainly to eastern Britain in open country and especially near the coast. (Map: page 218)

5 Great Grey Shrike

3 ♂ Red-backed Shrikes

4 ♀

2 ♀ Golden Orioles

1 ♂

Hilary Burn

(Eurasian) Jay *Garrulus glandarius*

The Jay is more often heard than seen. Its harsh calls are often the first sounds one hears on entering a wood and are sure to alarm other woodland species.

Although Jays may be found in most types of woodland, it is in oak woods that they are most numerous. They feed on acorns in autumn and regularly store any they cannot eat at once. Not all the acorns stored by Jays are recovered and, as a result, many take root and become young oaks. Thus Jays are responsible for the regeneration of our oak woods.

Not only acorns are eaten, of course: Jays also feed on insects, as well as other fruits and seeds. In spring, they raid the nests of other species and take eggs and young. It is this feeding behaviour which has made Jays unpopular with gamekeepers, who regularly shoot or trap them.

In spite of persecution, the Jay has managed to colonise new areas, and it appears to be becoming more numerous in towns, where there have been reports of Jays taking food which has been hung up for small birds such as tits.

Jays are usually rather sedentary, but in some years, such as 1983, large numbers (including flocks of several hundred) may wander in search of food if the acorn crop has failed.

(Black-billed) Magpie *Pica pica*

The Magpie's liking for eggs and young birds caused it to be shot and trapped by gamekeepers, especially during the 19th century. Numbers recovered, although there was another temporary decline in eastern Britain after the Second World War, linked to the use of organochlorine chemicals in farming. The species spread into towns and cities and Magpies may now be more numerous in some towns than on modern farms where hedges have been removed and old grassland ploughed. In some urban areas they have been suspected of reducing the populations of small song birds, but there is no evidence that Magpies have caused any long-term harm.

The arrival of the Magpie in Ireland can be traced back to a few individuals which crossed the Irish Sea in about 1676, and arrived in Co. Wexford; from then on, the Magpie successfully colonised the whole of Ireland.

Magpies are easy to locate as they are not only large and noisy, but build large, untidy, domed nests made of sticks in tall trees or hedges. Eggs, of course, comprise only a small part of their diet: they also feed on insects, small mammals, carrion, grain and fruit.

Jay (1)

Slightly larger than feral Rock Dove – 34 cm. Secretive. Colourful with pinkish-brown body, black-and-white wings with blue patch, and white rump which contrasts with black tail. Wings are rounded, and flight rather jerky. Call is a harsh screech. *Resident in woodland in many parts of the British Isles. Also visits some town parks and gardens.* (Map: page 218)

Magpie (2)

Size of Rook – 46 cm. Black-and-white with long tail. Wings are rounded and tail often looks wedge-shaped. Call is a harsh 'chack, chack'. *Resident in most of the British Isles except parts of northern Scotland. Usually found where there are small woods or large hedges. Breeds in some towns and often visits large gardens.* (Map: page 218)

Jay

Magpie

Jay

juvenile

2 Magpies

1 Jay

Hilary Burn.

(Red-billed) Chough *Pyrrhocorax pyrrhocorax*

The Chough (pronounced 'chuff') is by far the rarest of our breeding crows and has declined in recent years. Once it regularly nested in Cornwall, and is incorporated into that county's coat of arms. The last pair nested there in 1960, but recently a few birds have returned. The removal of rough, unimproved coastal grassland grazed by cattle and sheep and the scarcity of dung-feeding insects has contributed to the decline.

Its strangely shaped bill is a valuable tool: it enables the Chough to probe into the ground to find ants, the larvae of other insects and spiders.

(Eurasian) Jackdaw *Corvus monedula*

The Jackdaw's liking for bright, shiny objects is well known, and this may even have given it the Latin specific name, *monedula*, meaning 'money-bird', perhaps because of the habit of pet Jackdaws to take coins.

Jackdaws nest in holes in trees or in cliffs, but they also nest in ruined buildings, church towers and chimneys. They usually nest in colonies, and have a complicated system of communication using different attitudes and calls. They are very intelligent and Jackdaws in captivity have learnt quite complicated tricks.

Although they often feed alongside other crows, Jackdaws have a shorter bill and take most of their food from on, or near, the surface. They feed largely on insect larvae, but also take young birds, eggs, slugs and worms.

Rook *Corvus frugilegus*

On mild winter days, Rooks may be seen returning to their tree-top rookeries and starting to rebuild their nests. In their search for material, they often steal twigs from neighbouring Rooks' nests.

Traditionally many Rooks nested in elm trees, but since Dutch Elm Disease swept Britain, most have been forced to use other trees. Rookeries in Wales average 25 nests, England and Northern Ireland average around 30, but Scotland averages over 80 nests. In 1975, the largest rookery in Britain (Aberdeenshire) contained over 2,000 nests.

When Rooks gather food for their young, they store it in an expandable pouch under their bill. They feed by probing into the ground, and take worms, insects and grain. For years, they have been considered a pest and persecuted, but they may be helpful to farmers as many of the insects they eat are harmful to crops.

In winter, Rooks will regularly visit their rookeries, but in the evenings they often join vast communal roosts which include migrant Rooks from the Continent.

Chough (1)
Larger than Jackdaw – 39 cm. Black, with long curved red bill and red legs. Call is a ringing 'chow'. Flight is buoyant. Often performs aerobatics around cliffs. *Resident on rocky coasts of western Britain and Ireland. Sometimes breeds in inland quarries.* (Map: page 218)

Jackdaw (2)
Smaller than Rook – 34 cm. All-black except for grey back to head; pale eye. Often seen in flocks, and mixes with Rooks and Starlings. Flight is rather pigeon-like. Frequently performs aerobatics. Wings look rather pointed, except when soaring. Calls are a sharp 'jac' or a ringing 'kyow'. *Breeds in a variety of habitats, including woods, sea cliffs, quarries and town centres.* (Map: page 219)

Rook
Slightly smaller than Carrion Crow – 46 cm. Adult's (**3**) all-black plumage looks purple at close range. Face is greyish-white, bill appears long and pointed. Has steep forehead and loose feathers at top of legs. Juvenile (**4**) is similar to adult, but with dark, feathered face. Similar to Carrion Crow in flight but has longer head, rounded tail, narrower wings and faster wingbeats. Call is a loud 'kaah'. *Feeds on farmland. Breeds in colonies in woods or copses.* (Map: page 219)

Choughs

Rooks

Jackdaw

Carrion
Crow
juvenile

juvenile

1 Choughs

juvenile

Rooks

2 Jackdaw

3 adult

Hilary Burn

Carrion Crow *Corvus corone*

This is one of the most widespread breeding species in the British Isles; it is found in many different habitats, from town parks to remote islands.

The all-black form of the Carrion Crow *C.c. corone* is found in Asia and parts of western Europe; in between is the form *C.(c.) cornix* known as the 'Hooded Crow' which, in the British Isles, is common in northern Scotland, the Isle of Man and Ireland. Where the two races meet, they regularly interbreed and intermediates are common.

While Carrion Crows are sedentary here, they are migratory in parts of northern Europe and some cross the North Sea which accounts for Hooded Crows appearing in eastern England in winter, although this has happened less frequently in recent winters.

Although Carrion Crows may sometimes be seen in small flocks, they are more often seen singly or in pairs. They do not nest in colonies like Rooks.

First-years and migrants may flock together in winter and large communal roosts are formed sometimes, often in woodland. Rooks and Jackdaws may join these roosts.

Carrion Crows eat a wide range of food, including insects, worms, grain and fruits. They often feed on dead animals (carrion) and will also catch and kill small animals and birds as well as taking eggs. They have been observed dropping shellfish on to roads and then eating the contents after the shells have been smashed by passing traffic. Carrion Crows have also been seen to break the foil caps on milk bottles in order to get at the cream.

(Common) Raven *Corvus corax*

The Raven features in legends from Britain, Ireland and many other countries and is often associated with death. Perhaps this grim reputation is not surprising as it is a carrion eater and must have been commonly seen around battlefields and gallows in olden times. As Ravens not only feed on carrion, but also kill mammals and birds and take eggs, they have been persecuted by gamekeepers, but during this century numbers have started to recover.

Ravens may have four or five nest-sites within their territories. Most will be on crags or sea cliffs, but increasingly trees are being used. Each winter one of these sites will be selected and eggs may be laid as early as February. Sometimes old Raven's nests are taken over by Peregrines.

Where Ravens are plentiful, they will sometimes feed in flocks or gather together in communal roosts in the evenings outside of the breeding season.

Carrion Crow
Slightly larger than Rook – 47 cm. Powerful bill and no white on face. In flight, the tail is square and wings are broad. Flight is strong. Carrion Crows found in most of Britain (**1**) have all-black plumage, but the race found in Ireland and northern and western Scotland, known as the 'Hooded Crow' or 'Hoodie' (**2**), has a grey body. In parts of Scotland, the two races regularly interbreed. Call is a hoarse, croaking 'craah'.
Found throughout the British Isles. (Map: page 219)

Raven (3)
Larger than Carrion Crow – 64 cm. Largest member of crow family. Has large head, huge bill and shaggy throat feathers. In flight, head projects farther in front of wings than does Carrion Crow's and tail is wedge-shaped. Often performs aerobatics while giving its croaking 'prruk, prruk' call.
Resident in western Britain and Ireland, especially around sea cliffs and in upland areas with crags. (Map: page 219)

Carrion Crows

Ravens

Magpie

2 'Hooded Crow'

hybrid

1 Carrion Crow

3 Raven

(Common) Starling *Sturnus vulgaris*

It is not unusual, in early summer, to come across a pale blue egg lying, unbroken, on a lawn or some other area of short grass. The egg will be a Starling's and have been dropped there by a Starling which, for a reason that is not understood, removed it from a nearby nest.

Starlings are often unpopular with people who feed garden birds as, during the winter, they travel around in flocks and gorge themselves on food which was intended for smaller birds. Starlings are, however, rather more interesting than most people realise.

They are superb mimics and their own, typically jumbled songs contain lots of phrases which are copied from other species or other sounds. Curlews, Lapwings, Song Thrushes, Golden Orioles and chickens are all mimicked, as are barking dogs, human whistles and even telephones.

Holes in trees, especially old woodpecker holes, are often used as nest-sites by Starlings, but they also use holes in cliffs and walls and nest under the eaves of houses. The nest-holes are often obvious because of the tell-tale white droppings beneath the entrances.

Gardeners should welcome Starlings probing, with their bills slightly open, into a lawn in their search for leatherjackets (the larvae of the cranefly) and other insects. They feed on a variety of other foods, including worms and spiders during the breeding season, and fruit, berries and other vegetable matter at other times of year.

The Starling has been an adaptable and successful species. In past centuries, it was not so widespread as it is now, but in the last hundred years it has become one of our most common birds. In 1890, it was introduced into New York and 65 years later it had colonised most of North America. In recent years, however, the British Starling population has declined. The reason for this is not clear, but it is possible that agricultural changes are adversely affecting Starlings in the same way as they are affecting several other familiar farmland birds.

For a really exciting spectacle, one has only to locate a local Starling roost at dusk. As early as June, when some Starlings have finished nesting, small flocks may be seen heading for the roost as dusk approaches. The roost may be in woodland, in a reedbed or in a city centre, like the once famous roost in Leicester Square, London. Later in the year, more Starlings arrive from Europe, and some roosts have numbered over one million individuals. Before they settle down for the night, they may be seen in large feeding flocks or swooping down to bathe communally before performing some marvellous aerobatics over their roost. Such concentrations often attract birds of prey, such as Sparrowhawks.

Starling
Smaller than Blackbird – 21.5 cm. Rather short tail. Black plumage appears purple or oily green at close quarters. In winter (**1**) many of its feathers have pale tips, giving spangled appearance. Bill is yellow in summer (**2**), horn-coloured in winter. Juvenile (**3**) is brown, with pale throat. Juvenile moulting into adult plumage (**4**) has curious combination of the two plumages. Song is a mixture of scratchy whistles and warbles, often including imitations of other bird calls. Flight is fast and direct, and pointed wings have triangular shape. Except when nesting, is usually seen in flocks and often gathers in vast communal roosts.
Resident throughout the British Isles, except in exposed upland areas.
(Map: page 219)

1 *winter*

3 *juvenile*

2 ♂

juvenile

2 *summer*

Starlings

Hilary Burn

House Sparrow *Passer domesticus*

The House Sparrow has benefited enormously from man's activities. Although it probably originated in the steppes of Asia, accidental and intentional introductions by man, to such places as North and South America, South Africa, Australia and New Zealand, have probably made the House Sparrow now the world's most widespread bird species. It is, however, not the most numerous species in the British Isles. It is scarce in remote places where there are no houses to give shelter, and it often depends on man or his animals. Its nest-sites are in any kind of hole, often in a building, but sometimes in trees even in the middle of a wood, or it will build a large, untidy, domed nest in a tree or hedge: House Sparrows often take over House Martins' nests.

The House Sparrow eats a wide range of foods and quickly exploits new sources: for example, it learnt to copy tits and to hang on peanuts and other food suspended from bird tables.

House Sparrows have been found nesting in almost every month of the year, but generally they breed between May and August, and often rear three broods. Nests are sometimes close together in loose colonies, and after nesting House Sparrows will flock together. It is at this time that they may do some damage, by feeding on grain in agricultural areas.

Surprisingly, the British population is in decline. House Sparrows in the countryside experience the same food shortages as other farmland species. Why urban populations are falling is more mysterious.

(Eurasian) Tree Sparrow *Passer montanus*

The recent decline of the Tree Sparrow is paralleled by declines of Corn Bunting, Linnet and Sky Lark and may be linked to changes in agriculture. Tree Sparrows have, however, experienced similar declines in the past and it is possible that large-scale immigration from the Continent swells our population at irregular intervals.

In Britain this is the sparrow of woods and fields, rather than towns and gardens. It nests in holes in trees, in cliffs and sometimes in buildings. It will also take over Sand Martin holes. After breeding, Tree Sparrows generally travel in flocks and often mix with House Sparrows, finches and buntings.

In parts of Europe and Asia, Tree Sparrows may be found around towns, like House Sparrows in Britain, and in some places they are considered to be serious pests.

Being smaller than House Sparrows, they will sometimes use nestboxes, and may 'evict' a pair of Blue Tits to take over their box. Most Tree Sparrows nest in colonies which may fluctuate in size from year to year.

House Sparrow
14.5 cm. A very familiar species. Male (**1**) has brown, streaked upperparts, grey crown, black throat and whitish cheeks, grey rump and white wing-bar. Female (**2**) is duller, without the bold head markings, but often shows pale stripe over eye. Juvenile (**3**) is similar to female. Call is a loud 'chirrup'.
Common resident. Seldom far from houses or farms.
(Map: page 219)

Tree Sparrow (4)
Smaller than House Sparrow – 14 cm. Similar to male House Sparrow, but has brown crown, smaller black bib, black spot on whitish cheeks and partial white collar. Female is similar to male. Call is 'tek, tek', shorter and sharper than the 'chirrup' of House Sparrow.
Resident in England, Wales and lowland Scotland.
(Map: page 219)

Corn Bunting

Chaffinch

Yellowhammer

Reed
Buntings

4 Tree
Sparrows

juvenile

adult

3 *juvenile*

1 ♂

House Sparrows **2** ♀

HilaryBurn

Chaffinch *Fringilla coelebs*

This is one of our most numerous breeding species. Numbers increase in winter when additional Chaffinches, mainly from Norway and Sweden, move south to the Netherlands, cross the sea and arrive in southeast England. On their return journey, they are likely to take a more direct route and fly straight to Scandinavia.

Our resident Chaffinches do not travel far from their breeding territories. Migrants can be recognised because they remain in flocks which usually contain mainly males or mainly females.

Chaffinches are well equipped to feed on a wide variety of food. They have a typical seed-eater's bill which can deal with beech mast (the fruit of the beech tree), grain, and small seeds from common weeds, but is sufficiently pointed to help them catch insects in the breeding season. Insects may be picked off leaves, taken from the ground or caught in the air.

The Chaffinch's song is very variable. It differs noticeably from one part of the country to another, and there are even small differences between the songs of those living in different Scottish glens.

The female, which has the advantage of camouflage, builds the nest and incubates the eggs. The male uses his bright colours in a courtship display. After moulting, the male has buff tips to his bright feathers which make him more like the female, but these tips wear away, and by spring he has bright plumage again.

Brambling *Fringilla montifringilla*

The Brambling takes over from the Chaffinch as the common finch in northern Europe. In northern birch woods it may be the most abundant species, except for the Willow Warbler.

The number of visiting Bramblings varies from year to year and flocks are very mobile. The chief food is beech mast; when it is plentiful, there are likely to be more Bramblings around, often joining Chaffinch flocks.

We get rather fewer Bramblings than some other parts of Europe where huge concentrations may form where mast is abundant. During the winter of 1951–2, it was estimated that 70 million gathered around a single Swiss town when the surrounding beech trees were loaded with mast.

Chaffinch

Slightly larger than House Sparrow – 15 cm. Male (**1**) is colourful, with pinkish breast, two large white wing-bars and white outer tail feathers. Female (**2**) also has white wing-bars and outer tail feathers, but is more uniform brown. Call is loud 'tink' rather like Great Tit's. Song is a loud musical rattle ending in a flourish.
Common breeding species wherever there are trees and bushes. In winter may be found in many habitats, especially open farmland.
(Map: page 219)

Brambling

Size of House Sparrow – 14.5 cm. Similar to Chaffinch, but with orange sides to breast and bold white rump. Has no white shoulder patch or white in the tail. Male in spring (**3**) has black head. Female (**4**) is duller with grey patch on back of head. Call is a harsh 'tswark'.
Winter visitor to most parts of Britain, but rather scarce in parts of Ireland. A few pairs nest most years, mainly in Scotland. (Map: page 220)

Brambling

Chaffinch

3 Brambling
♂ *spring*

4 ♀

Bramblings

♂ *winter*

2 ♀

Chaffinches

1 ♂

HilaryBurn.

(European) Greenfinch *Carduelis chloris*

These birds often come into gardens in winter, especially if peanuts are on the menu! They are able to hang on most nut-dispensers and often drive away other species.

The Greenfinch's powerful bill is used for breaking open seeds which it finds throughout the year. Young Greenfinches are fed on regurgitated food.

Unlike Chaffinches, Greenfinches nest in loose colonies and defend only small territories around their nests. They will search for food away from the colony in small flocks. The reason for this difference is, presumably, that Chaffinches feed their young on insects which are found throughout their territory: Greenfinches need seeds which may be very plentiful in only a few places.

In winter, some additional Greenfinches arrive here from the Continent and flock sizes increase. Often they join with House Sparrows, Yellowhammers and other species.

In spring, they may be seen singing and displaying over their small territories. They then have a very distinctive rather slow, deliberate, wavering display-flight, which helps to show off their vivid yellowish wing- and tail-flashes.

(European) Goldfinch *Carduelis carduelis*

In the last century, Goldfinches were common cage-birds, 132,000 being caught in one year near Worthing, Sussex. Fortunately, Goldfinch trapping is now illegal, although it continues in some other parts of Europe.

The favourite food of Goldfinches is thistle seeds, which they can reach with their rather long, slim bills. They are able to cling to swaying stems and will use their feet to grasp their food and draw it towards them.

Many of our Goldfinches migrate to the Continent in autumn, while only a few arrive here from farther north. In spring, Goldfinches may be seen singing and displaying on a branch and as they sing, with wings drooped, they swing from side to side.

(Eurasian) Siskin *Carduelis spinus*

The planting of ornamental and commercial conifer trees has helped the Siskin to colonise new areas in Britain and Ireland. It feeds on seeds, especially favouring pines, birch and alder.

Siskins are very agile, and will hang on the thinnest twigs in order to reach their food. This habit of hanging on food has helped them to take advantage of a new source of food: hanging nut-dispensers which have been put out in gardens for tits.

Greenfinch

Size of House Sparrow – 14.5 cm. Large finch with heavy-looking bill. Male (**1**) is brighter green below than above with bright green rump and yellowish-green flashes in wings and tail. Female (**2**) is duller with streaked back, but similar flashes in wings and tail. Juvenile is similar to female, but more streaked. Has twittering flight call. Song is twittering with long-drawn-out, nasal 'dzwee'. *Common throughout most of the British Isles and visits gardens in winter.* (Map: page 220)

Goldfinch

Smaller than House Sparrow – 12 cm. Adult (**3**) has red face and a vivid yellow wing-bar on its black wings. Juvenile (**4**) is similar, but without the red face. Flight is bouncing. Call is a tinkling twitter. Musical song is similar to call but longer. *Common resident in most parts of the British Isles except the north of Scotland.* (Map: page 220)

Siskin

Smaller than Greenfinch – 12 cm. Small, streaky greenish-yellow finch with yellow rump, yellow wing-bar and short, forked tail. Male (**5**) has black cap and bib. Female (**6**) is duller than male without any black on head. Call is a clear 'tsuu' and a hard twittering. *Breeds in conifer woods especially in northern Scotland. Winter visitor to much of southern Britain and Ireland, especially feeding on alder and birch.* (Map: page 220)

Siskin

5 *summer* ♂

winter ♂

Siskins

Siskin
juvenile

Goldfinches

4 *juvenile*

Siskins

6 ♀

Redpoll

Greenfinch

House Sparrow

3 Goldfinches

2 ♀

Greenfinches

juvenile

1 ♂

Hilary Burn.

(Common) Linnet *Carduelis cannabina*

Linnets were popular cage-birds in the 19th century and continual trapping reduced the numbers in the countryside. With protection the population recovered, but since the mid-1970s it has fallen again. This recent decline is attributed to changes in farming practice.

Once one has learnt the calls of our common finches, one soon discovers that the Linnet is found not only on farmland but also on rough ground near town centres, and it may even nest in large gardens where there are mature shrubs.

Linnets feed mainly on seeds of weeds. They often breed in small colonies and start to nest in April, when seeds become available after the winter. Early nests are usually in evergreen bushes such as gorse, because at that time other shrubs do not have any leaves.

Linnets may join flocks of other seed-eaters when a particular food becomes available: Chaffinches, Bramblings, Greenfinches, Tree Sparrows and buntings may feed with Linnets. In some places food is so plentiful that there is far more than any one bird can eat and so there is no reason why others should not share it.

Twite *Carduelis flavirostris*

The British Isles is home for a significant but declining proportion of the European Twite; western Norway is the only other area where this species is common.

Twites take over from Linnets in upland areas in summer, but also breed near sea-level around rocky coasts. In winter, some Twites move from the uplands, visiting farmland and gathering in large flocks in some coastal areas such as The Wash in East Anglia.

(Lesser) Redpoll *Carduelis cabaret*

Britain and Ireland are almost at the southern edge of the Redpoll's range and those that breed here are smaller and darker than those farther north.

Redpolls are most common where there are birch trees as their seeds are an important food along with seeds from sallow, alder and many other plants. Some insects are also eaten. Redpolls have colonised many parts of the country in recent years, although numbers peaked in the 1970s and have since fallen. Their initial spread was helped by the increase in young conifer plantations and the abundance of mature birch trees where they often nest.

Most Redpolls in northern Britain move south for the winter and some cross the Channel to the Continent. Many more leave in years when there is a poor crop of birch seed.

Linnet
Smaller than House Sparrow – 13 cm. Male (**1**) has reddish-brown back, greyish head and red forehead and breast. Female (**2**) lacks any red and is more heavily streaked. Both sexes show white flashes in their wings. Has bouncing flight and twittering flight call.
Found in most parts of the British Isles except for parts of northwest Scotland.
(Map: page 220)

Twite
Smaller than House Sparrow – 13 cm. Linnet-like, with longer, more forked tail. Brown, with dark streaks, more stripy back, and less white in wings and tail than Linnet. Dark bill in summer, pale yellowish in winter. Male (**3**) has pink rump in summer. Call is a harsh 'cheueet'. Song is similar to Linnet's.
Breeds in upland areas of Scotland and the Pennines, and also on the west coasts of Scotland and Ireland. Winter visitor to the east coast. (Map: page 220)

Redpoll
Size of Blue Tit – 11.5 cm. Small and active, often feeding at tops of trees. Dark, streaked back and paler underparts. Male (**4**) has red forehead and breast and black chin. Female (**5**) is similar but the red is duller. Flight is bouncing and usual call is a metallic 'chi-chi-chi-chi'. Song is like call, but with buzzing trills.
Found in most parts of the British Isles, but scarce in the southwest of England.
(Map: page 220)

Snow Bunting

Twites

Chaffinch

Reed
Bunting

3 Twite ♂

Redpoll

1 ♂

Linnets

2 ♀

4 ♂

5 ♀

Redpolls

Hilary Burn.

Common Crossbill *Loxia curvirostra*

These birds feed on conifer seeds. Their feet are used for holding cones and their strangely shaped but powerful bill is adapted for extracting the seeds.

Conifer seeds form in cones in autumn, but the cones do not open and release their seeds for between 3 and 22 months, depending on the species of tree. This means there is food available for the crossbills throughout the year. The cone crop, however, varies from year to year and each year crossbills move until they locate a new supply of cones and will, then, often stay to nest wherever they happen to be.

As well as moving annually, the Common Crossbill population 'erupts' in some years: perhaps because of the failure of the pine crop, perhaps because of over-population, large numbers leave traditional conifer woods and move far afield, even to areas with no conifers. Some of these crossbills die, others survive and populate new forests for a time, others return to their traditional areas. In England, many conifer plantations have been temporarily colonised after crossbill eruptions.

Scottish Crossbill *Loxia scotica*

The remains of the old Caledonian forest of the Scottish Highlands are the home of the Scottish Crossbill, which is currently accepted as a true species, not a race of the Common Crossbill, as was previously thought.

The Scottish Crossbill has a larger, deeper bill than the Crossbill, and this adaptation helps it to extract seeds from pine cones, whereas the Common Crossbill feeds mainly on seeds from the softer spruce cones.

(Common) Bullfinch *Pyrrhula pyrrhula*

It is unfortunate that this attractive finch is considered a pest in areas where fruit is grown: it has been trapped and killed in large numbers. Bullfinches do, however, take many buds – up to 30 per minute – and can spoil a fruit crop. Like several other farmland birds, the Bullfinch has suffered a marked decline in recent years.

Bullfinches are generally seen in pairs and not in flocks. They seldom move far, although in recent years some have shown signs of 'erupting' when their chief winter food, ash seed, is in short supply; it is at such times that most damage is done on fruit farms.

Various seeds are eaten and it is in early spring, when other food is scarce, that they turn to buds. Small snails are also eaten, their shells being broken in the Bullfinch's powerful bill. The young are fed on seeds and insects, which are carried to the nest in two pouches in the floor of the Bullfinch's mouth.

Common Crossbill
Larger than House Sparrow – 16 cm. Large head, short tail and crossed bill: tips of upper and lower mandibles overlap. Male (**1**) is brick-red (sometimes yellow or orange) with dark wings and tail. Female (**2**) is grey-green with brighter green rump. Juvenile (**3**) is like female, but more streaked. Call is a loud, hard 'chip, chip, chip'.
Breeds in East Anglia, the New Forest, Northumberland, Scotland and a few other places.
In some years is found in many other areas as well.
(Map: page 220)

Scottish Crossbill (4)
Larger than House Sparrow – 16.5 cm. Slightly larger than Common Crossbill, with larger, heavier bill. Call is loud 'chup, chup, chup'. Otherwise very similar to Common Crossbill.
Lives in the old pine woods of the Scottish Highlands.
(Map: page 221)

Bullfinch
Larger than House Sparrow – 15 cm. Plump, neat, with short black bill. Tail, wings and cap are black. Rump is white. Male (**5**) has pinkish-red breast. Female (**6**) has brownish breast. Juvenile (**7**) is similar to female, but lacks black cap. Call is a piping 'dew'.
Resident almost anywhere that there are tangled bushes for nesting. (Map: page 221)

Common Crossbills

2 ♀

1 ♂

3 juvenile

4 Scottish Crossbills

♀

♂

Bullfinches

5 ♂

6 ♀

7 Bullfinch juvenile

Hilary Burn

Hawfinch *Coccothraustes coccothraustes*

In summer, Hawfinches feed mainly high up in trees and are very difficult to observe. In winter, they often feed on fallen fruits on the ground, but they are very timid and, again, are difficult to watch. They are most likely to be discovered by hearing their Robin-like calls from high up in tall trees where Robins are unlikely to be.

Some Hawfinches breed in small colonies, while others nest singly. Hawfinches feed on seeds and in summer they also take insects. The massive bill and powerful muscles help the Hawfinch to crack open hard seeds, such as hornbeam, and even cherry stones in order to eat their kernels. The force required to crack a cherry stone is estimated at over 27 kg.

Lapland Bunting (Lapland Longspur) *Calcarius lapponicus*

In winter, it is not unusual to come across small flocks of finches and buntings feeding on the seashore or on nearby turf. Sometimes a Lapland Bunting will join one of these flocks, but care is needed in identification, as females, and males in winter, may be confused with Reed Buntings.

Although Lapland Buntings have occasionally nested in Scotland, most winter visitors come to us from northern Scandinavia, as their name suggests.

Snow Bunting *Plectrophenax nivalis*

This is the most northerly breeding songbird. It breeds in the far north of Europe, Asia and North America, on both mountains and barren tundra. Food, in the form of insects and seeds, is plentiful, but the summer is short. After breeding, the Snow Bunting moults its feathers and grows new ones before migrating south. The moult is so fast that, in the far north, these birds may become flightless for a short period.

In early spring, the Snow Bunting regularly searches for food in frozen snow, and the ice crystals wear away the feathers around the bill. This species may be unique in having a second partial moult so that new face feathers are grown before the breeding season.

In winter, many Snow Buntings remain in upland areas, but others join flocks, especially along sandy coasts of eastern Britain. Travelling in flocks, they feed in their characteristic way: each bird feeds quickly, runs along the ground, then flies to the front of the flock. This 'leap-frogging' means the flock moves forward, in one direction, at about the speed of a human walking quickly.

Hawfinch (1)

Larger than House Sparrow – 18 cm. Largest of our breeding finches, but very shy. Has massive bill and head. Pinkish-brown with black wings, white wing-flashes and white tip to its short tail. Female like male, but duller. Juvenile is less colourful with dark bars on underparts. Call is 'tik' or 'tzik', very similar to call of Robin.
Found in deciduous woods and cherry orchards, mostly in England and a few parts of Wales and Scotland.
(Map: page 221)

Lapland Bunting

Size of Reed Bunting – 15 cm. Male in summer (**2**) has black head and white eye-stripe. Bill is yellow. In winter male resembles female (**3**), which is like female Reed Bunting, but with reddish-brown nape, and two pale wing-bars enclosing rufous patch. Call is a hard 'tick-i-tick', often followed by musical 'teu'.
Has recently nested in Scotland, otherwise a rare, mainly autumn visitor to the east coast. (Map: page 221)

Snow Bunting

Larger than House Sparrow – 16.5 cm. A stockily built bunting with white underparts and a lot of white in its wings. Male in summer (**4**) is white with black back and black centre to its tail. Male in winter (**5**) is much browner. Female (**6**) and juvenile show less white than male, but more than any similar species. Call a musical 'teu'.
A few breed in Scotland. Winter visitors elsewhere, especially in north and east.
(Map: page 221)

1 Hawfinches

Reed Bunting

Skylarks

5 Snow Bunting

2 ♂

3 ♀

♂ winter

Lapland Buntings
autumn ♂

6 ♀

Snow Buntings

4 ♂

Hilary Burn

Yellowhammer *Emberiza citrinella*

This is a familiar farmland species. Its distinctive song, and its habit of singing from the top of a bush, or some other obvious perch, make it easy to see in spring and summer when the male is defending his breeding territory. After nesting, however, the territories are abandoned and Yellowhammers may be seen in flocks, often mixed with other buntings, finches and sparrows. In winter, they roost communally in thick bushes or, sometimes, reedbeds.

Yellowhammers feed on seeds, but also eat insects and fruits. Although common on most types of farmland, they are most numerous on highly productive land, especially where there are thick hedges containing a few trees. They are also found on heathland and on the edge of woods.

The population of our Yellowhammers does not show the spasmodic fluctuation which is typical of many of our small perching birds. They do not seem to be badly affected by severe winter weather, yet they do not usually travel far from their breeding areas. Yellowhammers have even been observed roosting amongst low vegetation underneath 30 cm of snow. Since the first edition of this book, the Yellowhammer has shown a remarkable decline in the west. In Northern Ireland this has resulted in the species becoming virtually extinct in 20 years; elsewhere it is still present, but in smaller numbers. The decline has been linked with agricultural intensification.

Cirl Bunting *Emberiza cirlus*

The Cirl Bunting is most numerous in sheltered valleys, and among the vineyards of the Mediterranean region; those found in Britain are on the northern edge of their range.

The attractive male Cirl Bunting prefers to sing from a prominent perch, often a tree in a hedgerow. The drab female is much easier to overlook. Although the male often sings again on fine days in winter, the species is generally hard to observe then, as small groups travel around the local farmland.

It is likely that the Cirl Bunting colonised Britain comparatively recently, as the first nest was found in Devon in 1800. It has never been very common, but was, for a time, much more widespread than it is now, extending north to north Wales, for instance. It is now very rare except on the south Devon coast. In recent years, conservationists and farmers have ensured that some stubble fields remain unploughed in autumn to provide winter food for Cirl Buntings in winter. This, and some supplementary feeding, has helped the population to recover to about 450 pairs.

In winter, Cirl Buntings prefer to feed close to hedgerows where there is cereal stubble and plenty of weeds. They feed on grain, especially barley, and weed seeds.

Yellowhammer
Larger than House Sparrow – 16.5 cm. Rather slim and long-tailed. Male in spring (**1**) has bright yellow head and breast. Female (**2**) is duller. Both male and female have white outer tail feathers and chestnut rumps. Juvenile resembles dull female and is more streaky. Call is a metallic 'chip'. Song is 'chitti, chitti, chitti, chitti, chee-eez', said to sound like 'little bit o' bread and no cheese'. *Found in open country in most parts of Britain and Ireland.* (Map: page 221)

Cirl Bunting
Slightly smaller than Yellowhammer – 16 cm. Male (**3**) has black throat, black line through eye and greyish-green band across breast, with rest of underparts yellow. Female (**4**) and juvenile are like female Yellowhammer, but rump is brown, not chestnut. Call is a thin 'zit'. Song is a rattle of one note repeated: similar to Lesser Whitethroat's or to the beginning of Yellowhammer's song. *Rather rare. Resident in southern and southwestern England.* (Map: page 221)

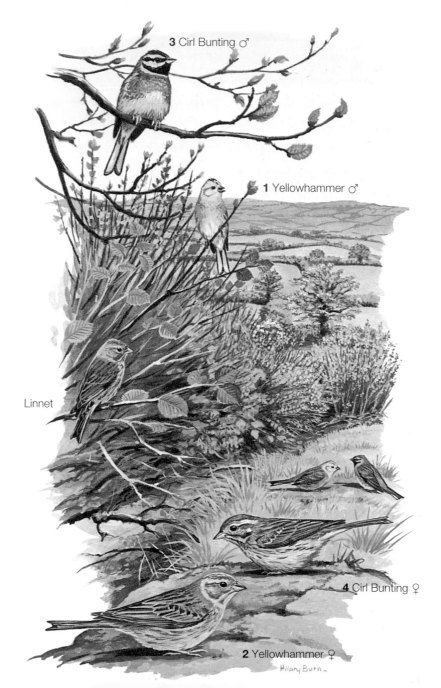

3 Cirl Bunting ♂

1 Yellowhammer ♂

Linnet

4 Cirl Bunting ♀

2 Yellowhammer ♀

Hilary Burn

Reed Bunting *Emberiza schoeniclus*

Many of the wetlands of Britain and Ireland have been drained and most of the species which depend on them have become rarer. The Reed Bunting, however, is an exception. From about 1950, for a reason that is not really understood, the Reed Bunting moved into many drier areas such as young conifer plantations and barley fields, as well as continuing to nest in traditional areas near lakes and rivers. Perhaps this change had been forced on the Reed Bunting by a lack of wet sites, the species modifying its requirements to suit the changing environment. Whatever the reason, the Reed Bunting became established in many places to which it had previously only been a rare visitor.

From 1975, the situation changed again and numbers began to decline. This may be due partly to climate and partly to agricultural changes. By the 1990s, the population had returned to the levels of the 1960s.

The chief food is seeds, but insects are also eaten in summer. Outside the breeding season, Reed Buntings flock together and often join flocks of other buntings and finches which roam over farmland in their search for food. Recently, Reed Buntings have become more common in gardens and now sometimes visit bird tables in winter.

Corn Bunting *Miliaria calandra*

This large, rather plain bunting is often unnoticed by beginner birdwatchers, yet it is quite easy to see in spring and summer as it sings from power lines, gate posts or small bushes. Indeed, the Corn Bunting appears to depend on the farmland which man has created.

Corn Buntings spend much of the winter in flocks and may gather in large roosts in the evenings. Males often return to their territories as early as January, but females may remain in their flocks until April or May. Some male Corn Buntings are polygamous, meaning that they have more than one mate in the breeding season.

Nests are often built on the ground in cornfields and this is one farmland species which does not seem to mind the removal of hedges. Its distribution in Britain is patchy, but may, in part, be linked to the production of barley. Since 1981, there has been a widespread decline and a contraction of its range in Britain: it has virtually disappeared from Wales, southwest England and parts of Scotland. The biggest decline is in eastern England.

Reed Bunting
Slightly larger than House Sparrow – 15 cm. Male (**1**) has black head and white collar, sparrow-like body and white outer tail feathers. Female (**2**) lacks black head markings. Male in autumn is more like female. Call is a loud 'tseeo'. Simple song is a very plain 'chink, chink, chink chittichick'.
Widespread resident in the British Isles. Often found near water but also in drier places.
(Map: page 221)

Corn Bunting (3)
Larger than Yellowhammer – 18 cm. Largest bunting, with large head and heavy bill. Brown with darker streaks, those on breast forming dark patch. Often perches on wires, fence posts and other obvious places. Legs often dangle during short flight away from song post. Call is a short, sharp 'quit'. Song is a short wheezy jangle, said to sound like the rattle of keys.
Resident mainly on arable farmland in many parts of the British Isles. Very local in Ireland and rare in Wales.
(Map: page 221)

3 Corn Bunting

Skylark

Corn Bunting

Reed
Buntings

1 ♂

2 ♀

Hilary Burn

The Rarities

Common Crane *Grus grus* (**1**)
Larger than Grey Heron – 110–120 cm. Grey body with loose feathers over tail. Dark head with white band running from eye and down neck. Flies with neck outstretched. Call is a loud 'krooh'.
Annual migrant which has occasionally over-wintered. Since 1981, a few have been breeding and over-wintering.

White Stork *Ciconia ciconia* (**3**)
Larger than Grey Heron – 100–115 cm. White with black flight feathers, red bill and long red legs.
Decreasing in north and west Europe. A few reach the British Isles each year. Likes damp water-meadows and other waterside habitats.

Purple Heron *Ardea purpurea* (**5**)
Slighter, smaller, shorter-winged and generally more rufous than Grey Heron – 78–90 cm. Black crown. Bold black stripes on buff face and neck. In flight, long coiled neck bulges below body, and large feet extend beyond tail.
Breeds in southern Europe. Irregular visitor to lakes and reedbeds in southeast England.

Little Bittern *Ixobrychus minutus* (**7**)
Larger than Lapwing – 33–38 cm. Very secretive. Crown, back and flight feathers black, buff underparts and oval patch on wing. Female duller and more streaked than male.
A few reach margins of lakes or rivers in southern Britain each year; bred in 1984.

Glossy Ibis *Plegadis falcinellus* (**2**)
Smaller than Grey Heron – 55–65 cm. Rich chestnut plumage looks black from a distance. Bill is long and decurved. Flies with neck outstretched.
Nearest colonies are in southern Europe, but individuals are nomadic and wild birds sometimes reach the British Isles. May visit reedbeds and other wet places.

Little Egret *Egretta garzetta* (**4**)
Smaller than Grey Heron – 55–65 cm. Small white heron with black bill and legs and bright yellow feet.
Increasingly frequent visitor from southern Europe which first nested in Britain in 1996. Likes shallow margins of rivers, lakes and coastal marshes.

Night Heron *Nycticorax nycticorax* (**6**)
Smaller than Grey Heron – 58–65 cm. Adult has black crown and back, white forehead and cheeks and grey wings and rump. Juvenile is brown and spotted, rather like Bittern.
Frequent vagrant from Europe to southern Britain. Some zoos keep free-flying individuals.

1 Common Crane

2 Glossy Ibis

3 White Stork

5 Purple Heron

4 Little Egret

6 Night Heron

7 Little Bittern ♂

juvenile

Hilary Burn

Ring-billed Gull *Larus delawarensis* (**1**)
Smaller than Herring Gull – 43–47 cm. Larger and bulkier than Common Gull with head shape and expression more like Herring. Adults have paler back and smaller white spots on black wing-tips. Bill yellow with black band. First-winter differs from Common, by paler back, prominent pattern of round spotting on hind-neck and large black eye.
Breeds in North America. May sometimes be seen in British Isles with other gulls, especially in western coastal areas.

Ring-necked Duck *Aythya collaris* (**3**)
Size of Tufted Duck – 37–46 cm. Small diving duck with 'triangular' head. Drake is glossy black with grey flanks and white patch between flanks and breast. Female is grey-brown with white 'spectacles' and pale face.
Native of North America which is seen increasingly frequently in Britain and Ireland in winter. Some move from lake to lake, making it difficult to know how many are involved.

Spotted Crake *Porzana porzana* (**5**)
Smaller than Moorhen – 22–24 cm. Small, compact rail with greenish or greyish brown plumage, obviously spotted with white. Buff under tail. Very secretive and difficult to observe. Song, 'hweet', sounding rather like a series of whip-lashes, usually heard at dusk or after dark.
Widespread in Russia and west to Sweden. Small numbers probably breed in Britain most years and others arrive in late summer. Found in swamps and fens.

Buff-breasted Sandpiper *Tryngites subruficollis* (**7**)
Similar size to Common Sandpiper, but with longer neck and legs – 18–20 cm. Like small Ruff with longer body and squarer head. Underparts usually pale buff. No wing-bar and plain rump. Plover-like flight.
Breeds in the Arctic, North America and Russia, and winters in South America. Rare visitor to the British Isles where it visits dry open areas.

Wilson's Phalarope *Phalaropus tricolor* (**9**)
Smaller than Redshank – 22–24 cm. More at home on land than other phalaropes and has longer bill and yellow legs. Most frequent visitors are first-winters with pale plumage, white underparts and a dark mark through eye.
Breeds in western Canada and winters in South America. A few vagrants reach the British Isles most years where they visit marshes and other wet areas.

White-winged Black Tern (White-winged Tern)
Chlidonias leucopterus (**2**)
Smaller than Common Tern – 20–23 cm. Similar to Black Tern with shorter bill and shorter, less forked tail. Feeds by picking food from water surface. Breeding plumage is black body and underwing coverts, with silver-white upperwings, rump and tail. Juvenile is separated from Black Tern by dark back, white rump, paler wings and no dark shoulder patches.
Breeds in southwest Europe, west and east Asia. Occasional spring and autumn visitor to lakes in southern Britain.

Surf Scoter *Melanitta perspicillata* (**4**)
Similar size to Common Scoter – 45–56 cm. Dark sea-duck with no wing markings and massive bill. Drake is black with white patches on forehead and nape. Large bill is swollen and multi-coloured. Female is black-brown with two pale patches on side of head.
Breeds in the north of North America and is a rare winter visitor to British and Irish coasts, especially in the north.

King Eider *Somateria spectabilis* (**6**)
Slightly smaller than Eider – 47–63 cm. Round-headed. Drake has white breast and mostly black body. Head is pearl-grey with orange-red bill and bare shield on forehead. Duck resembles Eider but has warmer plumage, more feathers between bill and eye and rounder head.
An Arctic species which winters around the coast of Scandinavia and sometimes reaches British coasts; regular around Shetland.

Black-winged Stilt *Himantopus himantopus* (**8**)
Smaller body than Redshank, but longer bill and much longer legs – 35–40 cm. White with black back and wings. Extraordinary long legs are pink and trail in flight. Call is shrill 'kek, kek'.
Breeds in southern Europe, Asia and North Africa. Is a rare annual visitor to Britain and has nested three times in the last 50 years. Feeds in shallow fresh or brackish water.

White-rumped Sandpiper *Calidris fuscicollis* (**10**)
Smaller than most Dunlins – 15–17 cm. Rather like large stint with long body, long wings, short straight bill and white rump. Slight wing-bar. Pale underparts, greyish streaked breast, and brown back with white edges to coverts.
Breeds in Arctic Canada and winters in South America. Occasional late summer/autumn visitor to marshes, mainly near the coast.

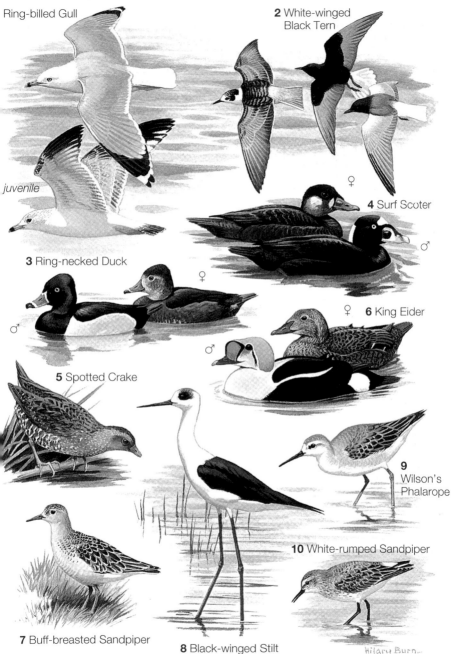

Ring-billed Gull

2 White-winged Black Tern

juvenile

4 Surf Scoter ♀ ♂

3 Ring-necked Duck ♂ ♀

6 King Eider ♀ ♂

5 Spotted Crake

9 Wilson's Phalarope

10 White-rumped Sandpiper

7 Buff-breasted Sandpiper

8 Black-winged Stilt

Hilary Burn

White-tailed Eagle *Haliaeetus albicilla* (**1**)
Similar size to Golden Eagle – 70–90 cm, but more
bulky, with shorter, wedge-shaped tail, massive bill
and longer neck. Looks huge in flight; broad
rectangular wings, deeply fingered at the ends and
protruding head. Adult is brown with white tail.
Juvenile darker brown and lacks white tail.
Reintroduced on to west coast of Scotland.
Resident, but some move away from breeding
areas in winter.

Red-footed Falcon *Falco vespertinus* (**3**)
Smaller than Kestrel – 29–31 cm. Hunts prey by
hovering, chasing in flight and pouncing from a
perch. Similar to Hobby with longer tail. Adult male
is sooty-grey with red 'trousers'. Female has grey
upperparts barred with black, and orange crown
and nape. Underparts are pale buff with barred
flight feathers and tail, pale throat, dark eye-patch
and 'moustache'.
Breeds in eastern Europe and Russia. Occasional
late spring migrant to the south and east of the
British Isles. Likes flat, open, often wet habitats.

Alpine Swift *Apus melba* (**5**)
Larger than Swift – 20–22 cm. Large powerful-
looking swift with relatively short tail, brown
plumage except for white underparts, which are
divided by a brown breast-band.
Breeds in southern Europe and sometimes
reaches southern England, especially in spring.

Woodchat Shrike *Lanius senator* (**7**)
Size of Red-backed Shrike – 18 cm. Larger head
and broader wings than Red-backed. Adult has
black mask, chestnut crown and nape, white bars
on dark wings and white underparts. Juvenile is
scaly brown, with paler rump and scapulars.
Breeds in central and southern Europe and some
reach Britain each year, especially coastal areas
with low trees and bushes in spring.

(European) Honey-buzzard *Pernis apivorus* (**2**)
Size of Buzzard – 51–57 cm. Secretive. Buzzard-
like, but with smaller, cuckoo-like head, slender
neck, thin-looking tail and trailing edges of wings
much straighter. Grey head and grey-brown
upperparts. Underparts vary from pale to dark;
some adults are boldly patterned and always have
dark carpal patch, dark trailing edges to wings and
dark band on tip of tail. Juvenile is also variable
and lacks the bold patterns of adults.
Very scarce summer visitor to British woodland.

Snowy Owl *Nyctea scandiaca* (**4**)
Much larger than Barn Owl – 53–66 cm. Round-
headed mostly white with a cat-like face. Adult
male is all white with very few dark marks.
Female is also white, but heavily barred, with all-
white face.
Has bred in Shetland and a few are seen most
years. Very occasionally other Snowys from the
Arctic arrive in Britain.

European Bee-eater *Merops apiaster* (**6**)
Size of Mistle Thrush – 28 cm. Catches insects
in the air. Often hunts from overhead cables.
Brilliant multicoloured plumage. Adults have long
central tail feathers. Call is liquid 'quilip', often
given in flight.
Breeds in southern Europe. Is a regular visitor to
the British Isles in spring and has nested twice in
the 20th century.

(Spotted) Nutcracker *Nucifraga caryocatactes* (**8**)
Slightly smaller than feral Rock Dove – 33 cm.
Brown plumage speckled with white. Plain brown
crown and wings. White undertail-coverts and
white tip to tail. Recalls small Jay with broad wings
in flight. Tends to perch on tops of trees and feed
more in the open than Jay.
Breeds in northern and central Europe where it
feeds on pine seeds. Shortage of food results in
occasional irruptions when small groups visit
eastern Britain.

2 Honey Buzzard

1 White-tailed Eagle

3 Red-footed Falcon ♂

♀

juvenile

♂

4 Snowy Owl

5 Alpine Swift

6 European Bee-eater

7 Woodchat Shrike

juvenile

8 Nutcracker

Hilary Burn

Short-toed Lark *Calandrella brachydactyla* (**1**)
Smaller than Sky Lark – 13 cm. Rather pipit-like. Generally unobtrusive on ground, and has a jerky walk. Back is sandy with darker streaks. Underparts are whitish with a few streaks on breast and dark marks at sides of breast. Short thick bill, rounded head and almost no crest. White outer-tail features in flight. Call is 't-trip', more rippling than Sky Lark.
Summer migrant to southern and eastern Europe. Some reach Britain in spring and autumn.

Pallas's Leaf Warbler *Phylloscopus proregulus* (**3**)
Size of Goldcrest – 9 cm. Very small and active warbler with large head which resembles Firecrest. Often hovers when feeding. Olive-green plumage. Yellow supercilia meet on forehead, dark eye-strip and yellow central crown stripe. Double wing-bar and pale yellow rump.
Breeds in Asia. Annual visitor to south and east coast of England in autumn. Seen in trees and bushes, often with tits and goldcrests.

Red-breasted Flycatcher *Ficedula parva* (**5**)
Smaller than Spotted Flycatcher – 12 cm. Secretive. Warbler-like, but frequently cocks tail like Wren. Plump. Grey-brown above, whitish below. Two white patches at base of tail. Male has orange-red throat.
Breeds from Denmark, through Europe to the Middle East. Regular passage migrant each autumn.

Common Rosefinch *Carpodacus erythrinus* (**7**)
Sparrow sized – 14.5 cm. Stocky and thick-necked, similar shape to Bullfinch. Plain grey-brown upperparts and whitish underparts. Black eye in pale face. Thick Bullfinch-like bill. Adult male has brick-red head, shoulders and breast after his second year. Song is a haunting 'te-chew-we-chew'.
Breeds in northern and eastern Europe. Annual visitor to Britain and now breeds here occasionally.

Ortolan Bunting *Emberiza hortulana* (**9**)
Slightly smaller than Yellowhammer – 16 cm. Slim and long-winged. Back is sparrow-like. Adult male has grey-green head and breast, pale ring around eye, yellow throat, white cheek stripe, rufous underparts and yellow-brown rump. Reddish bill and legs. Male in autumn, female and juvenile are more like Yellowhammers, but eye-ring and pink bill and legs separate the species. Call is a liquid 'quilip'.
A summer visitor to much of Europe. Occurs on south and east coasts of British Isles, mainly in autumn.

Richard's Pipit *Anthus novaeseelandiae* (**2**)
Larger than Meadow Pipit – 18 cm. Rather thrush-like. Larger, darker and more heavily streaked than other pipits. Brown and buff with heavy streaking on upperparts. Strong bill, long tail and long legs. Hind claw is exceptionally long. Wagtail-like flight.
Breeds in central Asia. Some individuals reach southern and eastern Britain mainly in the autumn. Frequents grassy areas.

Tawny Pipit *Anthus campestris* (**4**)
Larger than Meadow Pipit – 16.5 cm. Wagtail-like with slim body and long tail. Adult is sandy coloured and rather plain except for a line of black spots on the median coverts. Juvenile has dark scallop-shaped marks on upperparts and spotting on flanks.
Breeds in Europe, North Africa and Russia. Occasional visitor especially to the south coast of England in autumn.

European Serin *Serinus serinus* (**6**)
Smaller than Redpoll – 11 cm. Tiny, active and Canary-like. Long wings without wing-bars and short, notched tail. Heavily striped yellowish-green body and yellow rump. Female duller than male. Juvenile is buff with pale yellow rump. Call is a liquid, twittering trill.
Common breeding species in southern Europe, which rarely breeds in southern England. Likes gardens, parks and wood edges.

Little Bunting *Emberiza pusilla* (**8**)
Resembles female Reed Bunting, but is smaller – 13.5 cm, more compact, with clear eye-ring, shorter, more pointed bill, rufous sides to face, rufous crown, less rufous on back, whiter underparts with fine streaking. May appear rather pipit-like.
Breeds from Finland to Siberia. An autumn passage migrant mainly to the east coast of Britain.

1 Short-toed Lark

2 Richard's Pipit

3 Pallas's Leaf Warbler

4 Tawny Pipit

5 Red-breasted Flycatcher ♂

6 European Serin

7 Common Rosefinch

8 Little Bunting ♂

9 Ortolan Bunting ♂

Hilary Burn

Use of the Maps

These distribution maps show breeding ranges (hatched) and wintering ranges (pale blue). The information is the most up-to-date available, and the maps' compiler wishes to acknowledge the enormous debt owed to the work of over 10,000 birdwatchers summarised in *The Atlas of Breeding Birds in Britain and Ireland* (1976) and *The Atlas of Breeding Wintering Birds in Britain and Ireland* (1986), which show the results of surveys by the British Trust for Ornithology and the Irish Wildbird Conservancy.

For easy cross-reference, each map includes the page number of the text as well as the name of the species.

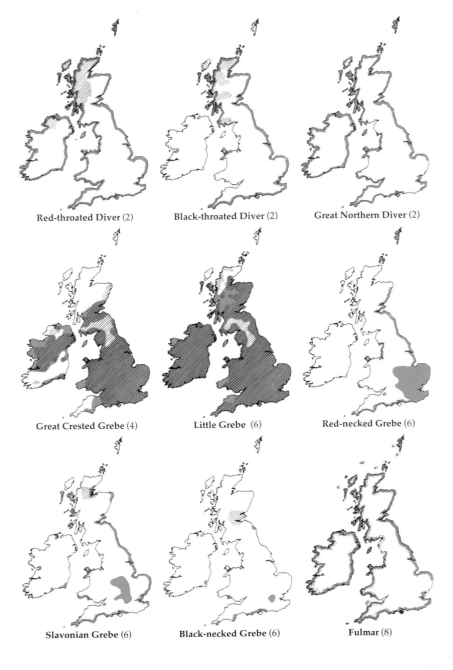

Red-throated Diver (2)

Black-throated Diver (2)

Great Northern Diver (2)

Great Crested Grebe (4)

Little Grebe (6)

Red-necked Grebe (6)

Slavonian Grebe (6)

Black-necked Grebe (6)

Fulmar (8)

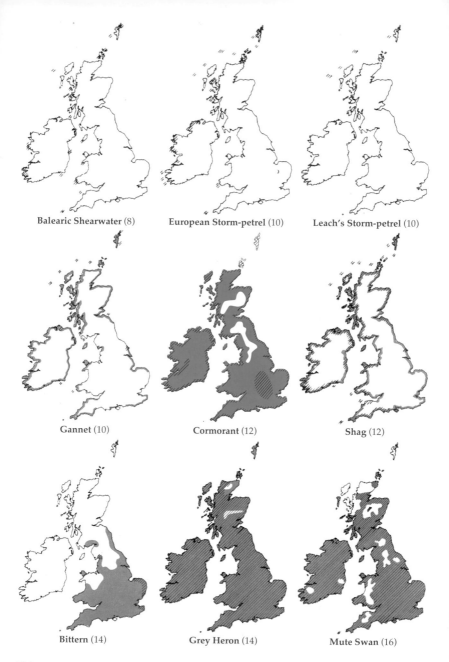

Balearic Shearwater (8)

European Storm-petrel (10)

Leach's Storm-petrel (10)

Gannet (10)

Cormorant (12)

Shag (12)

Bittern (14)

Grey Heron (14)

Mute Swan (16)

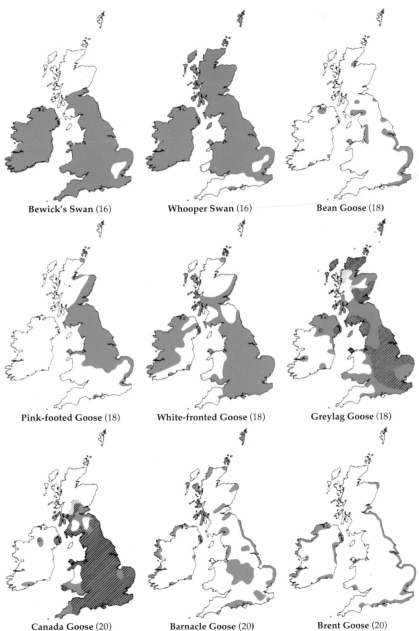

Bewick's Swan (16)

Whooper Swan (16)

Bean Goose (18)

Pink-footed Goose (18)

White-fronted Goose (18)

Greylag Goose (18)

Canada Goose (20)

Barnacle Goose (20)

Brent Goose (20)

Egyptian Goose (22)

Shelduck (22)

Mandarin Duck (22)

Mallard (24)

Wigeon (26)

Teal (26)

Garganey (26)

Gadwall (28)

Pintail (28)

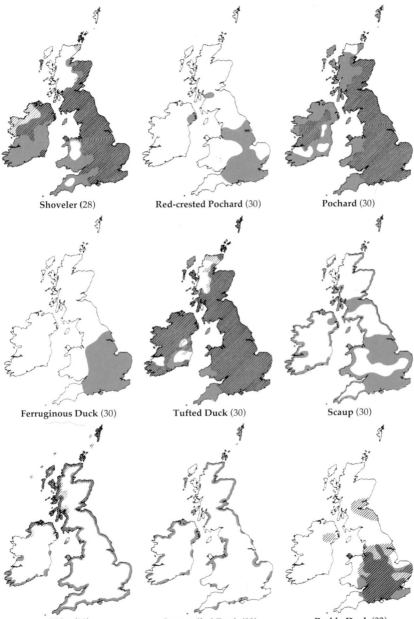

Shoveler (28) **Red-crested Pochard** (30) **Pochard** (30)

Ferruginous Duck (30) **Tufted Duck** (30) **Scaup** (30)

Eider (32) **Long-tailed Duck** (32) **Ruddy Duck** (32)

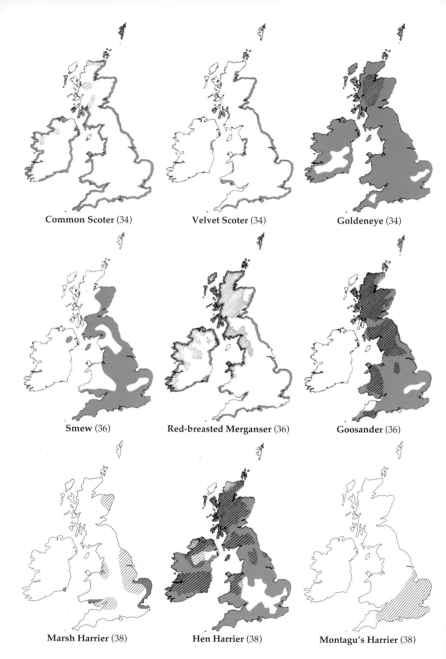

Common Scoter (34)

Velvet Scoter (34)

Goldeneye (34)

Smew (36)

Red-breasted Merganser (36)

Goosander (36)

Marsh Harrier (38)

Hen Harrier (38)

Montagu's Harrier (38)

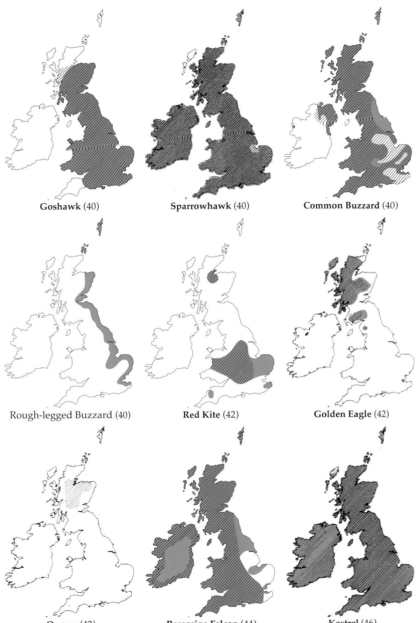

Goshawk (40)

Sparrowhawk (40)

Common Buzzard (40)

Rough-legged Buzzard (40)

Red Kite (42)

Golden Eagle (42)

Osprey (42)

Peregrine Falcon (44)

Kestrel (46)

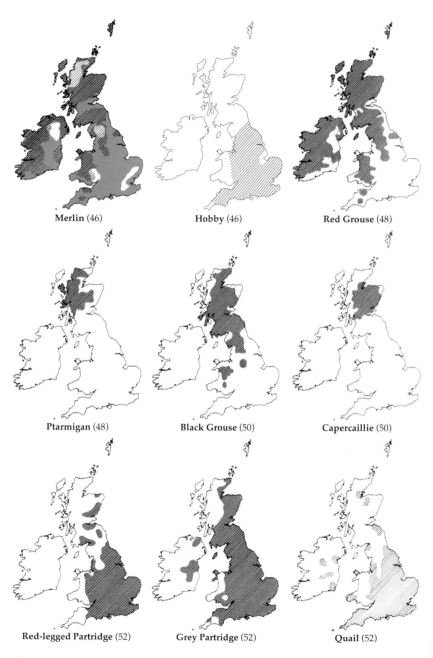

Merlin (46) **Hobby** (46) **Red Grouse** (48)

Ptarmigan (48) **Black Grouse** (50) **Capercaillie** (50)

Red-legged Partridge (52) **Grey Partridge** (52) **Quail** (52)

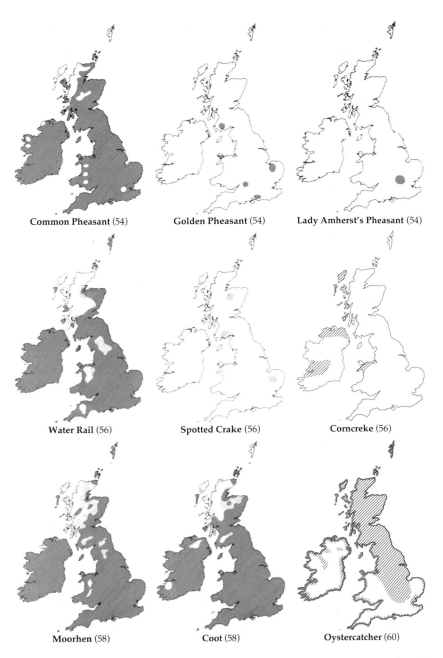

Common Pheasant (54)

Golden Pheasant (54)

Lady Amherst's Pheasant (54)

Water Rail (56)

Spotted Crake (56)

Corncreke (56)

Moorhen (58)

Coot (58)

Oystercatcher (60)

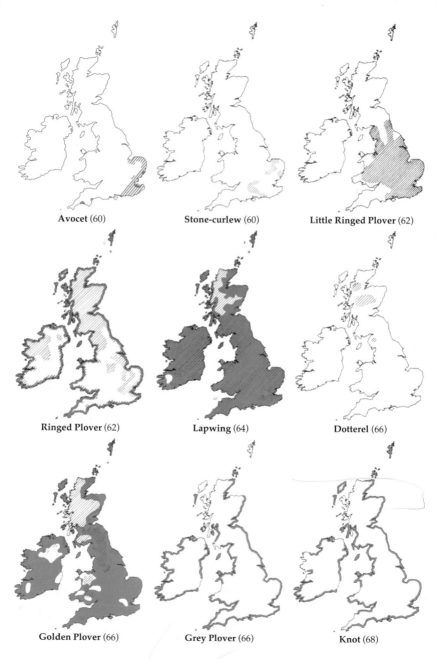

Avocet (60)

Stone-curlew (60)

Little Ringed Plover (62)

Ringed Plover (62)

Lapwing (64)

Dotterel (66)

Golden Plover (66)

Grey Plover (66)

Knot (68)

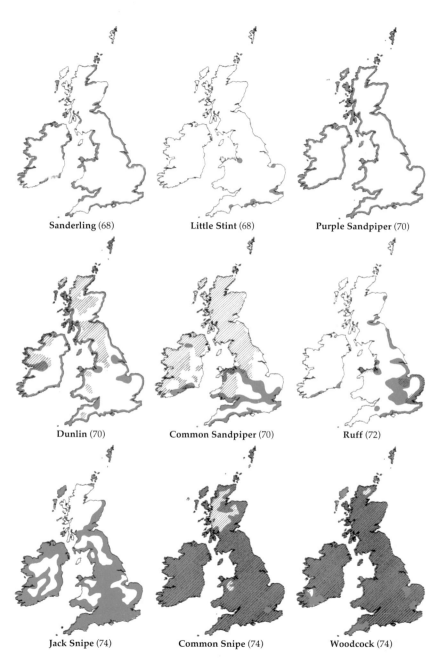

Sanderling (68)

Little Stint (68)

Purple Sandpiper (70)

Dunlin (70)

Common Sandpiper (70)

Ruff (72)

Jack Snipe (74)

Common Snipe (74)

Woodcock (74)

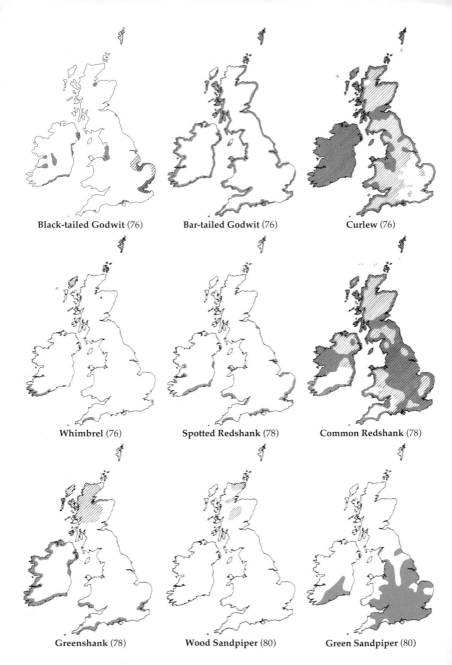

Black-tailed Godwit (76)   **Bar-tailed Godwit** (76)   **Curlew** (76)

Whimbrel (76)   **Spotted Redshank** (78)   **Common Redshank** (78)

Greenshank (78)   **Wood Sandpiper** (80)   **Green Sandpiper** (80)

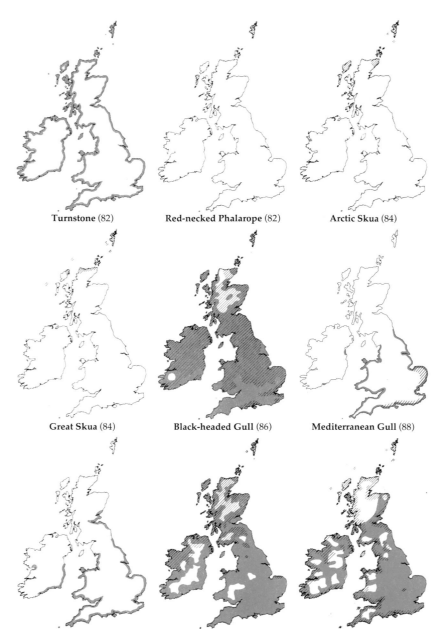

Turnstone (82)

Red-necked Phalarope (82)

Arctic Skua (84)

Great Skua (84)

Black-headed Gull (86)

Mediterranean Gull (88)

Little Gull (88)

Common Gull (88)

Lesser Black-backed Gull (90)

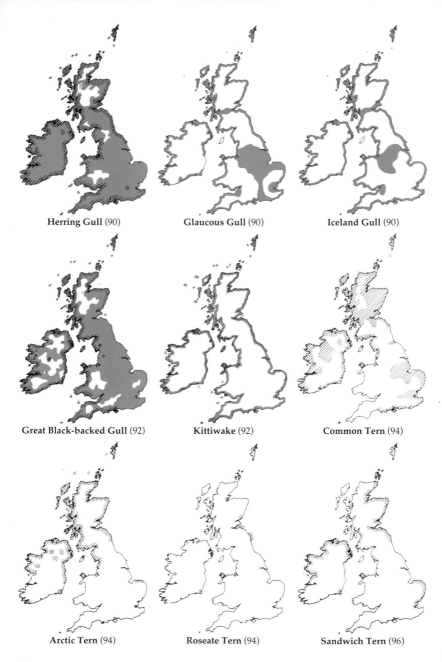

Herring Gull (90)

Glaucous Gull (90)

Iceland Gull (90)

Great Black-backed Gull (92)

Kittiwake (92)

Common Tern (94)

Arctic Tern (94)

Roseate Tern (94)

Sandwich Tern (96)

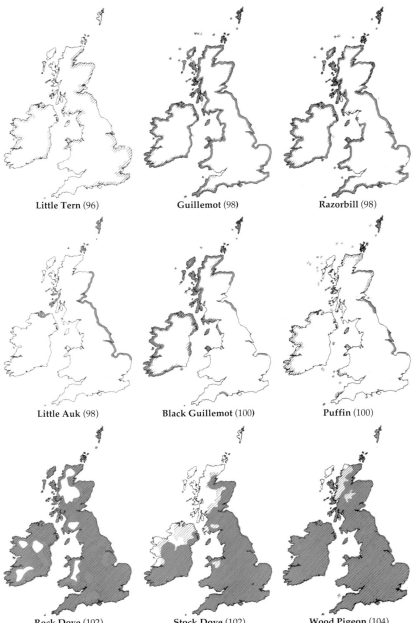

Little Tern (96) **Guillemot** (98) **Razorbill** (98)

Little Auk (98) **Black Guillemot** (100) **Puffin** (100)

Rock Dove (102) **Stock Dove** (102) **Wood Pigeon** (104)

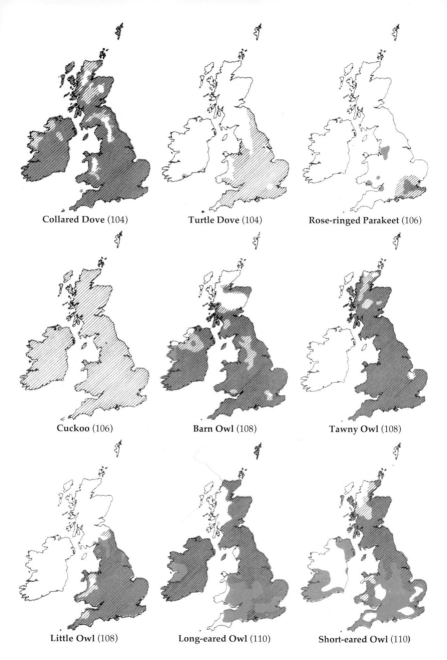

Collared Dove (104)

Turtle Dove (104)

Rose-ringed Parakeet (106)

Cuckoo (106)

Barn Owl (108)

Tawny Owl (108)

Little Owl (108)

Long-eared Owl (110)

Short-eared Owl (110)

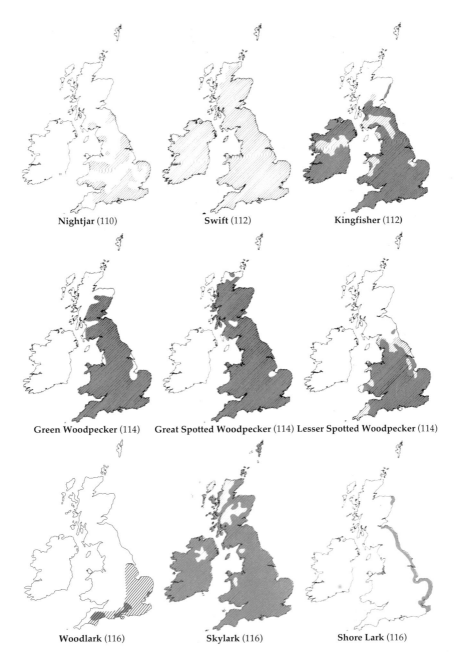

Nightjar (110)

Swift (112)

Kingfisher (112)

Green Woodpecker (114)

Great Spotted Woodpecker (114) **Lesser Spotted Woodpecker** (114)

Woodlark (116)

Skylark (116)

Shore Lark (116)

Sand Martin (118) Swallow (118) House Martin (118)

Tree Pipit (120) Meadow Pipit (120) Rock Pipit (120)

Water Pipit (120) Yellow Wagtail (122) Grey Wagtail (122)

Pied Wagtail (122)

Waxwing (124)

Dipper (124)

Wren (124)

Dunnock (126)

Robin (126)

Nightingale (128)

Black Redstart (128)

Common Redstart (128)

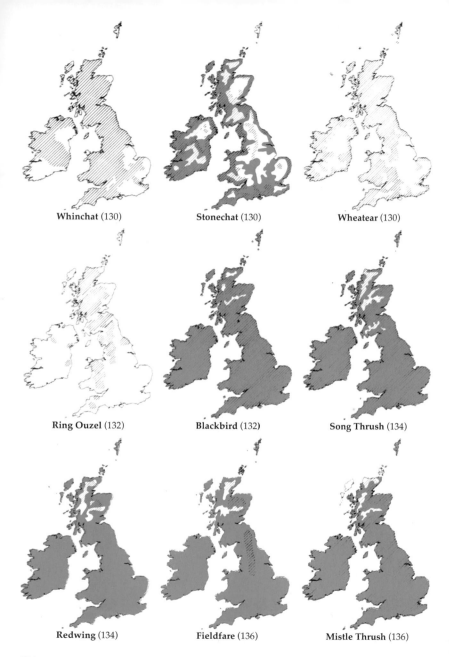

Whinchat (130) **Stonechat** (130) **Wheatear** (130)

Ring Ouzel (132) **Blackbird** (132) **Song Thrush** (134)

Redwing (134) **Fieldfare** (136) **Mistle Thrush** (136)

214

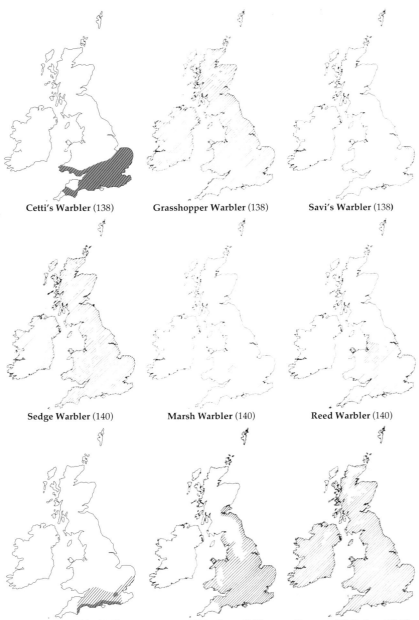

Cetti's Warbler (138)

Grasshopper Warbler (138)

Savi's Warbler (138)

Sedge Warbler (140)

Marsh Warbler (140)

Reed Warbler (140)

Dartford Warbler (142)

Lesser Whitethroat (142)

Common Whitethroat (142)

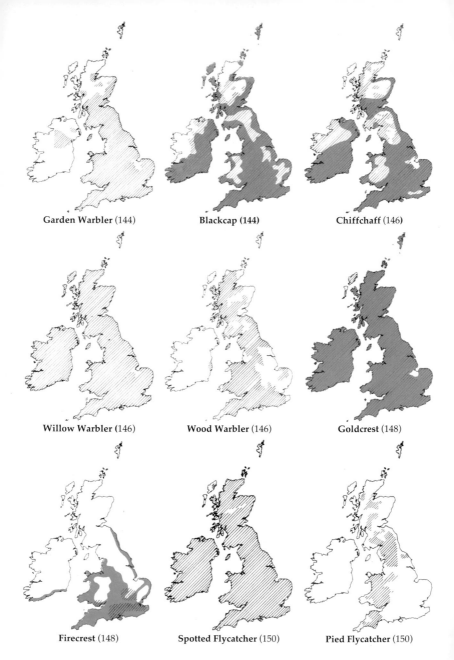

Garden Warbler (144) **Blackcap (144)** **Chiffchaff (146)**

Willow Warbler (146) **Wood Warbler** (146) **Goldcrest** (148)

Firecrest (148) **Spotted Flycatcher** (150) **Pied Flycatcher** (150)

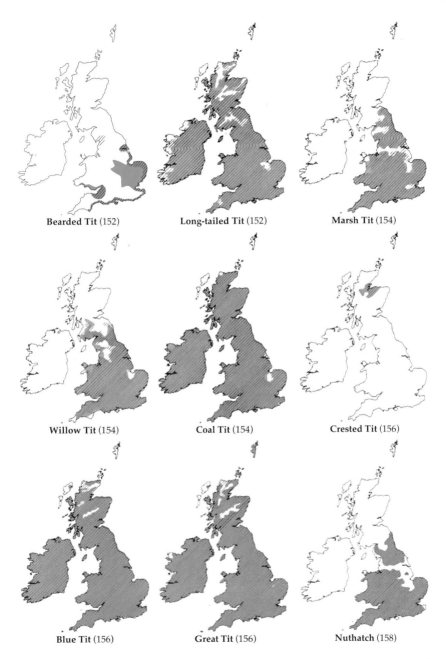

Bearded Tit (152) **Long-tailed Tit** (152) **Marsh Tit** (154)

Willow Tit (154) **Coal Tit** (154) **Crested Tit** (156)

Blue Tit (156) **Great Tit** (156) **Nuthatch** (158)

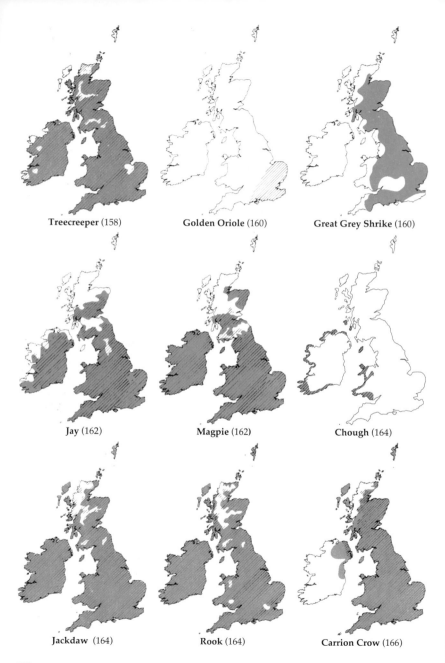

Treecreeper (158)

Golden Oriole (160)

Great Grey Shrike (160)

Jay (162)

Magpie (162)

Chough (164)

Jackdaw (164)

Rook (164)

Carrion Crow (166)

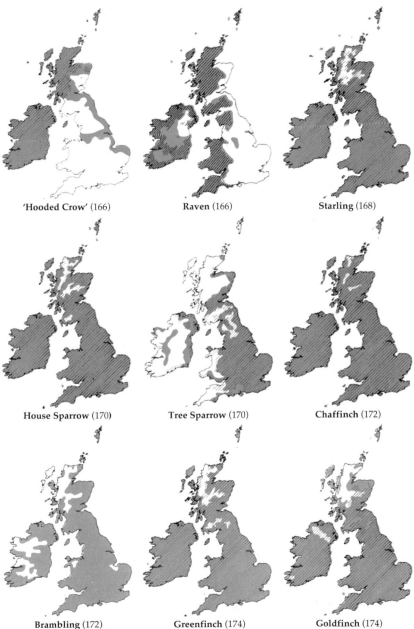

'Hooded Crow' (166)

Raven (166)

Starling (168)

House Sparrow (170)

Tree Sparrow (170)

Chaffinch (172)

Brambling (172)

Greenfinch (174)

Goldfinch (174)

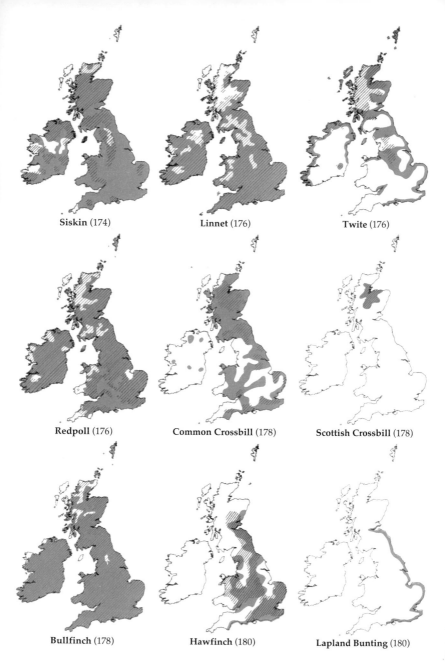

Siskin (174) **Linnet** (176) **Twite** (176)

Redpoll (176) **Common Crossbill** (178) **Scottish Crossbill** (178)

Bullfinch (178) **Hawfinch** (180) **Lapland Bunting** (180)

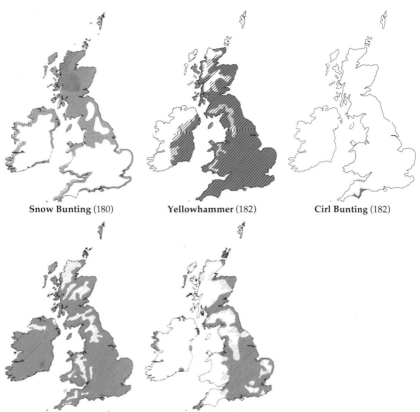

Snow Bunting (180) **Yellowhammer** (182) **Cirl Bunting** (182)

Reed Bunting (184) **Corn Bunting** (184)

221

Where to Watch Birds on RSPB Reserves

The Royal Society for the Protection of Birds owns or manages 430 square miles of nature reserves throughout the United Kingdom. These sites are managed for wildlife in general and for birds in particular. Where practical, visitors are welcome, and on the larger more popular reserves there are often buildings which house nature centres, shops and other facilities. On smaller or more remote reserves, however, facilities may be limited or non-existent.

The following brief guide gives an indication of what you can expect to find – both for birds and for people. Opening times and charges are liable to change and it is recommended that visitors telephone the reserve or check on the RSPB website, *www.rspb.org.uk* before setting out.

RSPB and Wildlife Explorer members are admitted free although there may be a small charge to attend events taking place on the reserves.

North of England

Bempton Cliffs, East Yorkshire
On cliff road from village of Bempton which is on the B1229 road from Flamborough to Filey. Tel: 01262 851179.

Open every day from March to November; weekends only from December to February. The reserve has over 3 miles/5 km of sheer chalk cliffs, rising to 400 feet/120 m. Bempton is one of the best places in England to see breeding seabirds (over 200,000). Five viewing points give spectacular views of Puffins, Gannets, Guillemots, Razorbills, Kittiwakes and Fulmars between April and mid-August. At other times there are migrants and possibly seals and porpoises.

Cliff-top walks of up to 1 mile/1.6 km (two viewpoints are suitable for wheel-chairs/pushchairs).

Facilities: Visitor centre, car park (charge for non-RSPB members), picnic area, shop, snacks/light refreshments, toilets (facilities for disabled visitors), binocular hire and special events during spring and summer (charge for guided walks).

Public transport: Rail – Bempton 1.5 miles/2.5 km. Bus – Bridlington to Bempton 1.5 miles/2.5 km.

Blacktoft Sands, East Yorkshire
On the A161 east of Goole through Reedness and Ousefleet. Tel: 01405 704665.

Open daily. Closed 25 December. Charge for non-RSPB members. Over 474 acres/192 ha of tidal reedswamps, saltmarsh, mudflats and brackish lagoons. Blacktoft has a wide variety of special birds, including Bearded Tits, Marsh Harriers and Avocets. In spring and autumn, many more migrants may be seen.

Facilities: Car park, picnic area, toilets (with adapted facilities for disabled visitors), small shop, binocular hire, six hides (five of which are wheelchair accessible), and special events for members and non-members.

Public transport: Bus stop opposite reserve entrance. Buses from Goole two/three hourly Monday–Saturday. The reserve is on a National Cycle Network route.

Campfield Marsh, Cumbria
3 miles/5 km west of Bowness-on-Solway. Tel: 016973 51330.

Open at all times. On the Solway estuary, the reserve has saltmarsh, wet grassland and areas of open water. At high tide, thousands of wading birds, including Oystercatchers, Knots, Grey Plovers and Bar-tailed Godwits roost. In the winter, wildfowl use the grassland and open water area. The wader roost can be seen from the lay-bys along the road edging the estuary and saltmarsh.

Facilities: Car park, wheelchair access, guided walks and special events.

Public transport: Bus – there are infrequent services to Bowness-on-Solway from Carlisle.

Fairburn Ings, West Yorkshire
4 miles/6.5 km north of M62, immediately to west of A1; 5 miles/8 km north-east of Castleford, signposted from Allerton Bywater off A656. Tel: 01977 603796.

Car park open daily. Two public paths are open at all times. Visitor centre open weekends and Bank Holidays. Easily accessible from the A1, Fairburn is a good place to see waterbirds at close quarters throughout the year. In winter up to 100 Whooper Swans. In summer breeding waders include Redshanks, Snipe and Lapwings. In spring and autumn, migrants such as Black Terns and Little Gulls visit.

Facilities: Car park, picnic area, small shop and visitor centre, snacks/light refreshments, toilets with adapted facilities for disabled visitors, hides (one of which is pushchair accessible).

Public transport: Rail – Castleford 5 miles/8 km. Bus – Allerton Bywater (1.5 miles/2.5 km from visitor centre), frequent from Castleford to Leeds. Infrequent service to Fairburn and Newtown from Castleford, Pontefract and Selby.

Haweswater, Cumbria

From the M6 (J39 or J40) follow road to Bampton and then Haweswater or Mardale. Tel: 01931 713376.

Open at all times; observation point 9 am to 6 pm April to August. This is the only place in England where Golden Eagles nest. An observation point is open during the breeding season. It is reached from the car park at the western end of Haweswater, 1.25 miles/2 km along an uneven path.

Facilities: Car park, observation point.

Public transport: Rail – Penrith (10 miles/16 km).

Hodbarrow, Cumbria

2 miles/3 km from Millom. Tel: 01229 778011.

Open at all times. Large numbers of waders and wildfowl can be seen on the freshwater lagoons. In the summer Common, Little and Sandwich Terns nest on the reserve and can be seen well from the hide on the sea-wall.

Facilities: Car park, hide (wheelchair accessible).

Public transport: Rail and bus – Millom (2 miles/3 km).

Leighton Moss, Lancashire

2 miles/3 km north of Carnforth. Signposted from the A6 north of Junction 35 of the M6. Tel: 01524 701601.

Reserve and visitor centre open daily (closed 25 December) (charge for non-RSPB members). Large reedbed and shallow meres provide suitable habitat for a variety of wildlife including breeding Bitterns, Bearded Tits, Marsh Harriers, Otters and Roe and Red Deer. A number of nature trails, ranging from 1 mile/1.6 km to 3.5 miles/5.6 km in length.

Facilities: Visitor centre, shop, tea-room, car park, picnic area, toilets (suitable for disabled), binocular hire, seven hides (four accessible to wheelchairs).

Public transport: Rail – Silverdale 200 yards/185 m. The reserve is on a National Cycle Network route.

Marshside

2 miles/3 km north of Southport town centre on the coastal road (Marine Drive). Daytime tel: 01704 233003.

The reserve can be viewed from the roads alongside the reserve. Hide open daily when staffing allows (groups should book in advance). Part of the internationally important Ribble Estuary, Marshside has some of the best lowland wet grassland in the north-west of England. It is an important winter refuge for Pink-footed Geese, Wigeon, Black-tailed Godwits and Golden Plovers and in spring has nesting Lapwings and Redshanks.

Facilities: Car park, hides (wheelchair access), guided walks and special events (charge for events), toilets at Churchtown Health Centre, toilets (for disabled visitors) at Southport Pier.

Public transport: Rail – Southport Chapel Street. Bus – Marshside Road stop 100 yards/90 m from reserve, routes 4, 4A and 104.

Morecambe Bay, Lancashire

Hest Bank foreshore is 2 miles/3 km north-east of Morecambe on the A5105. Tel: 01524 701601.

Hest Bank is open at all times. During migration and in winter, the reserve's sandflats and saltmarshes are vital feeding grounds for thousands of waders and wildfowl. At high tide, they are pushed back on to the saltmarshes, giving excellent views from Hest Bank (tide tables available from Leighton Moss). Do not go on to the saltmarsh or intertidal area – there are dangerous channels and quicksands.

Facilities: Tea room, shop and toilets at Leighton Moss reserve. There are trails to Eric Morecambe (wheelchair/pushchair accessible) and Allen Hides.

Public transport: Rail – Morecambe for Hest Bank and Silverdale for other areas. Buses to Hest Bank are approximately every two hours, on the Morecambe to Carnforth service.

Central England

Church Wood, Buckinghamshire

About 3 miles/5 km from J2 M40. In Hedgerley village take the small private track beside village pond next to pub. Park in the village. Tel: 01295 253330.

Open at all times. This small reserve forms part of the Chiltern woodlands and is a mixture of beech, ash and oak. Some parts of it are hazel coppice. Woodpeckers, Nuthatches and Blackcaps are among the birds breeding in the wood. In the spring the woodland floor is covered with flowering bluebells. Two marked paths (shorter 0.5 mile/0.8 km, longer 1.25 miles/2 km).

Public transport: Rail – Gerrards Cross. Bus – Slough to Hedgerley.

Coombes Valley, Staffordshire

Off the A523 road to Ashbourne, 3 miles/5 km south-east of Leek. Take minor road to Apesford (as signposted) for 1 mile/1.6 km. Tel: 01538 384017.

Open daily (closed 25/26 December). Nature trails through this beautiful steep-sided, wooded valley which is home for Pied Flycatchers, Redstarts and Wood Warblers in summer. Other woodland species and Dippers are resident. It is also excellent for butterflies, including the rare High Brown Fritillary.

Facilities: Car park, toilets, information centre (open weekends and weekdays during busy periods), one hide.

Public transport: Rail – Stoke-on-Trent 13 miles/21 km.

Gayton Sands, Dee Estuary, Cheshire

Parkgate is reached from the A540 Chester to Hoylake road, via the B5135. Tel: 0151 336 7681.

Open at all times. High tide is the best time to visit Gayton Sands. From the Old Baths car park near The Boathouse public house at Parkgate, you can watch large flocks of wading birds driven up on to the saltmarsh. In autumn and winter there are flocks of Pintails, Teals, Wigeons and Shelducks. Visitors should not walk on to the saltmarsh as the tides are dangerous.

Facilities: Car park, picnic area, guided walks and special events, wheelchair access.

Public transport: Rail – Neston 2 miles/3 km. Bus – Parkgate every hour.

Highnam Woods, Gloucestershire

3 miles/5 km west of Gloucester on the A40 Gloucester to Ross-on-Wye road. Tel: 01594 562852.

Open at all times. Bluebells, primroses and Nightingales in spring. A winter feeding-station at the hide attracts tits, finches and woodpeckers. Nature trail is 1.5 miles/2.5 km in length – and can be muddy.

Facilities: Car park, hide (accessible to wheelchairs).

Public transport: Rail – Gloucester 3 miles/5 km. Bus – Gloucester to Cinderford.

The Lodge, Bedfordshire

1 mile/1.6 km east of Sandy on the B1042 to Potton. Tel: 01767 680551.

Open daily (charge for non-RSPB members). The reserve, with its attractive mixed woodland and heathland, supports a wide variety of birds and wildlife, including woodpeckers, Nuthatches, tits and finches. The formal and wildlife gardens, run by organic methods, are also open to the public. Unfortunately there is no access to the house. Nature trails vary in length and one is wheelchair and pushchair accessible, as are the gardens.

Facilities: Car park, picnic area, hide (with wheelchair access), shop, snacks/light refreshments, toilets (suitable for disabled visitors), baby changing facilities, binocular hire, cycle facilities, dogs on leads on public footpaths, information centre.

Public transport: Rail – Sandy 1 mile/1.6 km. Bus – frequent Bedford/Sandy service 1.5 miles/1.6 km. The reserve is within 5 miles/8 km of a National Cycle Network route.

Nagshead, Gloucestershire

West of Parkend village, signposted off unclassified road to Coleford. Tel: 01594 562852.

Open at all times. Information centre open weekends. The reserve is famous for its breeding Pied Flycatchers. The nestboxes in which they nest have been monitored continuously since 1948. The wood is also home to Hawfinches, Buzzards and all three species of British woodpeckers. Two trails: 1 mile/1.5 km and 2.25 miles/3.5 km in length.

Facilities: Car park, information centre, hides.

Public transport: Rail – Lydney 6 miles/9.5 km and Gloucester 22 miles/35 km. Bus – Gloucester to Coleford service stops at Coalway, 2 miles/3 km from reserve.

Sandwell Valley, West Midlands
Off Tanhouse Avenue, via Hamstead Road, Great Barr. Tel: 0121 357 7395.

Open every day. Just outside Birmingham and close to the M6, Sandwell Valley is enjoyable for all the family. In summer birds breeding around the marsh, lake and wader scrape range from waders such as Little Ringed Plovers to ducks and songbirds such as Whitethroats. Other birds visit on migration and in winter ducks and waders find refuge.

Facilities: Car park, picnic area, visitor centre, snacks/light refreshments, toilets (suitable for disabled visitors), small shop. Hides (two with wheelchair access).

Public transport: Rail – Hamstead 2 miles/3.2 km. Bus – frequent services from Birmingham (16) and West Bromwich (406). The reserve is on a National Cycle Network route.

Symond's Yat, Gloucestershire
3 miles/5 km north of Coleford on B4432 signposted from Forest Enterprise car park. Tel: 01594 562852.

Open daily, April to August. The Peregrine viewing point at Symond's Yat Rock is a joint project run by the RSPB and Forest Enterprise, who own the site. Between April and August, telescopes are set up to give close views of the nesting Peregrines. The rock is a spectacular site high above the River Wye.

Facilities: Car park, toilets (suitable for disabled visitors), picnic area, drinks and light snacks.

There is no public transport to or near the site.

Eastern England

Berney Marshes, Norfolk
Located within the Halvergate grazing marshes. Tel: 01493 700645.

Open at all times along footpaths or by boat. This 900 acre/364 ha grassland supports breeding wading birds such as Lapwings, Redshanks and Snipes. In winter, a large flock of wintering wading birds, geese and wildfowl visit the reserve. There is a viewing screen and platform which overlook pools used by roosting and feeding birds such as Wigeons, Golden Plovers and Bewick's Swans in the winter.

Facilities: Picnic area next to Berney Arms public house, one viewing screen.

Public transport: Rail – request stop to Berney Arms halt.

Breydon Water, Suffolk
West of Great Yarmouth. Trails start from the Asda car park near Great Yarmouth railway station. Tel: 01493 700645.

Access at all times along public footpaths. Located next to Great Yarmouth, this estuary is the most important estuary on the east coast between the Wash and the Thames. In the winter large numbers of waders and wildfowl use the estuary, including up to 12,000 Golden Plovers, 12,000 Wigeons and up to 32,000 Lapwings.

The reserve is best viewed between November and February on a rising tide. Footpaths on the north and south shore.

Facilities: Parking at the Asda car park, hides; boat trips are organised on the first Sunday of every month. Telephone for more details.

Public transport: Rail – Great Yarmouth.

Fowlmere, Cambridgeshire

7 miles/11 km south of Cambridge between Fowlmere and Melbourn. Tel: 01763 208978.

Open at all times (donation from non-RSPB members). Fowlmere's reedbeds and pools are fed by natural chalk springs and a chalk stream that runs through the reserve. Special birds include Kingfishers and Water Rails, breeding Sedge, Reed and Grasshopper Warblers and a winter roost of Corn Buntings. One circular trail 1.5 miles/2.5 km in length, part of which is wheelchair/pushchair accessible.

Facilities: Car park, picnic area, hides (one accessible to disabled visitors), guided walks and special events.

Public transport: Rail – Shepreth (2 miles/3 km). The reserve is between 5 and 14 miles (8 km and 22.5 km) from a National Cycle Network route.

Frampton Marsh, Lincolnshire

4.5 miles/6.5 km south of Boston and 3 miles/4.5 km east of Kirton along minor roads along the north shore of the Wash. Tel: 01205 724678.

Open at all times. A public footpath/bridleway extends along the sea bank, which affords good views over the reserve and surrounding area. It supports a good variety of wintering and breeding birds. In the summer, Redshanks breed in large numbers, along with Oystercatchers, Skylarks and Reed Buntings. In the winter, Dark-bellied Brent Geese occur in internationally important numbers and Hen Harriers, Merlins and Short-eared Owls are frequently seen. Twites winter on the reserve too and Lapland Buntings are occasional visitors. Throughout the year the reserve hosts an important high-tide wader roost for species such as Grey Plovers and Dunlins.

Facilities: Car park and footpaths.

Public transport: Rail – the nearest railway station is at Boston (approximately 6 miles/11 km away). Bus – there is a very limited weekday bus service running from Boston to Frampton church (approximately 2 miles/3.2 km away).

Frieston Shore, Lincolnshire

5 miles/8 km east of Boston from the A52. Turn off the A52 at Haltoft End towards Freiston. Pass through the village and follow the road for about 3 miles/4 km. The southern car park is on the right over the concrete ramp.

The reserve is open at all times. Freiston Shore offers a wealth of birds throughout the year. Hen Harriers, Short-eared Owls, Dark-bellied Brent Geese and Twites can be seen in winter. If you are lucky you may see a Lapland Bunting. Redshanks, Avocets and other breeding waders can be seen in summer. There are two car parks. The northern one overlooks the realignment site that will revert to saltmarsh after the old sea bank is breached in the summer of 2002. The southern car park gives excellent views across the lagoon. The mature saltmarsh and sea can be viewed from the sea banks, a short walk from either car park. These banks may be muddy at times.

Facilities: Two car parks, at TF398424 and TF408435.

Public transport: The reserve is adjacent to a Lincolnshire County Council cycle route and 5 miles/8 km from a National Cycle Network route (route 1).

Havergate Island, Suffolk

For boat trips meet at Orford Quay. To book write to The Warden, 30 Mundays Lane, Orford, Woodbridge, Suffolk IP12 2LX.

Visiting is by prior arrangement only. Open April to August – first and third weekends of the month and every Thursday. September to March – first Saturday of the month. Boat charge for members. This small island in the River Ore is an important breeding place for Avocets, and Sandwich and Common Terns. Access to the island is by boat only. There is one trail, 1.5 miles/2.5 km in length.

Facilities: Car park, toilets, picnic area, binocular hire, hides.

Public transport: Rail – Woodbridge (10 miles/16 km). Bus – infrequent service to Orford.

Minsmere, Suffolk

Signposted from A12 and Westleton. Tel: 01728 648281.

Open daily except Tuesdays (charge for non-RSPB members). Minsmere, on the Suffolk coast, is one of the RSPB's oldest and most important nature reserves. Nature trails take visitors through a variety of habitats, including marshes, reedbeds, heath and woodland. Between 85 and 100 species of birds breed regularly, including Avocets, Nightjars, Bearded Tits, Marsh Harriers and Bitterns. Wildfowl and waders in winter and migrants in spring and autumn make Minsmere ideal for enthusiasts and families at all times of year. There are two 2 mile/3.2 km nature trails which remain dry underfoot for most of the year.

Facilities: Car park, eight hides (four accessible for disabled visitors), picnic area, visitor centre, tea-room, toilets (suitable for disabled visitors), shop, binocular hire.

Public transport: Rail – Darsham (4 miles/6.5 km), Saxmundham (6 miles/9.5 km). Bus – Eastern Counties frequent service from Ipswich/Aldeburgh to Leiston (5 miles/8km). Nearest stop Theberton (3 miles/5km), service twice daily. The reserve is between 5 and 14 miles (8 km and 22.5 km) from a National Cycle Network route.

North Warren, Suffolk

Car park situated just north of Aldeburgh on the coast road. Tel: 01728 688481.

Open at all times. A delightful reserve on the Suffolk coast consists of grazing marshes, reedbeds, heathland and woodland. Thousands of wildfowl use the marshes in winter while summer brings breeding Marsh Harriers, Woodlarks, Nightjars, Nightingales and Bearded Tits.

Facilities: Car park, guided walks and special events.

Public transport: Rail – Saxmundham 6 miles/9.5 km. Bus – regular service to Aldeburgh. The reserve is between 5 and 14 miles (8 km and 22.5 km) from the National Cycle Network route 1.

Ouse Washes, Cambridgeshire

Signed from Manea village (2.5 miles/4 km), which is 6 miles/9.5 km east of Chatteris on the A142/A141 between Ely and March. Tel: 01354 680212.

Hides always open. Visitor centre open daily except 25 and 26 December (charge for non-RSPB members). The Ouse Washes was created by fenland drainage schemes of the 17th century and provides an excellent introduction to the wildlife of the fens. The winter floods attract thousands of ducks and swans, which can be seen from the hides along the banks. In the summer, Redshanks, Black-tailed Godwits, Snipe and many wildfowl breed.

Facilities: Car park, toilets, picnic area, ten hides (one is wheelchair accessible), binoculars for hire, guided walks and special events, wheelchair access, information centre.

Public transport: Rail – Manea stop (3 miles/5 km), infrequent service.

Snettisham, Norfolk

Between King's Lynn and Hunstanton, signposted from the A149 at Snettisham. Tel: 01485 542689.

Open at all times. Snettisham at high tide during the autumn and winter is the site of one of Britain's great wildlife spectacles. The Wash's rising tide pushes tens of thousands of waders and ducks up the beach and on to the reserve's pools. From November to early February, up to 40,000 Pink-footed Geese roost on the reserve. They are best viewed either early in the morning or late afternoon. At other times, many thousands of birds feed on the reserve and in the summer you can see nesting gulls and terns. Tide tables are available from the reserve.

There is one trail, about 3.5 miles/5.5 km long. Disabled visitors may, by arrangement with the warden, drive to the first hide.

Facilities: Car park, hides (one wheelchair accessible).

Public transport: Rail – King's Lynn (13 miles/21 km). Bus – nearest stop 2 miles/3.2 km, service every half hour from King's Lynn. The reserve is within 5 miles/8 km of a National Cycle Network route.

Stour Estuary, Essex

1 mile/1.6 km east of Wrabness on B1352 Manningtree to Harwich road. Tel: 01255 886043.

Open at all times (donation from non-RSPB members). A coppiced wood close to the edge of the Stour Estuary. In the spring, Nightingales and other birds fill the woods with their songs. The flowers of spring are particularly beautiful. To see estuary birds, the best time to visit is during the autumn and winter when wildfowl and waders reach peak numbers. Two trails: the shorter is 1 mile/1.6 km in length and wheelchair/pushchair accessible during dry weather; the longer trail is 5 miles/8 km long.

Facilities: Car park (with height restriction), hides, guided walks and special events.

Public transport: Rail – Wrabness 0.5 mile/0.8 km. Buses from Colchester to Harwich via Wrabness pass the reserve car park.

Strumpshaw Fen, Norfolk

0.75 mile/1.2 km south-west of Strumpshaw and signposted from Brundall High Street off the A47 east of Norwich. Tel: 01603 715191.

Open daily (charge for non-RSPB members). Strumpshaw Fen is in the heart of the Norfolk Broads. A number of nature trails lead you through the varied habitats, including reedbeds and woodland. In the summer, there is a special trail in the flower-filled meadow and you may see a Marsh Harrier or a Swallowtail butterfly. In winter, a variety of wildfowl visit the reserve. The shortest trail is 1.5 miles/2.5 km, the longest 3.25 miles/5 km.

Facilities: Car park, toilets (suitable for disabled visitors), hides, picnic area, guided walks and special events.

Public transport: Rail – Brundall (1.5 miles/2.5 km). Bus – services from Norwich stop 0.5 mile/0.8 km from reserve on Brundall to Strumpshaw road.

Titchwell Marsh, Norfolk
5 miles/8 km east of Hunstanton on the A149. Tel: 01485 210779.

Open every day except 25/26 December (car park charge for non-RSPB members). On the beautiful North Norfolk coast, 5 miles/8 km east of Hunstanton, Titchwell offers a wealth of birds throughout the year. A firm path, suitable for wheelchairs and pushchairs, runs from the visitor centre to the sandy beach, past reedbeds, saltmarsh and shallow lagoons. A new path and boardwalk, also wheelchair and pushchair accessible, passes through areas of fen and wet woodland (carr) to the Fen Hide.

Facilities: Car park, visitor centre, hides (accessible to wheelchairs), cycle facilities, picnic area, servery selling light refreshments, toilets (suitable for disabled visitors), binocular hire.

Public transport: Bus – request stop opposite reserve entrance (Hunstanton–Wells-next-the-Sea route). The reserve is between 5 and 14 miles (8 km and 22.5 km) from a National Cycle Network route.

Wolves Wood, Suffolk
2 miles/3.2 km east of Hadleigh on the A1071 to Ipswich. Tel: 01255 886043.

The reserve is open at all times. This reserve is one of the few remaining areas of the ancient woodland that used to cover East Anglia. The RSPB is continuing the traditional coppicing method of management, which means that the wood has a wide variety of birds, plants and mammals. In the spring this is a good place to hear Nightingales. One trail, 1 mile/1.6 km in length.

Facilities: Car park, guided walks and special events.

Public transport: Nearest bus stop Hadleigh, hourly services from Ipswich.

South East England

Ardur Estuary
In the heart of Shoreham-by-Sea town centre. Tel: 01273 775333.

Open at all times. This small (25 acre/10 ha) estuary reserve is in the heart of Shoreham-by-Sea and is particularly good for watching small wading birds and other waterbirds in winter. The intertidal mudflats and saltmarshes attract a wide range of wading birds including Redshanks, Ringed Plover and Dunlins. More unusual wading birds such as Avocets and Whimbrels are also occasionally seen. Grey Herons and Little Egrets are regular visitors along with Cormorants and Shelducks.

Facilities: Public car park in Shoreham town centre.

Public transport: Rail – station ¼ mile/400 m. Bus – numerous local bus services from Brighton and Worthing. The reserve is on a National Cycle Network route.

Blean Woods, Kent

Signposted from Rough Common, north-west of Canterbury off the A2 to Dover or A290 to Whitstable. Tel: 01227 462491.

The paths are open at all times. Blean Woods is one of the largest areas of ancient broadleaved woodland in southern Britain. Woodpeckers are plentiful, while in the summer there are about 30 pairs of Nightingales and two pairs of Nightjars. The reserve is one of the few places in Britain where you can find the Heath Fritillary butterfly. Four trails, ranging from 1 to 7 miles/1.6 to 11 km (most are suitable for pushchairs and one is suitable for wheelchairs, but all trails may be muddy at times). The stone track along the reserve boundary is flat and can be used at all times.

Facilities: Car park, picnic area, guided walks and special events.

Public transport: Rail – Canterbury East (2 miles/3 km), Canterbury West (1.75 miles/3 km). Bus – Canterbury to Rough Common stops outside reserve entrance.

Dungeness, Kent

Signposted off the Lydd to Dungeness road 10 miles/16 km east of Rye and 1 mile/1.6 km south of Lydd. Tel: 01797 320588.

Open daily (charge for non-RSPB members). Situated on a shingle foreland extending into the English Channel, Dungeness reserve is important in spring and autumn for migrants, with always the chance of a rarity. Breeding colony of gulls and terns in summer and, in winter, large numbers of wildfowl.

Facilities: Car park, picnic area, hides (with wheelchair access), visitor centre, snacks/light refreshments, shop, toilets (suitable for disabled visitors), binocular hire, wheelchair and pushchair access to the 2 mile/3.2 km nature trail.

Public transport: Rail – Rye 10 miles/16 km and Folkestone 16 miles/25 km. Bus – Service 12 from Folkestone or Lydd stops at the reserve entrance on request. The reserve is between 5 and 14 miles (8 km and 22.5 km) from a National Cycle Network route.

Elmley Marshes, Kent

Signposted off the A249 to Sheerness on the Isle of Sheppey, 1 mile/1.6 km beyond the Kingsferry Bridge. Tel: 01795 665969 or 01273 775333.

Open daily (closed Tuesdays). The wet grassland at Elmley Marshes attracts thousands of ducks, geese and waders in the winter. Hen Harriers, Merlins, Peregrines and Short-eared Owls can also be seen during the winter. In the summer, the reserve is important for breeding waders, including Avocets.

Facilities: Car park, toilets, five hides (1.25 mile/2 km walk to the nearest hide and 6 mile/9.5 km round trip to the farthest hide (arrangements can be made for disabled and elderly visitors).

Public transport: Rail – Swale request stop (3 miles/5 km). Bus – nearest bus stop at Queenborough (4 miles/6.5 km).

Fore Wood, East Sussex

On the edge of Crowhurst, 2 miles/3 km south-west of Telham on the A2100. Please park at Crowhurst village hall (opposite the church). Turn right out of the hall and walk up the lane for 0.5 mile/0.75 km. The reserve entrance gate is on the left at the top of the lane. Tel: 01273 775333 (RSPB S-E England Office).

Open at all times. This small woodland reserve is managed by coppicing. A wide range of woodland birds breed, including Nightingales, Spotted Flycatchers and Great and Lesser Spotted Woodpeckers. Bluebells and wood anemones are abundant in the spring. Stout footwear is recommended as the trail may be muddy.

Facilities: Two hides.

Public transport: Rail – Crowhurst 0.25 mile/400 m.

Langstone Harbour, Hampshire

Off the A27/A3(M) roundabout south-west of Havant. Tel: 01273 775333 (RSPB S-E England Office).

Good views of the reserve can be obtained from a number of viewpoints and car parks on the surrounding roads. Access by boat during daylight hours at designated landing area only. The reserve is made up of mudflats, creeks with saltmarsh and shingle islands in Langstone Harbour. Little Terns, Ringed Plovers and Redshanks breed. Over 7,000 Brent Geese winter here, along with Teals, Shelducks, Dunlins and Oystercatchers.

Public transport: Rail – Bedhampton 1 mile/1.6 km.

Nor Marsh and Motney Hill, Kent

View from Riverside Country Park off B2004, 1 mile/1.6 km north of Gillingham. Tel: RSPB 01634 222480; Riverside Country Park 01634 378987.

Open every day. There are no RSPB-run facilities but there is a full range in the nearby Riverside Country Park which overlooks the reserve. Nor Marsh is a saltmarsh island in the Medway Estuary. To the east is Motney Hill, another area of mud and saltmarsh. In the winter at both sites, large numbers of wildfowl can be seen, including Brent Geese, Pintails, Shelducks and Goldeneyes along with Grey Plovers, Knots and Avocets. Black-tailed Godwits in spring and autumn. Little Egrets on Nor Marsh in late summer. Walks to view Nor Marsh 1 mile/1.6 km round trip (wheelchair and pushchair access), Motney Hill 3.5 miles/5.5 km round trip (pushchair accessible).

Facilities: Car park, bicycle rack, toilets, baby-changing facilities, tea-room, picnic area, guided walks and special events.

Public transport: Rail – Rainham 2 miles/3 km, Gillingham 3 miles/5 km. Bus – Twydall Shopping Centre (8 minutes from Gillingham).

Northward Hill, Kent

Signposted from High Halstow, 4 miles/6.5 km north-east of Rochester. Tel: 01634 222480.

Paths open at all times. Visits to other parts of the reserve (including the heronry) are by prior arrangement only.

Northward Hill is a mixture of woodland and wet grassland. As well as Nightingales and Turtle Doves, the wood has the largest heronry in the UK, with around 150 pairs of Grey Herons nesting in the treetops. Waders such as Lapwings and Redshanks breed on the marshes below. In the winter, waders and wildfowl including Wigeons and Teals can be seen, along with Buzzards, Hen Harriers and Merlins. Three trails (shortest 0.3 mile/0.5 km) and public footpath to marshes (4 mile/6.5 km round trip).

Public transport: Rail – Strood 5 miles/8 km. Bus – services from Strood stop regularly in High Halstow.

Pulborough Brooks, West Sussex

Reserve is signposted off the A283 Pulborough to Storrington Road, about 2 miles/3 km south-east of Pulborough. Tel: 01798 875851.

Open daily (closed 25 December). Visitor centre open daily (closed 25/26 December) (charge for non-RSPB members). In the Arun Valley, this beautiful reserve is important for many species of wildlife. In winter, flooding of the meadows gives refuge to thousands of wildfowl and waders. Breeding species include Nightingales and waders. In the summer, there are many butterflies and dragonflies. The 2 mile/3.2 km nature trail leads through hedge-lined paths to a viewpoint and hides. Suitable for pushchairs and manual wheelchairs with a strong helper.

Facilities: Car park, hides (most wheelchair accessible), view point, shop, tea-room, toilets (suitable for disabled visitors), baby changing facilities, cycle facilities, binocular hire, battery-powered vehicle is available for hire, special events.

Public transport: Rail – Pulborough 2 miles/3.2 km. Bus – An hourly service (100) runs daily, except Sundays and Bank Holidays, between Pulborough Station and Steyning. Taxi – available from Pulborough station. The reserve is between 5 and 14 miles (8 km and 22.5 km) from a National Cycle Network route.

Rye Meads, Hertfordshire

2 miles/3 km from A10 and 6 miles/9.5 km north of M25 (J25) in Hoddesdon. Follow sign for Rye Park into Rye Road. Tel: 01279 793720.

Open daily but closed 25/26 December (charge for non-RSPB members). This reserve has reedbeds, open water and meadows that attract many different birds, including breeding Kingfishers and Common Terns. In winter there are good numbers of wildfowl and Water Rails and Bitterns may occasionally be seen. Rye House is particularly suited to family visits.

Facilities: Car park, picnic area, hides (most accessible to wheelchairs), closed-circuit TV on Common Tern colony and Kingfisher bank during the breeding season.

Public transport: Rail – Rye House 300 yards/275 m. Bus – regular service – 500 yards/460 m. The reserve is on a National Cycle Network route.

Tudeley Woods, Kent

Near to the A21 Tonbridge to Hastings road, off the minor road to Capel, 2 miles/3 km south of Tonbridge. Also signed off the B2017, east of Tudeley village. Tel: 01273 775333 (RSPB S-E England Office).

Open at all times. All three British woodpeckers live in the wood as well as Nuthatches and Treecreepers. The springtime carpet of bluebells and primroses is impressive. This is also a good time to listen to the songs of the many different warblers that nest on the reserve. In the summer look out for orchids and butterflies, including the White Admiral and Speckled Wood. The two trails can be very muddy after rain.

Facilities: Car park.

Public transport: Rail – Tonbridge (3 miles/5 km).

South West England

Arne, Dorset
East of Wareham off A351 to Swanage, taking turning signposted to Arne, or take road from Stoborough village. Tel: 01929 553360.

Only the Shipstal part of the reserve is open to visitors (at all times). An internationally important heathland reserve with breeding Dartford Warblers, Nightjars and Wood Larks. All six species of British reptiles and 22 dragonfly species have been recorded. The reserve overlooks Poole Harbour, where in winter there are large numbers of waders and wildfowl including Black-tailed Godwits, Brent Geese and Red-breasted Mergansers. A 1 mile/1.6 km path runs from the car park to Shipstal Point and the Poole Harbour shoreline. There are other paths around Shipstal Point.

Facilities: Car park (charge for non-RSPB members), toilets, picnic area, hides, guided walks and special events.

Public transport: Rail – Wareham 4 miles/6.5 km. Bus stop in Stoborough 3 miles/5 km, Poole to Swanage service, hourly.

Aylesbeare Common, Devon
5 miles/8 km east of J30 of the M5 at Exeter, 0.5 mile/0.8 km past the Halfway Inn on the A3052, turn right, signposted Hawkerland. Tel: 01395 233655.

Open at all times. A Devon heathland reserve that is important for Dartford Warblers, Nightjars and Stonechats. Its sheltered wooded fringes, streams and ponds abound with butterflies, dragonflies and damselflies in summer. Two trails, 2 miles/3 km and 0.75 mile/1 km in length, and many paths (one farm track which crosses the heath is suitable for wheelchairs and pushchairs).

Facilities: Car park, picnic area, guided walks and special events.

Public transport: Rail – Exeter Central or St David's 10 miles/16 km. Bus – half-hourly 52 and 52A Exeter to Sidmouth service stops past car park.

Chapel Wood, Devon
1.5 miles/2.5 km west of A361, 2 miles/3 km north of Braunton. Signposted from Spreacombe. Tel: 01392 824614.

Open at all times. This small but varied, mainly deciduous, woodland has a good range of woodland birds and also the remains of an old hill fort and a historic chapel with a well. One trail up to 1.5 miles/2.5 km in length.

Facilities: Parking in lay-by, guided walks and special events.

Public transport: Rail – Barnstaple 8 miles/13 km. Bus stop 1.5 miles/2.5 km (Headon Mills stop), Barnstaple, Braunton and Ilfracombe service.

Exe Estuary, Devon
Exminster Marshes, east of Exminster village, 5 miles/8 km south of Exeter; Bowling Green Marsh, on the outskirts of Topsham, 5 miles/8 km south-east of Exeter, signposted from Holman Way car park, Topsham. Tel: 01392 824614.

Access at all times, but restricted to public footpaths and roads at both sites. This reserve covers two separate areas of coastal grazing marsh on opposite sides of the estuary – Exminster Marshes and Bowling Green Marsh. In spring you can watch breeding Lapwings and Redshanks and in winter during floods and at high tide there are thousands of roosting and feeding Curlews, Lapwings and Wigeons.

Facilities: Car park, one hide suitable for wheelchair users (10–15 minutes from car park), roadside viewing at Bowling Green Marsh, guided walks and special events.

Public transport: Exminster Marshes: Rail – Exeter station 5 miles / 8 km. Bus – Exeter to Dawlish regular service stops at roundabout on A379 (Swan's Nest) most of the day. Bowling Green Marsh: Rail – Topsham station 5 minutes' walk. Bus – Exeter to Topsham regular service stops at Quay most of the day. A foot ferry is sometimes available between the two parts of the reserve.

Garston Wood, Dorset
On the road to Broad Chalke, 1 mile/1.6 km north of Sixpenny Handley which is reached from the main Salisbury to Blandford road (A354). Tel: 01929 553360.

Open at all times. This ancient coppiced wood is especially worth visiting in spring, when it has breathtaking carpets of bluebells, wood anemones and primroses. Listen too for the song of the Nightingale and Turtle Dove and look out for signs of badgers and fallow deer.

Facilities: Car park.

Public transport: Rail – Salisbury 12 miles / 21 km.

Hayle Estuary, Cornwall
In town of Hayle, 5 miles/8 km north-east of Penzance. Tel: 01736 711682.

Open at all times. This most south-westerly estuary in the United Kingdom is a good place to watch birds in autumn and winter. Because it never freezes, it is important for migrating and wintering wildfowl such as Wigeon, Teals and Shelducks and also for waders such as Dunlins, Curlews and Grey Plovers.

Facilities: Car park, hides, wheelchair access, guided walks and special events.

Public transport: Rail – Hayle, Lelant Saltings and Lelant. Bus – St Ives to Hayle service, Penzance to Truro service.

Lodmoor, Dorset
To the north-east of Weymouth, 1 mile/1.6 km from the town centre, along A353 road to Wareham. Tel: 01305 778313.

Open at all times. This reserve always has something of interest. There is a grazing marsh with dykes, shallow pools, reedbed and scrub. Bearded Tits and Cetti's Warblers are around all year and autumn migration can be spectacular, with hundreds of Swallows, martins and Yellow Wagtails, as well as a variety of waders. One circular trail 2 miles / 3 km in length.

Facilities: Car park, hides, guided walks and special events.

Public transport: Rail – Weymouth 1 mile / 1.6 km. Bus – frequent local service Overcombe Corner, Lodmoor Country Park.

Marazion Marsh, Cornwall
At Mount's Bay, opposite St Michael's Mount, 2 miles/3 km east of Penzance. Tel: 01736 711682.

Open at all times. This reserve has Cornwall's largest reedbed with breeding Reed, Sedge and Cetti's Warblers, and a huge variety of plants and insects. In August and September the reserve is noted for migrant Spotted Crakes and Aquatic Warblers.

Facilities: Car park, hides, guided walks and special events (May to September), wheelchair access.

Public transport: Rail – Penzance 2 miles/3 km. Bus – daily from Penzance, stopping at Marazion 0.25 mile/0.4 km from reserve.

Radipole Lake, Dorset
Next to the Swannery Car Park in Weymouth. Tel: 01305 778313.

Reserve trails open at all times. The hide and visitor centre are open daily. The reserve is close to the town centre and very easy to visit. Reedbeds with large, shallow pools, rough grazing pasture and scrub provide habitat for birds such as Bearded Tits and Cetti's Warblers all year, migrants in spring and autumn and wildfowl in winter. The 1 mile/1.6 km nature trail and the hide are wheelchair and pushchair accessible, and there is also an audio nature trail for the visually impaired.

Facilities: Car park, picnic area, visitor centre, shop, snacks/light refreshments, toilets (suitable for disabled visitors), binocular hire.

Public transport: Rail – Weymouth station 0.25 mile/0.4 km. Bus stop with regular service 0.25 mile/0.4 km. The reserve is on a National Cycle Network route.

West Sedgemoor, Somerset
Car park is signposted just off the A378 Taunton-Langport road, 1 mile/1.6 km east of Fivehead. Tel: 01458 252805.

Open at all times. The Somerset Levels and Moors are one of England's largest remaining wet meadow systems. Large numbers of waders breed here and the winter floods attract over 50,000 waterfowl including, Teals, Wigeons and Lapwings. Swell Wood, an ancient deciduous wood on the southern edge of the reserve, has one of the UK's largest heronries, which is best visited between March and June. One woodland trail, 1 mile/1.6 km in length.

Facilities: Car park, hides (one suitable for disabled visitors), guided walks.

Public transport: Rail – Taunton 11 miles (18 km). Bus – stop in Fivehead on A378 – Southern National Taunton to Yeovil service.

Wales

Carngafallt, Powys
0.75 mile/1.2 km south of Rhayader on A470. Tel: 01597 811169.

Open at all times. This reserve combines woodlands, farmland and heather uplands. Red Kites and Pied Flycatchers are just some of the birds that can be seen here. There are two way-marked trails: Dyffryn Wood – 2 miles/3.2 km and Cwm yr Esgob – 1 mile/1.6 km.

Public transport: Rail – Llandrindod Wells (12 miles/19 km). Bus – for information contact the Rhayader Tourist Information Centre, telephone 01597 810591.

Conwy, Gwynedd
Access from the A55 expressway. Leave the A55 at the exit signed to Conwy and Deganwy:

the reserve entrance is on the roundabout above the expressway. Tel: 01492 584091.

Reserve and visitor centre open daily except 25 December (charge for non-RSPB members). The Conwy reserve was created by the RSPB following the construction of the Conwy tunnel. Shallow pools next to the estuary provide ideal feeding and roosting places for ducks, geese and many waders. The nature trails range from 0. 5 to 2 miles / 0.8 to 3 km in length and are suitable for pushchairs and wheelchairs.

Facilities: Car park, picnic area, hides (accessible by wheelchairs), visitor centre, snacks / light refreshments, toilets (suitable for disabled visitors), shop, binocular hire.

Public transport: Rail – Llandudno Junction 0.5 mile / 0.8 km. Bus – 0.5 mile / 0.8 km every 20 minutes. The reserve is on a National Cycle Network route.

Cwm Clydach, Swansea
Ceig Cefn Parc, 2 miles/3.2 km north of Clydach at the New Inn public house on the B4291. Tel: 01792 842927.

Public paths and trails open at all times. This mixed broadleaved woodland is home to breeding Pied Flycatchers, Redstarts and Buzzards. The Lower Clydach river flows through the centre of the reserve. Two trails: 1 mile / 2 km, and 7 miles / 11 km. The shorter trail is suitable for wheelchairs and pushchairs.

Facilities: Car park, guided walks and special events, wheelchair access.

Public transport: Rail – Swansea. Bus – Swansea to Craig Cefn Parc stop at reserve entrance, service hourly.

Dinas and Gwenffrwd, Carmarthenshire
10 miles/16 km north of Llandovery on the minor road to Llyn Brianne. Tel: RSPB North Wales Office 01248 363800.

Reserve – open at all times. A boardwalk takes visitors through oakwoods and then the trail continues to the fast-flowing river. Special viewing facilities have been set up at the reserve to watch Red Kites. Some parts of the nature trail are rugged and steep. One trail, 2 miles / 3 km in length. The trail includes some rocky areas unsuitable for pushchairs and wheelchairs.

Facilities: Car park (charge for non-RSPB members), picnic area.

Public transport: Rail – Llandovery (10 miles / 16 km).

Lake Vyrnwy, Powys
10 miles/16 km west of Llanfyllin via the B4393 to Llanwddyn. Tel: 01691 870278.

Reserve open at all times. Shop and visitor centre open daily in summer and at weekends in winter. In the Berwyn hills, west of Llanfyllin, this reserve is popular with families and birdwatchers alike, as it has good facilities and a variety of birds. As well as the lake (reservoir), there are rocky streams with Dippers and Kingfishers and moorland with Ravens and Buzzards. The trails range from 1.5 to 3 miles / 2.5 to 5 km.

Facilities: Car parks, hides (one has wheelchair access), visitor centre, snacks / light refreshments, picnic areas, toilets (suitable for disabled visitors), shop, binocular hire.

Public transport to the reserve is very difficult. The reserve is between 5 and 14 miles (8 km and 22.5 km) from a National Cycle Network route.

Mawddach Valley, Gwynedd

Directions to the reserves can be obtained from a sign outside the Information Centre, 2 miles/3 km west of Dolgellau on the A493 next to the toll bridge at Penmaenpool. Tel: 01341 422071.

Open at all times. Information centre is open daily during the summer. The two reserves in the Mawddach Valley offer superb scenery and beautiful walks through oak wood and scrubland. In the spring Pied Flycatchers, Wood Warblers and Redstarts can all be heard in Coed Garth Gell. Ravens and Buzzards are present throughout the year.

Facilities: Car park, toilets.

Public transport: Rail – Morfa Mawddach 4 miles/6.5 km. Buses run along the A493 from Fairbourne.

Point of Air – Dee Estuary, Flintshire

Access from Talacre, which is signed off the A548, 2 miles/3 km east of Prestatyn. Tel: RSPB North Wales Office 01248 361037.

Open at all times. Overlooking the Dee Estuary this reserve is at its best in the winter, when thousands of wading birds and wildfowl feed on the mudflats. At high tides the birds are forced on to the saltmarshes, giving closer views. One trail, 0.5 mile/0.8 km in length.

Facilities: Hide, guided walks and special events.

Public transport: Rail – Prestatyn (2 miles/3 km). Buses daily from Flint or Prestatyn.

Ramsey Island, Pembrokeshire

Offshore from St David's. Boats from St Justinian's lifeboat station, 2 miles/3.2 km west of St David's. Tel: 01437 720065. Boats to the island by Thousand Islands; for bookings, contact 01437 721686.

Open daily, Easter to 31 October (closed Tuesdays). (Charge for non-RSPB members. Boat fares extra.)

This dramatic offshore island has 400 feet/120 m seabird cliffs and fine examples of coastal heathland. The seabird cliffs are occupied between April and July. Choughs and Wheatears breed on the island. In the autumn, a colony of breeding Grey Seals can also be seen. The longest trail is 3.5 miles/5.5 km, the shortest 2 miles/3.2 km.

Facilities: Information centre, toilets, drinks and light snacks available, picnic area, small shop, binocular hire, guided walks and special events.

Public transport: Rail and bus from Haverfordwest to St David's.

South Stack Cliffs, Anglesey

2 miles/3 km west of Holyhead on minor roads signed from Holyhead and Trearddur Bay. Tel: 01407 764973.

Open daily Easter to September. In summer, over 4,000 pairs of seabirds nest on the spectacular South Stack cliffs. From Ellin's Tower visitor centre, you can watch Puffins, Fulmars, Guillemots and Razorbills, and see live pictures of the birds nesting on the cliffs. Public footpaths run along the clifftop.

Facilities: Car park, picnic area, visitor centre, toilets, binoculars and telescopes, closed-circuit TV, guided walks.

Public transport: Rail – Holyhead 2 miles / 3 km. Bus – daily from Holyhead to South Stack. The reserve is within 5 miles / 8 km of a National Cycle Network route.

Valley Lakes, Anglesey
2 miles/3.2 km south of Caegeilliog. Tel: 01407 764973.

Open at all times. A small reserve with reed-fringed lakes and small, rocky outcrops. A variety of ducks and other waterfowl can be seen on the lakes. One trail, 2 miles / 3 km in length.

Facilities: Car park.

Public transport: Rail – Valley (4 miles / 6.5 km), Rhosneigr (7 miles / 11 km). Bus – Maes Awyr / RAF Valley daily from Bangor and Holyhead.

Ynys-hir, Cardiganshire
Signposted from Eglwys-fach, 1 mile/1.6 km off A487. Tel: 01654 781265.

Open daily. Visitor centre open daily in summer and at weekends in winter (charge for non-RSPB members). The reserve has a mixture of Welsh oak woodland, estuary, reedbeds and pools, and is attractive to birds all year round. In spring the wood is full of flowers and the song of birds such as Pied Flycatchers and Redstarts. In autumn and winter large numbers of ducks and geese feed on the saltmarsh and farmland. Nature trails range in length from 0.5 to 3 miles / 0.8 to 5 km.

Facilities: Car park, picnic area, hides, visitor centre, snacks / light refreshments, toilets, binocular hire, cycle facilities.

Public transport: Rail – Machynlleth 6 miles / 9.5 km. Bus – to Eglwys-fach (Monday to Saturday, limited Sunday services). The reserve is between 5 and 14 miles (8 km and 22.5 km) from a National Cycle Network route.

Scotland

Northern Scotland

Abernethy Forest, Loch Garten, Highland
10 miles/16 km east of Aviemore between Boat of Garten and Nethybridge off the B970. Tel: 01479 831476 .

Osprey Centre open daily from early April to the end of August (charge for non-RSPB members). Loch Garten is famous for nesting Ospreys. This famous nest may be seen and 'live' nest-side video pictures are relayed to the Osprey Centre, where staff are on hand to explain what is happening. In the surrounding Caledonian pine forest, special wildlife includes Crested Tits, Scottish Crossbills and Red Squirrels. The new Osprey Centre is built almost entirely from native Scots Pine timber, much of it from sustainably managed woods of the Abernethy Forest Nature Reserve.

Facilities: Car park, shop, closed-circuit TV, binoculars available, toilets (suitable for disabled visitors), information (fully accessible to disabled visitors).

Public transport: Rail – Aviemore 10 miles / 16 km. Bus – service to Aviemore to

Nethybridge stop 1.5 miles/2.5 km from Osprey Centre. The reserve is within 5 miles/8 km of a National Cycle Network route.

Culbin Sands, Highland
1.5 miles/2.5 km east of Nairn off the Lochloy road. Tel: 01463 811186.

Open at all times. Overlooking the Moray Firth, Culbin Sands forms one of the largest shingle and sand dune bars in Britain, behind which there is extensive saltmarsh. Large numbers of sea ducks can be seen offshore during the winter. Bar-tailed Godwits, Oystercatchers and Knots flock at high tide. Much of the reserve is remote, unspoilt and largely undisturbed.

Facilities: Car park.

Public transport: Rail and bus – Nairn 1.5 miles/2.5 km.

Fairy Glen, Highland
On the Black Isle, by Rosemarkie on the A832. Tel: 01463 811186.

Open at all times. Fairy Glen is a small area of broadleaved woodland set in an attractive steep-sided valley. A fast-flowing stream runs through the middle of the reserve with two waterfalls at the upstream end. Typical woodland and stream birds are present, including Dippers, Buzzards and Grey Wagtails. One trail, 1.5 miles/2.5 km in length.

Facilities: Car park.

Public transport: Bus – frequent services from Inverness to Cromarty stop at Rosemarkie.

Forsinard, Highland
On the A897 26 miles/39 km from Helmsdale. Tel: 01641 571225.

Visitor centre open daily, April to October. 5 miles/8 km escorted walks every Tuesday and Thursday, from Easter to the end of August. Comprising almost 21,000 acres/8,400 ha of blanket bog, the deep peatlands of Forsinard lie at the heart of the internationally important Flow Country of Caithness and Sutherland. Breeding birds include Golden Plovers, Dunlins and Merlins. Visitors are encouraged to access the site via our visitor centre at Forsinard railway station where there is a bog pool trail, Hen Harrier nest camera, regular guided walks and roadside viewing. One trail, 1 mile/1.6 km in length.

Facilities: Car park, toilets (suitable for disabled visitors), guided walks and special events, visitor centre at Forsinard station (wheelchair accessible).

Public transport: Rail – Forsinard station.

Fowlsheugh, Aberdeenshire
3 miles/5 km south of Stonehaven, the car park at Crawton is signposted off the A92. Tel: RSPB East Scotland Office 01224 624824.

Open at all times. The cliffs of Fowlsheugh reserve are packed with breeding seabirds in the spring and summer. Guillemots, Razorbills and Kittiwakes breed in large numbers, with smaller numbers of Fulmars, Herring Gulls, Puffins and Shags. In May, June and July, boat trips from Stonehaven visit the cliffs in the evening to watch the nesting seabirds.

Facilities: Car park.

Public transport: Rail – Stonehaven 3 miles/5 km. Bus – request stop at Crawton turn-off.

Glenborrodale, Highland

1 mile/1.6 km west of Glenborrodale on the B8007. Tel: 01463 715000.

Open at all times. On the rugged Ardnamurchan peninsula, Glenborrodale is an ancient oak wood on the north shore of Loch Sunart. In spring, Wood Warblers nest, along with a range of woodland birds such as Redstarts and Spotted Fly-catchers. There is always a good chance of seeing an Otter along the shore, and seals are common. One trail, 2 miles/3 km in length.

Facilities: Guided walks in summer from Ardnamurchan Natural History Centre.

Insh Marshes, Highland

1.5 miles/2.5 km from Kingussie on the B970. Tel: 01540 661518.

Open at all times. This is one of the most important wetlands in Europe. In spring, Lapwings, Redshanks and Curlews nest here as well as Oystercatchers, Snipe and Wigeon. In winter, the marshes flood, providing roosting and feeding for flocks of Whooper Swans and Greylag Geese. The best time for visiting is between November and June. Around half of all British Goldeneyes nest at Insh. Two trails, 2 miles/3 km and 2.5 miles/4 km in length. Due to the rough terrain, neither are accessible to wheelchairs or pushchairs, but there are good views of the reserve from the B970.

Facilities: Car park, hides, picnic area, information point.

Public transport: Rail – Kingussie 1.5 miles/2.5 km. Bus – frequent bus services from Inverness and Perth stop in Kingussie.

Killicrankie

4 miles/6.5 km north-west of Pitlochry on the B8097, signposted from Killicrankie on unclassified roads to Balrobbie Farm.

Open at all times. (Car parking fee for non-members.) Rising from the dramatic narrow gorge of the River Garry, the reserve climbs steeply through oak and birch woodland to heather moorland. There is a great variety of woodland and moorland birds including Buzzards, Redstarts, curlews and Black and Red Grouse. Ravens nest on the crags. The reserve is exceptionally rich in plant life, with a number of rare and unusual species, but also a colourful show of common plants throughout the spring and summer. Two trails (1.5 miles/2.5 km and 3 miles/5 km) both of which are steep and rough and unsuitable for wheelchairs and pushchairs.

Public transport: Rail – Pitlochry 4 miles/6.5 km. Bus to Killiecrankie from Pitlochry.

Loch of Kinnordy, Angus

1 mile/1.6 km west of Kirriemuir on the B951. Tel: 01224 624824.

Open daily (closed Saturdays in September and October). (Parking fee for non-members.) The lochs, mires and fens of the reserve are surrounded by farmland. It is one of the best places in Scotland for seeing Black-necked Grebes, which nest in the midst of a colony of Black-headed Gulls. Ospreys visit regularly in summer. Trail and boardwalk is wheelchair accessible.

Facilities: Car park, hides (2 are accessible by wheelchair), guided walks and special events.

Public transport: Rail – Dundee. Bus – frequent services from Dundee and Forfar to Kirriemuir.

Loch Ruthven, Highland
18 miles/29 km south-west of Inverness, reached via the A9 and B851 taking the turn at Croachy. Tel: 01463 715000.

Open at all times. This beautiful loch is fringed by sedges and birch woods with open moorland. It is the most important site in the UK for Slavonian Grebe. Ospreys can be seen regularly and there is also a chance of seeing a Peregrine or Hen Harrier.

Facilities: Car park, hide.

Public transport: Rail – Inverness 11 miles/18 km. Bus – services twice daily to Croachy, 1 mile/1.6 km from reserve.

Loch of Strathbeg, Aberdeenshire
Signposted from the A90 at Crimond. Tel: 01346 532017.

Open at all times (charge for non-RSPB members). This wetland reserve is an excellent place to see Pink-footed Geese and Whooper Swans during the winter. In the summer the meadows attract breeding waders, including Lapwings and Redshanks. On the small islands in the loch, Sandwich and Common Terns and a variety of wildfowl breed. Short trail between hides.

Facilities: Car park, hides (one is wheelchair accessible), toilets (suitable for disabled visitors), guided walks and special events, visitor centre and observation room.

Public transport: Bus – regular services from Peterhead and Fraserburgh stop at Crimond village (1 mile/1.6 km from visitor centre). Access to the whole reserve is difficult without a vehicle (4 miles/6.5 km from centre to hide).

Udale Bay, Highland
1 mile/1.6 km west of Jemimaville on the B9163. Tel: 01463 811186.

Open at all times. Udale Bay is an extensive area of mudflat, saltmarsh and wet grassland on the Cromarty Firth. From late summer to April the reserve supports large numbers of wildfowl and waders. Best visited within an hour of the high tide, when there can be spectacular views of flocks of waders. In autumn up to 5,000 Wigeons feed on the beds of eel-grass that grow in the bay. Late summer is good time to see fishing Ospreys.

Facilities: Car park, hide (wheelchair accessible).

Public transport: Rail – Dingwall 16 miles/26 km. Bus – Jemimaville four times a day.

Southern Scotland

Baron's Haugh, North Lanarkshire
To the south of Motherwell, close to the M74 (J14). Tel: RSPB Scottish Office 0131 311 6500.

Open at all times. A small urban nature reserve with a meadow, some marshland, woodland and the River Clyde. This diversity of habitats makes it valuable for wildlife and over 170 species of birds have been recorded here. You may see Kingfishers by the river and Whooper Swans on the flooded meadows (haugh) in the winter. Two trails: 0.5 mile/0.8 km and 2 miles/3 km (longer trail suitable for wheelchairs and pushchairs).

Facilities: Car park, hides (two with wheelchair access and can be reached by car).

Public transport: Rail – Motherwell and Airbles Road. Bus – Airbles Road.

Inversnaid, Stirling

15 miles/24 km west of Aberfoyle at the end of the B829 and an unclassified road. Tel: 0131 311 6500.

Open at all times. Inversnaid is set on the east shore of Loch Lomond. The woodland rises steeply from the shores of the loch and then gives way to open moorland. In the summer, Pied Flycatchers and Redstarts breed here, along with resident birds. Buzzards nest on the crags in the wood and Black Grouse can sometimes be seen on the moorland. One trail, 1 mile/1.6 km in length. There is a path through the woodland, but it is steep and rugged in places and is therefore not suitable for pushchairs or those with limited mobility.

Facilities: Car park, toilets (March to October only).

Public transport: Bus – daily post-buses from Aberfoyle and minibuses from Callander and Aberfoyle. Bus stop at Inversnaid Hotel about 0.5 mile/0.8 km from the reserve.

Ken-Dee Marshes, Dumfries and Galloway

Car park on minor road north from Glenlochar to the A762. Tel: RSPB Galloway Reserves Office 01671 402861.

Open at all times. The reserve is both a wetland and woodland site. In the winter, many wildfowl, including Greenland White-fronted Geese, can be seen on the reserve. During the spring, migrant Redstarts and Pied Flycatchers join the resident woodland birds to breed. Red Squirrels and Otters are also found on the reserve. One trail, 3 miles/5 km in length.

Facilities: Car park, hide.

Public transport: Rail – the nearest railway station is in Dumfries, 6 miles/8.5 km.

Loch Gruinart, Islay, Argyll and Bute

Signed from A847 Bridgend to Bruichladdich road, 3 miles/5 km. Tel: 01496 850505.

Visitor centre open daily (closed 25 December and 1 January). The reserve can be seen easily from the road, letting you birdwatch from a car. During the spring there are hundreds of breeding waders, Lapwings, Redshanks and Snipes, and the nights resound to the call of the Corncrakes. Hen Harriers nest on the moor, and hunting Golden Eagles and Peregrines occur all year round. Loch Gruinart is famous for the large numbers of Barnacle and White-fronted Geese that spend the winter on Islay. In the visitor centre a live video camera gives even closer views of the grazing geese.

Facilities: Car park, hide (wheelchair accessible), toilets (suitable for disabled visitors), binoculars for hire, guided walks, visitor centre (ground floor wheelchair accessible), closed-circuit TV.

Public transport: Ferry from Kennacraig to Port Askaig or Port Ellen by *Caledonian MacBrayne Ferries*. Flights from Glasgow to Islay. Bus – nearest stop 3 miles/5 km.

Lochwinnoch, Renfrewshire

18 miles/29 km south-west of Glasgow between Paisley and Largs on the A760. Tel: 01505 842663.

Reserve and centre open daily except Christmas and New Year holidays (charge for non-RSPB members). This is an ideal reserve for all the family as the trails, birdwatching hides and visitor centre are all easily accessible. The visitor centre, with its tower, gives good views over the marshland and loch, where in the winter you can see ducks, geese and swans. In the spring Great Crested Grebes can be seen displaying on the Aird Meadow and Sedge Warblers can be heard singing in the marshland. The two nature trails, 0.25 mile/0.4 km and 0.5 mile/0.8 km, are both suitable for wheelchairs and pushchairs.

Facilities: Car park, hides (all accessible to wheelchairs), picnic area, visitor centre, snacks/light refreshments, toilets (suitable for disabled visitors), shop, binocular hire.

Public transport: Rail – Lochwinnoch opposite reserve. Bus – request bus stop near reserve (regular service from Glasgow). The reserve is on a National Cycle Network route.

Mersehead, Dumfries and Galloway
18 miles/29 km south-west of Dumfries on the A710 just before Caulkerbush. First turn on left after Southwick Home Farm. Tel: 01387 780298.

Open at all times. Mersehead covers a large area of farmland, wet meadows, saltmarsh and mudflats on the north shore of the Solway. It is important for wintering wildfowl, including Barnacle Geese, Pink-footed Geese, Wigeons and Pintails. In summer Lapwings, Curlews, Redshanks and wildfowl breed here. A reedbed is also being created. Two trails, 1.5 miles/2.5 km and 3.5 miles/5.5 km in length.

Facilities: Car park, hide, toilets (suitable for disabled visitors), guided walks and special events, wheelchair access, information centre.

Public transport: Bus – daily rural service from Dumfries stops 1 mile/1.6 km from reserve on A710.

Mull of Galloway, Dumfries and Galloway
5 miles/8 km south of Drummore and well signposted. Tel: 01671 402861.

Open at all times. Visitor centre run by local Community Development Trust and the RSPB open from Easter to September.

The Mull of Galloway is the most southerly point in Scotland. The cliffs are home to thousands of breeding seabirds, including Guillemots, Razorbills and a few Puffins. The best time of year to visit is between April and July. On the small rocky outcrop, Scar Rocks RSPB reserve, over 2,000 pairs of Gannets breed. There is a variety of short cliff-top walks, but please take care.

Facilities: Car park, guided walks and special events.

There is no public transport near the reserve.

Vane Farm, Perth and Kinross
On the south shore of Loch Leven, 1 mile/1.6 km along the B9097 east of M90 (J5), signposted from motorway. Tel: 01577 862355.

Reserve open daily except Christmas and New Year holidays (charge for non-RSPB members). With wonderful views of Loch Leven from the visitor centre and the spectacular view from the top of Vane Hill, this is one of the most popular nature reserves in Scotland. Birds include Pink-footed Geese and Whooper Swans in winter, nesting Redshanks, Snipe, Lapwings and various ducks in summer, and

Peregrines, Buzzards and Sparrowhawks all year. Two trails: longest 1 mile / 1.6 km.

Facilities: Visitor centre (wheelchair accessible), hides, car park, cycle facilities, picnic area, coffee shop, toilets (suitable for disabled visitors), shop, binocular hire.

Public transport: Rail – Lochgelly 4 miles / 6.5 km, Cowdenbeath 4 miles / 6.5 km. Bus – nearest stops in Kinross (6 miles / 9.5 km) and Ballingry (5 miles / 8 km). The reserve is within 5 miles / 8 km of a National Cycle Network route.

Wood of Cree, Dumfries and Galloway

3 miles/5 km north of Minnigaff/Newton Stewart on the east bank of the river Cree. Follow signs through Old Minnigaff. Tel: RSPB Galloway Reserves Office 01671 402861.

Open at all times. The Wood of Cree is the largest ancient wood in southern Scotland. In spring, the wood is alive with the sound of bird song, as the resident birds are joined by Redstarts, Pied Flycatchers, Garden Warblers and other migrants. Otters, deer and Red Squirrels are resident.

Facilities: Car park, guided walks and special events.

Public transport: Bus – nearest bus to Newton Stewart 3 miles / 5 km away.

Western Isles

Balranald, North Uist, Western Isles

3 miles/5 km north of Bayhead. Turn for Hougharry off the A865. Tel: 01876 560287.

Reserve open at all times. Visitor centre open April–August. Sandy beaches and a rocky foreshore are separated from the machair and marshes by sand dunes; there are also shallow lochs. Many species of waders nest on the flower-rich machair and the croftland. The best times to visit are late May for the waders and Corncrakes and the end of June and July for the wild flowers. One trail: 3.5 miles / 5.5 km is not suitable for wheelchairs.

Facilities: Car park, information centre (wheelchair access), toilets, guided walks (May to August; Tuesdays and Thursdays).

Public transport: There is a post-bus service. Ferry – nearest port is Lochmaddy served by *Caledonian MacBrayne Ferries*. Airport – Benbecula via Glasgow.

Coll, Argyll and Bute

6 miles/9.5 km west of Arinagour, Isle of Coll. Tel: 01879 230301.

Open at all times. Please avoid walking through fields of hay and crops. The island of Coll has long, white shell beaches, sand dunes and machair grassland, all typical Hebridean habitats. The reserve is a stronghold for the rare Corncrake. There are also many other breeding birds on the reserve, including Redshanks, Lapwings and Snipe. In the winter large numbers of Barnacle and Greenland White-fronted Geese use the site.

Facilities: Car park information bothy at Totronald. Guided walks in summer.

Public transport: Coll is reached by ferry from Oban by *Caledonian MacBrayne Ferries*.

Orkney

Birsay Moors and Cottasgarth, Orkney
The reserve is between Dounby (3 miles/4.8 km) and Evie (2 miles/3.2 km) either side of the Hillside road, B9057, and to Burgar Hill off the A966 1 mile/1.6 km north of Evie. Tel: 01856 85017.

Open at all times. In the summer, Hen Harriers, Short-eared Owls and Arctic Skuas nest on the moorland. The Orkney vole is also common on the reserve. There is one hide that gives excellent views of Red-throated Divers in spring. There are no trails, but a network of peat-cutters' tracks gives easy access to pedestrians.

Facilities: There are three car parking areas.

Copinsay, Orkney
2 miles/3 km off the east coast of East Mainland. Tel: 01856 850176.

Open at all times, weather permitting. This uninhabited island was purchased as a memorial to the naturalist James Fisher. The cliffs of the reserve are home to a huge colony of breeding seabirds, including Fulmars, Guillemots, Razorbills and Kittiwakes.

Facilities: Old farmhouse on island may be available for basic overnight accommodation.

Public transport: Flights from Edinburgh.

Hobbister, Orkney
4 miles/6.5 km south-west of Kirkwall. Tel: 01856 850176.

Open at all times but access is limited to the land between the A964 and the sea. The reserve is a mixture of moorland, sandflats, saltmarsh and sea cliffs. Hen Harriers, Short-eared Owls and Red-throated Divers breed on the moorland. On the coast there are Red-breasted Mergansers and Black Guillemots.

Facilities: Car park.

Public transport: Flights operate from Edinburgh. Ferries operated by *P & O Scottish Ferries*.

Hoy, Orkney
On north-west part of Hoy. Tel: 01856 791298.

Open at all times. This Orkney reserve is a mixture of moorland and cliffs and includes the famous Old Man of Hoy rock stack. Great Skuas breed on the moor along with Red Grouse, Dunlins and Golden Plovers. Seabirds, including Guillemots, Razorbills and Kittiwakes, breed on the cliffs.

Facilities: Car park.

Public transport: Ferry – daily service from Stromness to Moness Pier or Bouton to Lyness service.

The Loons, Mainland, Orkney
3 miles/5 km north of Dounby on Orkney Mainland. Tel: 01856 850176.

There is no access to the marsh, but good views can be obtained from the road and hide. This marshland reserve is one of the best remaining marshes in Orkney.

In the summer Pintails and waders breed, while in the winter the flooded marsh attracts hundreds of ducks and smaller numbers of White-fronted Geese.

Facilities: Car park, hide.

Public transport: Ferry – operated by *P & O Scottish Ferries*. Flights from Edinburgh.

Marwick Head, Orkney

About 11 miles/17.5 km north of Stromness. Tel: 01856 721210.

Open at all times. The reserve is in the north-west corner of the Mainland, Orkney. Thousands of pairs of seabirds crowd on to the cliffs. The cliff top has spectacular displays of sea campion, thrift and spring squill.

Facilities: Car park.

Public transport: Ferry – operated by *P & O Scottish Ferries*. Flights from Edinburgh.

Mill Dam, Shapinsay, Orkney

1 mile/1.5 km north-east of Balfour village. Tel: 01856 711373.

Hide open at all times, but no access to the reserve. In winter, Whooper Swans can often be seen on this Orkney reserve along with Greylag Geese. In the summer Pintails breed on the marsh with other ducks, including Wigeons and Shovelers.

Facilities: Car park, hide (accessible by wheelchair).

Public transport: Ferry from Kirkwall by *Orkney Ferries*.

North Hill, Papa Westray, Orkney

On northern part of Papa Westray. Tel: 01857 644240 (April to August only).

Open at all times. During the breeding season, please contact the summer warden before visiting. The low cliffs of this Orkney reserve are home to breeding seabirds, including Guillemots, Razorbills and Kittiwakes. On the hill, a large colony of Arctic Terns nests close to Arctic Skuas, Eiders, Ringed Plovers and Oystercatchers.

Public transport: Ferry from Kirkwall by *Orkney Ferries*. Flights from Kirkwall, contact Loganair: tel: 01856 872494.

Noup Cliffs, Westray, Orkney

From Pierowall follow the minor road west to Noup Farm, then the track to the lighthouse at the north end of the reserve. Tel: 01857 644240 (April to August only).

Open at all times. These isolated cliffs have one of the UK's largest seabird colonies. On the 1.5 mile/2.5 km stretch of cliffs, over 44,500 Guillemots and 12,700 pairs of Kittiwakes breed, along with Razorbills and Fulmars.

Facilities: Car park.

Public transport: Ferry from Kirkwall by *Orkney Ferries*.

Trumland, Rousay, Orkney

Near Trumland House in the south of Rousay. Tel: 01856 821395.

Open at all times. Red-throated Divers, Merlins and Hen Harriers all breed on the heather moorland of this Orkney reserve. One trail on the reserve.

Facilities: Car park.

Public transport: Ferry from Tingwall by *Orkney Ferries*.

Shetland

Fetlar, Shetland
Take the public ferry to Fetlar from either Unst or Yell. Tel: 01957 733246.

Hide open April to October, no access to the statutory bird sanctuary April to August. During the summer, a wealth of birds breeds on this island reserve, including 90% of the British population of Red-necked Phalaropes. These fascinating waders can be seen from the RSPB hide or at the Loch of Funzie. Red-throated Divers, Whimbrels, and Arctic and Great Skuas also breed on the island.

Facilities: Hide (at Mires of Funzie), public toilets at ferry terminal, guided walks, information sign.

Public transport: Via ferry from Yell / Unst. Contact *P & O Scottish Ferries*. Flights from Edinburgh, Inverness, Aberdeen.

Loch of Spiggie, Mainland, Shetland
2 miles/3 km north of Sumburgh Airport, turn off the B9122 near Scousburgh. Tel: 01950 460800.

No access to reserve, but good views of loch from road. The large shallow loch attracts considerable numbers of wildfowl during the autumn and winter, including Whooper Swans, Wigeons and Teals. In the summer Arctic Terns, Arctic and Great Skuas, and Kittiwakes can be seen bathing in the loch.

Facilities: Car park, information sign.

Public transport: Ferry – contact *P & O Scottish Ferries* for information. Flights from Edinburgh, Inverness and Aberdeen. Bus – daily service between Lerwick and Sumburgh.

Sumburgh Head, Mainland, Shetland
Southernmost tip of Mainland Shetland, 2.25 miles/3.5 km from Sumburgh Airport. Tel: 01950 460800.

The reserve is always open. The cliffs around Sumburgh Head attract thousands of breeding seabirds, including Puffins, Guillemots, Shags and Fulmars. Gannets are regularly seen offshore. Whales and dolphins can also occasionally be seen.

Facilities: Car park, information signs and special events.

Public transport: Ferry – contact *P & O Scottish Ferries* for information. Flights from Edinburgh, Inverness and Aberdeen. Bus – daily service from Lerwick to Sumburgh Airport and Grutness.

Northern Ireland

Belfast Lough
Off A2 dual carriageway between Belfast and Holywood. Tel: 02891 479009.

Viewpoints open at all times, observation room open Tuesday–Sunday, closed Mondays and Christmas Day. The reserve is situated within the Belfast Harbour Estate on the shores of Belfast Lough. The mudflats are important feeding areas for a variety of waders and wildfowl. At high tide, flocks of waders such as Redshanks, Oystercatchers and Black-tailed Godwits can be seen from the hide and viewing points.

Facilities: Car park, hides, toilets, observation room, two sheltered viewpoints, both of which are wheelchair accessible.

Lower Lough Erne Islands, Co. Fermanagh
The forest is 6 miles/10 km east of Belleek off the A47 to Kesh. Tel: 013656 58835.

The reserve is a mix of coniferous forest and 40 diverse islands in Lower Lough Erne. Castlecaldwell Forest is open at all times. Lusty More is the only island open to the public – access by boat only. The breeding birds of the reserve include Snipe, Redshanks, Curlews and Sandwich Terns. In winter, Whooper Swans and geese can be found in the area.

Facilities: Limited facilities available at Castlecaldwell Forest Reserve nearby.

Lough Foyle, Co. Londonderry
The reserve can be accessed via a number of minor roads off the A2 between Limavady and Londonderry. Tel: (028) 9049 1547.

Open at all times. Various viewpoints give excellent views over the mudflats and adjacent fields. In early winter, the Lough is an outstanding place to see large numbers of waterfowl, including Brent Geese, Whooper Swans and Wigeons.

Public transport: Rail – Londonderry (8 miles/13 km). Bus – Ballykelly.

Portmore Lough, Co. Antrim
Leave M1 at J9 to Aghalee, then follow brown tourist signs to the reserve. Tel: (028) 9265 2406.

Open daily. The reserve lies on the south-western shore of Portmore Lough to the east of Lough Neagh and consists of wet grassland fringed by woodland and scrub. In the winter Greylag Geese and Whooper Swans visit the fields. In the summer Curlew and Snipe breed here. A wide variety of wildfowl can be seen from the hide. Tree Sparrows may be seen.

Facilities: Car park, hide, information centre, toilets, picnic area.

Public transport: There is no public transport to the reserve.

Rathlin Island Cliffs, Co. Antrim
Five miles/8 km off the coast from Ballycastle. The West Light viewpoint is about 4 miles/6 km from the harbour. Tel: (028) 2076 3948.

Open April to August. Visitors must contact the warden first. Rathlin Island is 5 miles/8 km off the north coast of Northern Ireland. From late May to early July, the spectacular cliffs on the reserve are home to thousands of breeding seabirds. The West Light platform gives magnificent views of Guillemots, Razorbills, Puffins and Fulmars.

Facilities: The West Light platform offers excellent, safe views of the seabird colony. Access is only under the supervision of warden staff. All amenities are at the harbour. There are no toilets at the viewpoint.

Public transport: Rail – Ballymoney (15 miles/ 24 km). Ferry from Ballycastle by *Caledonian MacBrayne Ferries*. Private minibus on island to West Light (telephone 028207 63909).

Ornithological Organisations

British Birds is the monthly magazine which builds up into a valuable work of reference. It was founded in 1907 and contains articles on identification and bird behaviour as well as reports of unusual species and bird news from Britain and the rest of Europe.

The British Birds Rarities Committee is responsible for examining reports of rare birds seen in Britain, and its annual report is published in *British Birds*.

British Birds, Fountains, Park Lane, Blunham, Bedford, MK44 3NJ
www.britishbirds.co.uk

The British Trust for Ornithology organises surveys and enquiries which are carried out by amateur ornithologists and administered by a team of professional biologists. The BTO also organises the ringing of birds in Britain. Publications include *BTO News* and the quarterly scientific journal *Bird Study*.

BTO, Beech Grove, Tring, Hertfordshire, HP23 5NR www.bto.org

The Royal Society for the Protection of Birds is the largest voluntary wildlife conservation body in Europe. The RSPB owns important reserves, carries out research, investigates conservation problems and helps to enforce the bird protection laws. There are RSPB members' groups in most parts of the United Kingdom and the Society actively promotes bird study in schools. Members receive the colourful quarterly magazine *Birds*.

RSPB, The Lodge, Sandy, Bedfordshire, SG19 2DL www.rspb.org.uk

The Wildfowl Trust manages wildfowl refuges at Slimbridge, Gloucestershire, and at several other centres. The Trust also owns collections of wildfowl for research and education and has encouraged the breeding of some rare species in captivity. The Wildfowl Trust publishes the magazine *Wildfowl World*, and *Wildfowl*, an annual collection of scientific papers.

The Wildfowl Trust, Slimbridge, Gloucester, GL2 7BT www.wwt.org.uk

RSPB Wildlife Explorers, the junior section of the RSPB, is the largest national organisation for young birdwatchers. The club publishes the colourful bi-monthly magazine *Bird Life* which contains articles by experts and by members and a separate magazine called *Wild Times* for younger members. Wildlife Explorers runs many projects and competitions and organises holiday courses and one-day events in many parts of Britain and Northern Ireland, and has a network of local members' groups. There is a club for teenage members called RSPB Phoenix with its own magazine, *Wingbeat*.

RSPB Wildlife Explorers, The Lodge, Sandy, Bedfordshire, SG19 2DL
www.rspb.org.uk/youth

Most of the above organisations will supply a free sample copy of their journals on request.

Index

Page numbers in *italic* refer to illustrations
Page numbers in brackets refer to maps

Auk, Little 98, *99* (209)
Avocet 60, *61* (204)

Bee-eater, European 190, *191*
Bittern 14, *15* (196)
   Little 186, *187*
Blackbird 132, *133* (214)
Blackcap 144, *145* (216)
Bluethroat 126, *127*
Brambling 172, *173* (220)
Bullfinch 178, *179* (221)
Bunting, Cirl 182, *183* (221)
   Corn 184, *185* (221)
   Lapland 180, *181* (221)
   Little 192, *193*
   Ortolan 192, *193*
   Reed 184, *185* (221)
   Snow 180, *181* (221)
Buzzard, Common 40, *41* (201)
   Rough-legged 40, *41* (201)
   Honey 190, *191*

Capercaillie 50, *51* (202)
Chaffinch 172, *173* (219)
Chiffchaff 146, *147* (216)
Chough 164, *165* (218)
Coot 58, *59* (203)
Cormorant *3*, 12, *13* (196)
Corncrake 56, *57* (203)
Crake, Spotted 56, 188, *189* (203)
Crane, Common 186, *187*
Crossbill, Common 178, *179* (220)
   Scottish 178, *179* (221)
Crow, Carrion 166, *167* (219)
   Hooded *45*, 166, *167* (219)
Cuckoo 106, *107* (210)
Curlew 76, *77* (206)

Dabchick *see* Grebe, Little
Dipper 124, *125* (213)
Diver, Black-throated 2, *3* (195)

Great Northern 2, *3* (195)
   Red-throated 2, *3* (195)
   White-billed 2
Dotterel 66, *67* (204)
Dove, Collared 104, *105* (210)
   Rock 102, *103* (209)
   Stock 102, *103*, *105* (209)
   Turtle 104, *105* (210)
Duck, Ferruginous 30, *31* (199)
   Mandarin 22, *23* (198)
   Long-tailed 32, *33* (199)
   Tufted 30, *31* (199)
   Ring-necked 188, *189*
   Ruddy 32, *33* (199)
Dunlin *69*, 70, *71*, *81* (205)
Dunnock *107*, 126, *127* (213)

Eagle, Golden 42, *43* (201)
Egret, Little 186, *187*
Eider 32, *33* (199)
   King 188, *189*

Falcon, Peregrine *45* (201)
   Red-footed 190, *191*
Fieldfare 136, *137* (215)
Firecrest 148, *149* (216)
Flycatcher, Pied 150, *151* (217)
   Red-breasted 150, *151*, 192, *193*
   Spotted 150, *151* (217)
Fulmar 8, *9* (195)

Gadwall 28, *29* (198)
Gannet 10, *11* (196)
Garganey 26, *27* (198)
Godwit, Bar-tailed 76, *77* (206)
   Black-tailed 76, *77* (206)
Goldcrest 148, *149* (216)
Goldeneye 34, *35* (200)
Goldfinch 174, *175* (220)
Goosander 36, *37* (200)
Goose, Barnacle 20, *21* (197)

Bean 18, *19* (197)
Brent 20, *21* (197)
Canada 20, *21* (197)
Egyptian 22, *23* (198)
Greylag 18, *19* (197)
Pink-footed 18, *19* (197)
White-fronted 18, *19* (197)
Goshawk 40, *41* (201)
Grebe, Black-necked 6, *7* (195)
    Great Crested 4, *5*, *7* (195)
    Little 6, *7* (195)
    Red-necked 6, *7* (195)
    Slavonian 6, *7* (195)
Greenfinch 174, *175* (220)
Greenshank 78, *79* (206)
Grouse, Black 50, *51* (202)
    Red 48, *49* (202)
Guillemot 98, *99*, *101* (209)
    Black 100, *101* (209)
Gull, Black-headed 86, *87*, *89* (207)
    Common 88, *89* (207)
    Glaucous 90, *91* (208)
    Great Black-backed 92, *93* (208)
    Herring 90, *91* (208)
    Iceland 90, *91* (208)
    Lesser Black-backed 90, *91* (207)
    Little 88, *89* (207)
    Mediterranean 88, *89* (207)
    Ring-billed 188, *189*
    Sabine's 88, *89*

Harrier, Hen 38, *39* (200)
    Marsh 38, *39* (200)
    Montagu's 38, *39* (200)
Hawfinch 180, *181* (221)
Heron, Grey 14, *15* (196)
    Night 186, *187*
    Purple 186, *187*
Hobby 46, *47* (202)
Hoopoe 112, *113* (211)

Ibis, Glossy 186, *187*

Jackdaw 164, *165* (219)
Jay 162, *163* (218)

Kestrel 46, *47* (201)
Kingfisher 112, *113* (211)

Kite, Red 42, *43* (201)
Kittiwake 92, *93* (208)
Knot 68, *69* (204)

Lapwing 64, *65* (204)
Lark, Shore 116, *117* (212)
    Short-toed 192, *193*
Linnet 176, *177* (220)

Magpie 162, *163* (218)
Mallard 24, *25*, *29* (198)
Martin, House *113*, 118, *119* (212)
    Sand 118, *119* (212)
Merganser, Red-breasted 36, *37* (200)
Merlin 46, *47* (202)
Moorhen *57*, 58, *59* (203)

Nightingale 128, *129* (213)
Nightjar 110, *111* (211)
Nutcracker 190, *191*
Nuthatch 158, *159* (218)

Oriole, Golden 160, *161* (218)
Osprey 42, *43* (201)
Ouzel, Ring 132, *133* (214)
Owl, Barn 108, *109* (210)
    Little 108, *109* (210)
    Long-eared 110, *111* (210)
    Short-eared 110, *111* (210)
    Snowy 108, 190, *191*
    Tawny 108, *109* (210)
Oystercatcher 60, *61* (203)

Parakeet, Rose-ringed 106, *107* (210)
Partridge, Grey 52, *53* (202)
    Red-legged 52, *53* (202)
Peregrine Falcon 44, *45* (201)
Phalarope, Grey 82, *83*
    Red-necked 82, *83* (207)
    Wilson's 188, *189*
Pheasant, Common 54, *55* (203)
    Golden 54, *55* (203)
    Lady Amherst's 54, *55* (203)
Pigeon, Wood *103*, 104, *105* (209)
Pintail 28, *29* (198)
Pipit, Meadow 120, *121* (212)
    Richard's 192, *193*
    Rock 120, *121* (212)

Tawny 192, *193*
Tree 120, *121* (212)
Water 120, *121* (212)
Plover, Golden *65*, 66, *67* (204)
Ringed 62, *63*, 204
Grey 66, *67* (204)
Kentish 62, *63*
Little Ringed 62, *63* (204)
Pochard 30, *31* (199)
Red-crested 30, *31* (199)
Ptarmigan 48, *49* (202)
Puffin 100, *101* (209)

Quail 52, *53* (202)

Rail, Water 56, *57* (203)
Raven 166, *167* (219)
Razorbill 98, *99*, *101* (209)
Redpoll 176, *177* (220)
Redshank, Common *77*, 78, *79* (206)
Spotted 78, *79* (206)
Redstart, Common 128, *129* (214)
Black 128, *129* (214)
Redwing 134, *135* (214)
Reedling *see* Tit, Bearded
Reeve *see* Ruff
Robin 126, *127* (213)
Rook 164, *165* (219)
Rosefinch, Common 192, *193*
Ruff 72, *73* (205)

Sanderling 68, *69* (205)
Sandpiper, Common 70, *71* (205)
Buff-breasted 188, *189*
Curlew 80, *81*
Green 80, *81* (206)
Pectoral 72, *73*
Purple 70, *71* (205)
White-rumped 188, *189*
Wood 80, *81* (206)
Scaup 30, *31* (199)
Scoter, Common 34, *35* (200)
Surf 188, *189*
Velvet 34, *35* (200)
Serin, European 192, *193* (220)
Shag 12, *13* (196)
Shearwater, Balearic 8, *9* (196)
Cory's 8

Great 8, *9*
Manx 8, *9*
Sooty 8, *9*
Shelduck 22, *23* (198)
Shoveler 28, *29* (199)
Shrike, Great Grey 160, *161* (218)
Red-backed 160, *161* (218)
Woodchat 190, *191*
Siskin 174, *175* (220)
Skua, Arctic 84, *85* (207)
Great 84, *85* (207)
Long-tailed 84, *85*
Pomarine 84, *85*
Skylark 116, *117* (212)
Smew 36, *37* (200)
Snipe, Common 74, *75* (205)
Jack 74, *75* (205)
Sparrow, Hedge *see* Dunnock
House 170, *171* (219)
Tree 170, *171* (219)
Sparrowhawk 40, *41* (201)
Spoonbill 14, *15*
Starling *125*, 168, *169* (219)
Stilt, Black-winged 188, *189*
Stint, Little 68, *69* (205)
Temminck's 68, *69*
Stonechat 130, *131* (214)
Stone-curlew 60, *61* (204)
Stork, White 186, *187*
Storm-petrel, Leach's 10, *11* (196)
European 10, *11* (196)
Swallow *113*, 118, *119* (212)
Swan, Bewick's 16, *17* (197)
Mute 16, *17* (196)
Whooper 16, *17* (197)
Swift 112, *113*, *119* (211)
Alpine 190, *191*

Teal 26, *27* (198)
Tern, Arctic 94, *95* (208)
Black 96, *97*
Common 94, *95* (208)
Little 96, *97* (209)
Roseate 94, *95* (208)
Sandwich 96, *97* (208)
White-winged Black 188, *189*
Thrush, Mistle 136, *137* (215)
Song 134, *135* (214)

Tit, Bearded 152, *153* (217)
   Blue 156, *157* (217)
   Coal 156, *157* (217)
   Crested 154, *155* (217)
   Great 156, *157* (218)
   Long-tailed 152, *153* (217)
   Marsh 154, *155* (217)
   Willow 154, *155* (217)
Treecreeper 158, *159* (218)
   Short-toed 158
Turnstone *71*, 82, *83* (207)
   Twite 176, *177* (220)

Wagtail, Grey 122, *123* (213)
   Pied 122, *123* (213)
   White 122, *123*
   Yellow 122, *123* (213)
Warbler, Aquatic 140, *141*
   Barred 144, *145*
   Cetti's 138, *139* (215)
   Dartford 142, *143* (215)
   Garden 144, *145* (216)
   Grasshopper 138, *139* (215)
   Icterine 144, *145*
   Marsh 140, *141* (215)
   Melodius 144, *145*

   Pallas's Leaf 192, *193*
   Reed 140, *141* (215)
   Savi's 138, *139* (215)
   Sedge 140, *141* (215)
   Willow 146, *147* (216)
   Wood 146, *147* (216)
   Yellow-browed 148, *149*
Waterhen *see* Moorhen
Waxwing 124, *125* (213)
Wheatear 130, *131* (214)
Whimbrel 76, *77* (206)
Whinchat 130, *131* (214)
Whitethroat, Common 142, *143* (215)
   Lesser 142, *143* (215)
Wigeon 26, *27* (198)
Woodcock 74, *75* (205)
Woodlark 116, *117* (211)
Woodpecker, Great Spotted 114, *115* (211)
   Green 114, *115* (211)
   Lesser Spotted 114, *115* (211)
Wren 124, *125* (213)
Wryneck 114, *115* (211)

Yellowhammer 182, *183* (221)

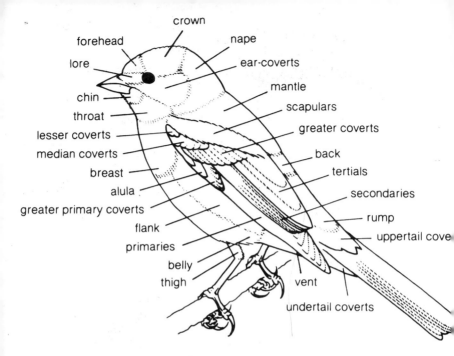

crown

forehead

nape

lore

ear-coverts

chin

mantle

throat

scapulars

lesser coverts

greater coverts

median coverts

back

breast

tertials

alula

secondaries

greater primary coverts

rump

flank

uppertail cove

primaries

belly

thigh

vent

undertail coverts

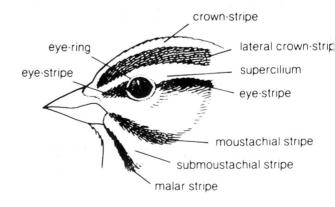

crown-stripe

eye-ring

lateral crown-strip

eye-stripe

supercilium

eye-stripe

moustachial stripe

submoustachial stripe

malar stripe